THE CHRONICLES OF PANCHITA VILLA
AND OTHER GUERRILLERAS

CHICANA MATTERS SERIES
Deena J. González and Antonia Castañeda, editors

Chicana Matters Series focuses on one of the largest population groups in the United States today, documenting the lives, values, philosophies, and artistry of contemporary Chicanas. Books in this series may be richly diverse, reflecting the experiences of Chicanas themselves and incorporating a broad spectrum of topics and fields of inquiry. Cumulatively, the books represent the leading knowledge and scholarship in a significant and growing field of research and, along with the literary works, art, and activism of Chicanas, underscore their significance in the history and culture of the United States.

The Chronicles of

Panchita Villa

and Other Guerrilleras

ESSAYS ON CHICANA/LATINA
LITERATURE AND CRITICISM

Tey Diana Rebolledo

 UNIVERSITY OF TEXAS PRESS
Austin

Requests for permission to reproduce material
from this work should be sent to:
Permissions
University of Texas Press
P.O. Box 7819
Austin, TX 78713-7819
www.utexas.edu/utpress/about/
bpermission.html

♾ The paper used in this book meets the
minimum requirements of ANSI/NISO Z39.48-
1992 (R1997) (Permanence of Paper).

LIBRARY OF CONGRESS
CATALOGING-IN-PUBLICATION DATA
Rebolledo, Tey Diana, date–
The chronicles of Panchita Villa and other
guerrilleras : essays on Chicana/Latina
literature and criticism / Tey Diana
Rebolledo.—1st ed.
    p.   cm. — (Chicana matters series)
Includes bibliographical references and index.
ISBN 0-292-70692-8 (alk. paper)—
ISBN 0-292-70963-3 (pbk. : alk. paper)
1. American literature—Mexican American
authors—History and criticism.
2. American literature—Hispanic American
authors—History and criticism.
3. American literature—Women authors—
History and criticism.   4. Hispanic American
women—Intellectual life.   5. Mexican
American women—Intellectual life.
6. Feminism and literature—United
States.   7. Women and literature—United
States.   8. Hispanic American women in
literature.   9. Mexican American women
in literature.   I. Title.   II. Series.
PS153.M4R427 2005
810.9'9287—dc22
                                        2005007620

Chapter 1, "The Chronicles of Panchita Villa:
Episode One," was originally published as
"The Chronicles of Panchita Villa: A Chicana
Guerrillera Literary Critic," in Jeanne Camp-
bell Reeseman, ed., *Speaking the Other Self:
American Women Writers* (Athens: University
of Georgia Press, 1997), 79–90.
    Chapter 4, "The Politics of Poetics: Or,
What Am I, a Critic, Doing in This Text
Anyhow?" by Tey Diana Rebolledo is re-
printed with permission from the publisher of
the *Americas Review* (Houston: Arte Público
Press—University of Houston, 1987).
    Selections from the works of Marjorie
Agosín, Ricardo Aguilar, Miriam Bornstein,
Ajedrez de Rosario Castellanos, Margarita
Cota-Cárdenas, José M. García-García, Inés
Hernández-Avila, Elena Milán, Ana Montes,

Marina Rivera, Raquel Sentíes, Alma Luz
Villanueva, and Helena María Viramontes are
reprinted by permission of the authors.
    Material quoted from *Face of an Angel,*
copyright © 1994 by Denise Chávez,
published by Warner Books and originally
in hardcover by Farrar, Straus and Giroux.
Reprinted by permission of Susan Bergholz
Literary Services, New York. All rights
reserved.
    Material quoted from *Loving Pedro
Infante,* copyright © 2001 by Denise Chávez,
published by Washington Square Press and
originally in hardcover by Farrar, Straus and
Giroux. Reprinted by permission of Susan
Bergholz Literary Services, New York. All
rights reserved.
    Material quoted from *So Far from God,*
copyright © 1993 by Ana Castillo, published
by Plume, an imprint of the Penguin Group
(USA) and originally in hardcover by W. W.
Norton. Reprinted by permission of Susan
Bergholz Literary Services, New York. All
rights reserved.
    Material quoted from *Loose Woman,* copy-
right © 1994 by Sandra Cisneros, published
by Vintage Books, a division of Random
House, Inc., and originally in hardcover by
Alfred A. Knopf, Inc. Reprinted by permission of Susan Bergholz Literary Services, New
York. All rights reserved.
    "It Occurs," copyright © 2003 by Sandra
Cisneros. Reprinted by permission of Susan
Bergholz Literary Services, New York. All
rights reserved.
    "Our Tejana," copyright © 1997 by San-
dra Cisneros. First published in the *San Antonio Express News,* August 17, 1997. Reprinted
by permission of Susan Bergholz Literary
Services, New York. All rights reserved.
    "Afternoon," copyright © by Sandra
Cisneros. Reprinted by permission of Susan
Bergholz Literary Services, New York. All
rights reserved.
    "Arise, Chicano"/"Levántate, Chicano,"
by Angela de Hoyos, translated by Mireya
Robles from *Arise Chicano and Other Poems,*
by Angela de Hoyos. M&A Editions, 2d
ed. © 1976. Reprinted by permission of the
publisher.
    "These Old Rags" from *When Living
Was a Labor Camp,* by Diana Garcia. © 2000
Diana Garcia. Reprinted by permission of the
University of Arizona Press.
    "Serpentine Voices" from *When Living
Was a Labor Camp,* by Diana Garcia. © 2000
Diana Garcia. Reprinted by permission of the
University of Arizona Press.
    "La Migra," excerpts from "Malinche's
Tips," and excerpts from "Llantos de La
Llorona: Warnings from the Wailer," from
Agua Santa/Holy Water by Pat Mora, copy-
right © 1995 by Pat Mora. Reprinted by
permission of Beacon Press, Boston.

To my daughter
Tey Marianna Nunn
Whose courage and vision are always inspiring

For my grandmother, Concepción (Concha) Galindo

And, as always, to my compañero
Michael M. Passi
Who Knows Why

CONTENTS

PREFACE

I have been studying and teaching Chicana/Latina literature for more than twenty years. During this time I have given many presentations and lectures on various aspects of this important literature. Often, after the lecture, the paper would be put away, awaiting the day when
I would have time to polish it, insert the proper footnotes and references,
and get the bibliography right. Of course, over the years sometimes life
would get in the way. There were classes to teach, books to read, friends
to talk to. Different projects would spring up and capture my enthusiasm.
But recently while cleaning my study, I realized that there were many
papers, mostly unpublished, that would in some way reflect my growth
as a scholar and my ideas about this literature, the place of our criticism,
about how and where our literary criticism has affected or not affected the
mainstream canon, and our struggle for representation.

At times the ideas contained in this collection are incomplete; they
are just the seeds for something that might be developed more fully later.
However, it seems to me that these essays, although imperfect, do represent a restless questioning about the place of Chicana/Hispana literature
and its critics and about our responsibilities as teachers and thinkers. The
essays are not meant to be overly academic, although I hope that they are
scholarly, too. If they sound conversational, it is because that is precisely
what they are: a conversation with the writers and readers out there. There
is much that is personal in these essays, because in some ways the growth of
Chicana literature has also been my growth as a teacher, scholar, and a person. And who I am is based on my childhood, my often conflicting sense
of exclusion from and at the same time inclusion within the mainstream,
and all the cultural and social events in the last twenty years.

I have a debt of gratitude to my students who have listened to me,
discussed with me, and who have greatly contributed to my intellectual
growth and understanding. And to Theresa May, who has encouraged me

all these years. Thanks go also to the Bogliasco Foundation Institute for the Arts and Humanities, a wonderful refuge where the ideas for this book were generated. And, as always, I am indebted to the writers and critics I have had the privilege to know. I have loved reading your books and talking with you over the years. And especially I value your friendship. So thanks, Margarita, Pat, Erlinda, María, Norma, Lucha, Teresa, Demetria, Denise, Sandra, Clara, Helena María, Gloria, Cherríe, Ana, Lorna Dee, Angela, Naomi, Patricia, Emma, Bernice, Miriam, Rina, Marina, Alma, Raquel, Antonia, Vangie, Inés, Carmen, Gina, Carla, Xelina, Alicia, Diana, Adaljiza, Marjorie, and Cordelia. And in special thought Estela Portillo Trambley, una de las primeras.

Hey, That's MY Story!

A CONVERSATION WITH MY PERUVIAN FATHER
AND MY MEXICAN MOTHER — LITERATURE
AND IDENTITY

I sit reading my father's short stories in the collection *La Llama y el Indio,* published in 1949, stories he had written over a period of several years. Some of the characters resemble me, some my beautiful mother. Sometimes the characters are a synthesis between my younger sister and myself, and even our faithful dogs Fino and Nusta make an appearance: Fino's habit of chasing cars and subsequent death because of it, and Nusta, the blond spaniel's color. There is much creative license, but I can still recognize us. And I certainly recognize my father's voice. I begin to understand also why my mother was jealous of my father's first wife, who tragically died. A short story about a trip on a Spanish train, which demonstrated the warmth and generosity of the Spanish people, also demonstrated my father's love for his wife, Lucía Alonso.

But Lucía died and later my grieving father went to Mexico (perhaps to distract himself from his sadness) and there he met my mother. She was divorced in a time when women did not divorce, had two children, and was working in El Palacio de Hierro, a high-end Mexico City store, selling mantillas. My father apparently was buying mantillas for the Spanish Club at New Mexico Normal College in Las Vegas, New Mexico, where he was teaching, saw my mother, one of the most beautiful women I have ever seen, and they ran away together. Several stories arose from this: one version is that my father wrote letters to my mother, and she and a friend thought they were funny and answered them. He then went to Mexico and she ran away with him, the federales hot on their tracks because she had her children, and she was not supposed to leave Mexico with them. Another version has them getting married right away with the taxi driver and a stranger as witnesses to their civil marriage, a cigar band standing in for the wedding ring. No one still alive knows what was true. But what I do know is that they were married on April 24, 1936, that his first wife, Lucía Alonso died in 1935, and that I was born on April 29, 1937. For

Cesareo Rebolledo and children (left to right): Lelia, Cesareo, Alina, and Washington Antonio (my father). Circa 1908.

many years I would perversely tell people that my parents were married on April 24 and I was born on the 29th.

What does this have to do with identity and the Chronicles of Panchita Villa? My father was Peruvian, although for years he told people he was a Chilean. There are many stories about this, too. He was trying to escape being inducted into the Peruvian military, his mother was a Chilean, and so forth. It is true that his grandfather was a Chilean who somehow (and family history is unclear about this) "left a gift" for my paternal great-grandmother, Pasión Alzamora, in the form of my grandfather, Cesareo Rebolledo. The family secret is that they were not married (shhh! don't tell). I never knew my paternal grandmother, who died quite young. There is a sad photograph of her family, all dressed in black, my father staring somberly into the camera. My grandfather was a cruel man, my cousins tell me. They had some land in Peru, and he treated the servants and workers badly. He treated my gentle father cruelly also. One night, because my father was afraid of the dark, Cesareo made him sleep in a spooky barn, all by himself. But my grandfather must have been a man of ideas—he named his sons after important men: the first was Napoleon ("Napo"), my father was Washington ("Washito"), the next Cesareo, after himself, and the last Renán, after the French philosopher. In 2003, while visiting Huaraz, Peru, where my father was born, we saw my family's lands, now mostly washed away and destroyed by earthquakes and aluviones. To cross over the raging Santa River, the locals use the time-honored and scary method of climbing into a basket and being taken by rope and pulley to the other side. "There," a man pointed, "is where the Alzamoras lived." The Chilean name of Rebolledo is forgotten.

My mother was a Mexican, born to a Mexican mother and an English grandfather (who the family says refused to speak Spanish—really? for seventy or more years?). My grandmother, Concepción Galindo, better known as Concha, was one of five beautiful Galindo sisters. We have many photographic portraits to attest to this. She was older when she married my grandfather, a solterona it was rumored because she was almost (gasp) thirty when she married. She had studied medicine in Chicago, had worked as a journalist it was said, and was appointed by President Porfirio Díaz to some important post, according to a plaque somewhere in the family. If she had not married before, it was because she didn't want to. Unfortunately, I cannot attest to any of this; I only knew her as an old lady dressed in black. However, there is a family picture in which she is showing off her long hair—hair she grew to detest, but my grandfather didn't let her cut it. She convinced her children to chew gum and stick it in her hair so she *had* to cut it. Actually this story never made sense to me, but I wrote the following poem about it.

El pelo de mi abuela

El pelo de mi abuela Concepción Galindo
se le caía hasta las caderas.
Por alguna razón,
mi abuelo, el venerable don Arturo,

Concepción Galindo.

no quería que se lo cortara,
ese cabello, largo,
risado y voluminoso
como en la fotografía.

Mi abuela, gordita,
chaparita,
siempre vestida de negro
cuando yo la conocía,
no parecía mujer vanidosa,

sensual y seductora,
sin embargo . . .
el abuelo sonreía
cuando ella
pasaba con su pelo suelto.
El cuento va
que un día,
ya muerto Arturo,
urgió a sus seis niños
mascar chicle
y pegarlo en su pelo
y
así
engomado, enredado y entumecido
tuvo que
cortárselo.

My Grandmother's Hair

The hair of my grandmother, Concepción Galindo,
fell down to her hips.
For some reason,
my grandfather, the venerable don Arturo,
did not want her to cut it,
that hair long, curly and
voluminous that you see
in the photograph.

My grandmother, chubby
and short,
was always dressed in black
when I saw her.
She didn't seem to be
a woman of vanity
nor sensual
nor seductive
nevertheless . . .
My grandfather
always smiled
when she passed by
with her hair loose.

The story goes
that one day,
Arturo dead,
she urged her six children
to chew gum
and stick it in her hair
and thus, sticky, tangled
and swollen
she had to cut it off.

Abuelita Concha made her living as a moneylender and was known in the family as a clairvoyant. I heard many spooky stories at the kitchen table about my grandmother's visions. It was said that family members and neighbors came to visit her shortly after they died to say good-bye. So when she had a vision, she would send someone to the house of the newly departed with her condolences. And they would always have just died. These stories scared me so that, like my father, I was always afraid of the dark. And I must say, even to this day I'm not so sure.

And so, what was I? Born in Las Vegas, New Mexico, to a Peruvian/Chilean father and a Mexican mother, I grew up speaking Spanish, quickly switching to English when I entered school. Well, when asked "Qué eres chula?" (What are you, cutie?), I would answer, "Pocha," which to me meant a mixture but which I later found out was derogatory. However, because we lived in New Mexico, had Spanish-speaking people all around us, and traveled often to Mexico to visit with my mother's family, I always identified with "lo mexicano." "Lo peruano" was relegated to my father's music ("Your father! Always listening to those huaynitos of his," my mother would say); a haunting flute filled strange music that enveloped our house when my father was home.

The Latin American side of my family didn't enter my life, really, until I was about twelve, when my father's sister and her husband came to visit from Peru. By that time we were living in New London, Connecticut, where my father was a professor at Connecticut College and life was very different from what it was in New Mexico. In 1951 we traveled to Peru, where I met my Peruvian family for the first time, fell in love with my fifteen-year-old cousin (isn't that what cousins are supposed to do?), and then my father died. His death effectively cut us off from that part of the family as my mother struggled to cope with two young children and her grief. In the years that followed we moved many times, and I went to college to study Spanish and literature. I became a historian, and it wasn't until I returned to graduate school in 1973 that I again became acquainted with literature. As I have detailed in other essays in this narrative, I became a Latin American literature specialist and then a Chicano literature specialist. Because the Mexican, then Mexican/American, aspect of my identity had always been so strong, it clearly helped me to identify with Chicano literature. These were the resonances and the spaces so important to my growing up. But what of that other part? That Peruvian/Chilean part, the Rebolledo part—not the Galindo/De la Torre part? And this is what I was trying to find in my father's stories, in the grammar book called *Amanecer* that he wrote for Spanish-speaking children. As I said before, I see my story and my father's story embedded in those books.

My mother, when first married to my father, must have had some time on her hands, or perhaps she was competing with him, as she wrote a novel. Never published, it languished in a trunk until it one day resurfaced in the possession of my sister Angeles. It is an interesting story of my mother's life in Mexico, and from it I included a section in the anthology *Infinite Divisions*. But it isn't my story—that is, it does not extend to the period in which I was born. Yet it is a family story, and in that sense it is mine, too.

While writing essays, every critic, especially those who are cultural critics, understands that our approach to literature and analysis is one based on our own particular perspective: who we are, what has molded us, the spaces and people surrounding us. And so in this collection I wanted to include essays on writers who have influenced me, molded me, and impressed me over the years. Perhaps this desire disrupts what might be a more coherent focus on just Chicana writers. However, I wanted to include the essays on the women writers from Latin America who have made my life meaningful and who, I thought, had taught us something about being women in difficult circumstances and about survival. Thus Rosario Castellanos, Alfonsina Storni, and Delmira Agustini are women I have long admired and wanted to include. Marjorie Agosín, who has written so beautifully about her family and their travails and who has so strongly defended social justice, also seemed to be a writer we could compare with those Chicana writers who wrote and struggled about many of the same things. These are all part of a larger story about transcendence and compassion, our heritage and family connections. They write about who they are and what has shaped them.

One day Margarita Cota-Cárdenas, about whom I have written extensively in this collection, and I were traveling by car from Phoenix to Tucson to attend a celebration honoring Dr. Dolores Brown, who had been our professor at the University of Arizona. Margarita was reading to me from her new novel, and when she finished reading a section, I said to her, "Hey, that's MY story!" The section recounted a story I had told her about an incident that happened to me at Connecticut College when I took part in a psychology experiment. They had deceived me about the nature of the experiment, and the results of that experiment, when they were revealed to me, were extremely disturbing. So disturbing, in fact, that I totally changed my life. (If you want to know what happened, you will have to read Margarita's novel, *Sanctuaries of the Heart*.) In any event, Margarita laughed and said, "I know, that's why I'm reading this to you!" You can't trust writers, you know; they steal things, and you should *never* tell them your best stories.

Several years later my husband and I were in Italy, traveling from Genova to Sorento. I had just finished a fellowship at the Institute for Arts and Letters at Bogliasco, and we were changing trains in Florence, where we had several hours to kill. We put our luggage in the left-luggage office, and my husband took our tickets out of his pocket and started to zip them into his bag. "Don't leave the tickets here," I said. "Someone could take them." Obligingly he put them back into his jacket pocket. As we were leaving the station to walk to the Duomo, we were swarmed by three young gypsy girls, one carrying a baby. First they asked for money, and then they surrounded Michael, fanning at him with their hands. The next thing I knew, Michael turned to me and said, "They have the tickets!" I became furious and, by this time being somewhat conversant in Italian, charged after the young women, grabbed the one with the baby (Michael says I slammed her into the wall, but I don't think that is true), and said, "Give me the tickets" in fairly good Italian. At first she refused, but I had a pretty firm grip on the baby she was carrying. She handed over one set of tickets. "Give me *all* the tickets," I emphasized, "or I'll take the bambino." Now I had almost lifted the baby out of her arms, so she gave me the rest of the tickets and ran off with her companions. We had collected a crowd by this time, including a man from England who told us that they had done exactly the same thing to him the day before and he had come back to see if he could find them. By then my adrenaline had started to subside, and I began to think of the consequences of my actions. What if the baby hadn't been hers and she had abandoned it? What if someone thought I was trying to steal the baby? (After all, I had read about an American in Guatemala who was accused of stealing babies to sell them for adoption.) We would have spent hours trying to explain to the carabinieri what had happened, perhaps even ended up in jail. In any event I reached the conclusion that my impulses might have led to drastic consequences. Safely back home from the trip, Michael and I told the story to several people, and every time it acquired embellishments.

One day several years later, we were invited to the home of friends for an Italian dinner. Stories were being told about trips to Italy, when someone told of a couple who had been robbed of their tickets by gypsies, whereas the wife grabbed a young gypsy with a baby, roughly slammed her against the wall, took the baby, and got the tickets back. I sat there with my mouth wide open as I heard the story, and of course, when it was over, said, "Hey, that's MY story!"

Well, stories, family and personal, as well as our experiences and our perceptions are what guide us as critics and readers. Many writers I know claim their poems and narratives are fiction, and I know this is true. But at the same time they are personal and autobiographical, and this is also true. Many of them have told me their stories, which I then see reflected in their writing. Sometimes they listen to our stories and use what makes sense to them.

In this collection I have tried to combine my personal and academic interests and my own experiences and perceptions. I have tried to reconcile all the many parts of me, the Latin Americana side, the Mexicana side, the Chicana side, the Americana side. This is not so much a melting pot as a green chile stew, with all the ingredients retaining their unique flavors. I am my mother's daughter, but my father's daughter as well, and I am the child of New Mexico as I am of Connecticut. I am a Mexicana, a Peruana, a Latina, and a Chicana (as well as an Americana). And so, in some sense, all of these essays are my stories. Hey!

Part One

On Criticism and Critics

ONE

The Chronicles of Panchita Villa

EPISODE ONE (1993)

Mother, father
there's no passing
the cup
I'm going to be a troublemaker
when I grow up.
—DEMETRIA MARTÍNEZ

The topic of this essay is Chicana literature, Chicana criticism, and the canon.[1] It is a subject about which I have written many times and which continues to evolve, depending on the historical moment, what has happened to Chicana literature and Chicana critics during the time immediately preceding, and how angry I am about the situation at any given time. In its various manifestations these thoughts have been called "Chicana Studies: The Missing Text," "Is There a Place for Chicana Studies in Women Studies?" "Lost in America," and once, when I was really angry, "Et tú, Bruta?" an aggressive play on the feminist betrayal of women of color, but doubly nasty because in Spanish Bruta is not only the feminine of Brutus, but also means "stupid" or "dumb." I am sorry to have to give yet another transformation of these ideas here, but I will try not to be offensively aggressive. The problem is that in all the years I have been speaking about this, I have not seen much change. Chicana critics have to continue to be guerrillera fighters.

To begin I want to clarify what canon I am discussing, as there are many literary canons of which Chicana literature might be a part, although the reality is that it is not part of many. Certainly we are not often mentioned in the larger context of Anglo European literature, nor are we considered within the context of Latin American literature. Neither are we included within the canon of general American literature. In the canons of Chicano and other minority literatures, the women writers have been more clearly and prominently recognized and included, particularly in recent years. Here I want to discuss the inclusion of Chicanas in the more narrowly focused feminist cannon: a place where a few Chicana writers such as Sandra Cisneros, Ana Castillo, and Gloria Anzaldúa are sometimes included and the rest of many fine writers, such as Pat Mora and Angela de Hoyos, excluded. And, in the main, it is a canon where most Chicana literary critics are excluded. In mainstream feminist journals such as *Signs*, very few, if any, Chicana critics have been published; and in other journals, such as *Critical Inquiry*, we cannot even imagine being included. Years ago, when I wrote a paper titled "Lost in America," I argued that we were lost because Chicana writers and critics were not included in mainstream anthologies, journals, or books. And until recently we were not really integrated in Chicano anthologies, which focused primarily on male writers. We were lost in women's studies because, except in exceptional cases, scholars in women's studies programs often felt that studying the latest French feminist theory or postmodern theory was more important than spending time in the study of minority women.

The problems facing Chicana writers are many. Until recently Chicana writers were cut off from the national market because of region and the newness of their literature. It has only been within the last fifteen years that we have begun to see their work consistently published even by Chicano publishers such as Arte Público, Third Woman, and the Bilingual Review Press. Before then, many Chicana writers self-published in chapbooks issued in small numbers and distributed among family and friends. There was no regional or national distribution of these texts. In the last several years some university presses have begun to publish Chicana writers and critics. Among these presses are the University of Arizona Press, the University of New Mexico Press, the University of Texas Press, and a few others. Lately some authors, beginning to make use of literary agents, have been able to break through into New York publishing houses, riding on the current interest in all things hot and Latino. This has happened both with their novels and poetry and, especially interesting and worthwhile, with children's books. Yet, except for these few big splashes, Chicana literature remains unknown. However, academics can no longer complain about a lack of literary texts and critical works written by Chicanas. In my research for *Infinite Divisions: An Anthology of Chicana Literature* (1993), I came across thousands of texts written by Chicanas, and creative work continues to emerge. While Chicana literature is fairly young, the high quality of the work shows that it is mature. But I want to discuss the problems that beset those of us in academia who are struggling to find a place for Chicana literature at least within academic circles, if not within the general public.

Another issue is the role of the Chicana critic. We all have faced the problem of working in what are thought of as "marginal areas": women and minority women. We are asked, What kind of a market can there be for that? Is it academically legitimate? Are the writers good enough? Do they have a sufficient body of work? Do you as a critic have enough theory? Does standard theory apply to minority writers? This is the sort of questioning that comes from one's department, college, colleagues. At the same time, we face the inquisition about political correctness and multiculturalism from the right, for example, the National Association of Scholars (the Nasties, I call them), who are trying to maintain power in the face of change. This makes us the target for an inquisition that can include public and private harassment (I know—a Chicana colleague and I have been the subject of such harassment) as well as other attempts at silencing.

Rather than discuss these issues in the abstract, I would like to talk on a more personal level. In 1985 I was invited to give a Last Lecture at the University of New Mexico. The Last Lecture Series was conceived as being the last, and perhaps most important, lecture that you would give during your lifetime. Clearly such a responsibility weighs heavily on your mind, even though you might not intend it to do so. Thus I approached my task with severity and enthusiasm. I titled my lecture "Meditations on Two Texts of Some Importance: *The Letter* of Sor Juana Inés de la Cruz and 'The Memoirs of Panchita Villa.'" Sor Juana's *Respuesta,* the seventeenth-century Mexican nun's feminist reply to patriarchal colonial Mexican society, is an important document in our Mexicana/Chicana intellectual history, one that defended women's right to knowledge and to education. In her *Respuesta* she not only saw knowledge as being female, and herself as the descendent of a long line of learned women, she had the temerity to claim that they were the originators of laws, propagators of Greek wisdom, and teachers of great philosophers and kings. She also asserted that a woman invented the Latin language, the basis of all writing and knowledge in the church. At one point, ordered by authorities to put away her books, she continued to make scientific observations: "But what could I tell, my lady, of the secrets of nature that I discovered while cooking? I observe that an egg binds and fries in butter and oil but breaks up in sugar syrup; that the yolk and white of the same egg are so opposed that each one separately will mix with sugar, but not both together . . . but, lady, as women, what wisdom may be ours if not the philosophies of the kitchen? Lupercio Leonardo spoke well when he said, 'How well one may

philosophize while preparing dinner. And I often say, when observing
these trivial details: 'Had Aristotle prepared victuals, he would have written
more'" (Peden, 62).[2] Sor Juana left an intellectual and cultural legacy that
has been eagerly taken up by Chicana writers and critics.

"The Memoirs of Panchita Villa," the other text referred to in my Last
Lecture, is also an ironically contrived text, patterned after a Mexican
novel of the 1930s. Martín Luis Guzmán wrote *The Memoirs of Pancho
Villa* to record the life and times of the Mexican revolutionary hero. Panchita Villa, our contemporary heroine, was also constructed as a literary
revolutionary, fighting against the academic establishment as a Chicana
and as a woman. The author is Concepción Galindo, better known in
her family as Concha (also the name of her grandmother). Concha was
born in a small town in northern New Mexico. She came from a family
of writers, and her mother wrote a novel about growing up during the
Mexican Revolution, a novel, to be sure, unpublished in the tradition
of so many women writers. Nevertheless, the novel influenced all three
daughters, who would go to the trunk, where it was generally stored, to
read about the time their mother, fleeing roving revolutionaries, was put
on a train where wounded and dying soldiers had been moved—her white
dress totally covered, to her horror, in blood. And about the time their
grandmother, the first Concepción, saved their grandfather from being
shot. In time this contemporary Concha grew up and became a university
professor. So in "The Memoirs of Panchita Villa" she details the struggle
that Chicana academics, intellectuals, and writers had to wage in order to
gain acceptance in the larger canonical worlds. In 1985 it was a chronicle
mainly against the narrow-mindedness of male-centered academic life and
intellectual inquiry. In the novel, the heroine, Panchita, questions various
people she meets. For example, she asks how minority women, students,
faculty, and staff are treated at universities? Welcomed or silenced? To the
males of her culture she asks whether there is also a place for Chicanas in
their revolution? Why is not the study of women and women's knowledge, especially that of minority women, considered valid? Now it is true
that in the intervening years some of this has changed, but unfortunately
two of her questions are still timely. In one, Panchita asks other women,
in particular feminists, "Why do you wish only to mirror and reproduce
yourself in terms of your scholarly interests?" And she asks why Chicanas
are not represented in the curriculum of women's studies and American
literature? Why, why, why, why, why? Because of its densely thick narration, its outlaw structure, we can clearly define the "Memoirs" as a novel
of questioning. And, as I was finishing my discussion of the "Memoirs,"

I said, "Well, enough is enough. It is true that some revolutions and some revolutionaries are more exciting than others. The type of everyday guerrilla warfare that Panchita engages in is on par with the observations of Sor Juana as she mixes egg yolks with sugar. But then perhaps if Aristotle had been a woman, he would have been a better revolutionary."

Then volume 2 of the "Memoirs" was written (it seems the author has at least six volumes in mind). Two central issues were addressed: how to include and integrate Chicana literary texts into the curriculum and into the canon and how to include and integrate Chicana critics into the canon. Since Panchita Villa has undertaken a thorough discussion of those issues, which you can read for yourself, here I will only add my own personal observations about Chicana literature and the feminist canon. Most women's studies programs are led by feminists who range in perspectives from traditional to liberal to radical. At times they remember that they need to include minority women in their courses and on their faculties. Certainly in recent years, with curriculum integration projects and with loud commentary from minority women, many programs have made significant inroads in inclusion. Many have not, and I truly believe, even with women who regard themselves as "liberals," there is still insensitivity and tokenism, and thus the necessity for us to constantly be educating. This attitude reminds me of a poem written in the early seventies by Marcela Lucero-Trujillo called "No More Cookies, Please," in which she states how tired she is of attending coffees with liberal feminists, constantly having to be nice and to explain herself, educating them (in Fisher, 402). For Chicana writers and critics, it seems to me, not much has changed. If any group of minority women has been able to cross boundaries, I believe it is Black women. More often than not, they are included in the curriculum, so their works are read. Chicanas are not half so well represented; Asian American and Native American women are almost invisible. We are still having trouble breaking into the mainstream, although a select few are doing quite well. We continue to be asked the questions, is the work any good? are the writers any good? are you any good? or are you good enough? (And since we ourselves ask these questions of ourselves often enough, it doesn't take much to discourage us.)

I want to outline several areas that for me continue to be problematic.

1. Integrating our research into mainstream books and journals. For a long time I have firmly believed in working on projects that would integrate our work into the larger canon. To this end I have published chapters in such works as *The Desert Is No Lady* and *For Alma Mater,* while continuing to publish extensively in Chicana/Chicano publications. Several years

ago I received a letter, however, which made me question the value of such integration. I would like to read you excerpts from it (names withheld), which will aptly illustrate what I am talking about. It may strike a familiar chord in some of you.

> Dear Professor Rebolledo:
>   My co-editor and I have just signed an advance contract with a University Press for a collection of essays on the fiction and/or autobiographies of twentieth-century British and American women writers. For some time now we have been searching for someone to write an essay on mothering in the fiction of a Chicana or Latina Woman writer.

(At this point and throughout I am going to do a Chicana deconstructionist analysis of this letter. To begin, I must mention that I did not know these women at all. I read that the volume is already put together since they have an advance contract. The editor at the press told them that they needed to find a Chicana or Latina, it doesn't matter which, so that their volume will not appear to be racist. They have already pre-selected the topic, mothering, but they don't know any Chicana or Latina critics, or really anyone who knows any, since they have been searching for some time. In addition, they don't know any universities where such knowledge might be found.)

"Your name was given to me by the Women's Studies Director at the University of . . . . She also suggested a possible novel *The Ultraviolet Sky* but we are certainly open to suggestion about this." (Here they have chosen the novel for me, but if I complain loud enough, they would be willing to change. After all, they have not read the novel, so it doesn't make all that much difference.)

"We are limiting each essay to 8250 words (23 pages, excluding bibliography), and our deadline is October 15, 1989. In fact it would be preferable if we could have an initial draft in September so that we can make editorial comments. Given the short notice, we do realize that this may be difficult to achieve." (Ah, yes, deadlines. The letter to me was dated July 14, with the 14th crossed out and the 18th written in; I received it on July 28. This gave me two months and a half to write a paper on a subject chosen for me. Because what I write might not be any good, they ask for it a little early so they can edit it—it might be really radical, or the more likely possibility is that, since I am a Chicana and speak other languages, it will be badly written in English, so changes will have to be made. It also assumes that I have nothing to do but write this paper. I was only involved in trying to finish books, write a paper for MALCS, finish a promised chapter for a book on Chicano colonial literature, get my classes organized, and coordinate the National Association for Chicano Studies Conference for 1990.)

The final paragraph: "Please let me know as soon as possible. You may phone me at home or at State University. But I am rarely in my office during the summer. You may, of course, also write to me at the above address. I do hope to hear that you will contribute an essay to this book."

(Deconstruction: Even though I have nothing to do with this project, she not only patronizes me but she places the burden of responsibility on me. I may phone her and, moreover, I should track her down. Barring not finding her, I can write to her, soon, immediately, with my excitement about having been invited to participate in this project.)

Now perhaps some of you will think I am overreacting to this letter. When you have received enough of them, you will see how serious this is. Question: What to do? I took the easy way out; I didn't answer. Advice from colleagues ranged from writing them an angry letter telling them "que se chinguen," to a letter educating them by refusing to participate but explaining why I am offended, to doing a Chicana deconstruction of it. This letter is serious because the project was from the start an unintegrated project without any input from minority writers about how best to combine these various papers and perspectives. It was tokenism at its worst because it was so genuinely insensitive and made so many assumptions about our work.[3]

2. It is very important to generate public programs, workshops, and other events on issues that minority women feel strongly about. But minority women have to be at the center of the planning for such programs. When they are, you can have great results. Erlinda Gonzales-Berry and I planned a program called "Redesigning the Traditional Literary Canon," invited female and male speakers, and collaborated between departments— and it was a great success. But there have been other programs that lacked this involvement, and they resulted in memorable disasters. One case in point is the Dark Madonna Conference held at UCLA several years ago and sponsored by the UCLA Center for the Study of Women and co-sponsored by many minority groups such as the African Studies Center, Chicano Studies, Hispanic Women's Council. It seemed a well-planned conference. On the night of the opening plenary session, with over 500 women in the audience, it quickly became apparent that all was not well. Of the six speakers on the podium, there were no minority women. (We

had all been relegated to sessions the next day.) The evening dragged endlessly on with discussions about women and uses of convention, garden
clubs, and so on. When time was allowed for questions, a woman stood
up and I recognized her, Roberta Fernández. She said, and I paraphrase,
"As you look at the audience, you can see that we are of all races. The
program was advertised as the Dark Madonna with an obviously Black
virgin and child on its cover. Why are there no minority women on the
plenary session?" As you can imagine, this left the persons on the stage in
total confusion with all sorts of embarrassing statements to be said, such as
well, there *are* minority women on the program tomorrow, we *tried* to include minority women (and they had invited quite a few of us), we didn't
think, and it's not *my* fault, I'm not the organizer. My point here is that
this happens again and again. When there are no minority women on the
planning committees, we are forgotten.

The bright note is that organizers of other conferences such as the Conference on American Women Writers do not fall into the above traps.
They energetically and conscientiously search out, invite, and integrate
minority women into their conferences.

3. I think that perhaps the greatest impact we have been able to make
vis-à-vis women's studies has been in curriculum integration. I am not so
sure about integration in the American literature and English curriculum.
At least at the University of New Mexico all the Women Studies courses
taught have to have a strong racial and ethnic component in them. Truly
integrating Chicanas on projects, however, has been a different story, even
on projects of curriculum integration. I have often worked with a regional
women's studies program on different projects and for many years have
been telling them that they need to have Chicanas on their advisory boards
and they need to consult with Chicanas on their projects instead of presenting them as faits accomplis. The program often makes attempts to be
inclusionary on their projects, inviting minority women to participate in
small numbers. Several years ago they received a grant from the Ford Foundation to participate in a curriculum integration project of a different sort:
to integrate the work of minority women into the women's studies curriculum. I was asked whether our program wanted to participate. I asked
what minority women were on the planning committee—well, none. I
asked who the project director was—well, an Anglo. I asked who the
coordinators were—well, an Anglo and a Chicano (male). I said no, no
thank you, that we didn't want to participate because we had no input. In
their January 1989 newsletter I read that of thirteen campus coordinators

for the project, only one was a Chicana, although two Chicanos were also included. Now if you think Chicanas have no input into the matter . . .

When one takes into consideration how these different projects are being put together and presented, it becomes clear that we Chicanas are not only not represented, but that others are speaking for us, others who may be sympathetic but who cannot presume to speak for us, not from our perspective. Once again, others are shaping our world view and presenting it as ours. Is this better than not being represented at all? I will leave this for you to cogitate.

What can Chicanas do about this besides complain? For one thing, at this time many Chicanas feel that we need to concentrate on our own research, our own classes, our own agendas. We need to finish our dissertations, our articles, our books. We need to be clear on our perspective and to look to other Chicanas as a source of support. When we are invited to be speakers, present papers, or collaborate on books, we must ask who the organizers are, who the planners are. Have they had input from minority women? Are they asking for ours? Are we invited at the beginning of the project so that we may take a role in shaping it? If the answers to our questions are not satisfactory, we might perhaps refuse to participate, particularly if we are being used as tokens and are matronized. If we are feeling generous, we might explain why we are refusing. We must express our concerns. If this is heard from enough of us, perhaps the message will sink in, and I won't be the only one who is difficult to work with.

If you feel I have exaggerated the exclusion of Chicana writers and critics from the canon, let me finish by outlining a recent incident. I received a call from an editor from a distinguished press in New York, asking me if I could review an anthology proposal for a book on American women writers from 1600 to the present. After I had agreed and received the proposal, I saw that there was not one Chicana or Latina writer included. However, there were 255 poems by Emily Dickinson (make no mistake, I think Dickinson is a fabulous writer) and 30 sonnets by Edna St. Vincent Millay. While African American women writers were generously included, Native American writers were scattered throughout, yet only two Asian American writers, Tan and Kingston, were present. No Hispana/Latina writers were included. And once again *The Yellow Wallpaper* was reproduced in its entirety (as it is endlessly). In my reply I said, "I have to tell you to begin, that I am totally shocked that in 1993 not one Chicana or Latina writer would be represented in an anthology of this magnitude. If the author would like to call this text the *Anthology of Anglo-American Women Writers*, then it might be acceptable, or perhaps it could be called *Emily Dickinson and Some Other Writers,* but to call it American Women Writers is truly a travesty . . . I think it would be an embarrassment for your press to publish this text as it stands. Moreover to simply tack on Chicana/Latina writers without meaningful integration would be an absurdity." To add insult to injury, I then received a form letter from the press thanking me for my review and asking if they could use any of my remarks for publicity.

Please do not misunderstand me: I am for working together to integrate works by women of color into the canon. But I am tired of being marginalized, matronized, and colonized. I want the texts to be fully integrated from the beginning in a meaningful way, texts that talk to each other in both the minority and traditional canon. I desire to see texts that are selected from a perspective of women of color and not the other way around.

What can you personally do about all this? Be thoughtful, include the work of women of color in your classes—place their work side by side with more traditional work. You might be surprised by the dialogue generated as the texts speak to each other. At a conference on American women writers, one of the keynote speakers noted that she thought we could not create a canon that would include minority writers because it would not be historically accurate. However, if one were to recognize that part of the Chicana tradition could (and should) include Mexican writers such as Sor Juana Inés de la Cruz (after all, the Southwest was part of Mexico until 1848) and stories from the oral traditions of Hispana/Mexicana and Native American writers, we could construct a much more creative (and historically significant) canon.

Other suggestions for more inclusive reading would be to buy (not photocopy) our books—encourage your students to buy our books. Selling books encourages publishers to publish more books. Invite us to lecture, include us from the beginning in your programming for conferences, enjoy our humor, our ironies, educate yourself, be revolutionary.

As I end, I would like to confess what you have already guessed, that "The Memoirs of Panchita Villa" results from another female tradition— apocryphal text—that is, that they are attributed to Concha Galindo, who in reality is me, that it is a not-yet-existent text; it is a discourse in progress. To finish, I would like to acknowledge all my revolutionary co-troublemakers who function on the Theory of Bad Conduct, who resist tradition and easy answers, who want to revolutionize the world to make it more just for all its people, who desire a system of knowledge and learning that is truly egalitarian, and who support teachers, texts, and critics who represent the other. I acknowledge those troublemakers who are not afraid to question established systems and who are on the edge of the wave of new learning. These are the colleagues who understand that revolution is the only real road to learning. And especially I want to acknowledge Sor Juana, who questioned and who clearly understood that language and knowledge are tools in the stairway to the pyramid of the mind.

I would like to end this discussion, which is just a beginning, with a poem by a Nuevo Mexicana writer, Gloria Gonzales:

> There is nothing
> so lonesome
> or sad
> that
> papas fritas
> won't cure.
>
> (REBOLLEDO, GONZALES-BERRY, AND MÁRQUEZ, EDS., 184)

TWO *The Chronicles of Panchita Villa*

EPISODE TWO (1997)

y la Chicana se levantó y se puso a hacer tortillas y revolución.
—MARÍA SAUCEDO

I dedicate this essay to my younger sister, Gloria Rebolledo Ingham, who died of uterine cancer in 1996, with a poem I wrote for her, titled "When I Had That Brain Operation."

> Four times my sister
> rode that seven person plane
> when I was sick.
> Tucson-Albuquerque.
> "I'm scared to fly
> on small planes," I said.
> She joked they'd
> had to pee before
> boarding.
> Service was a
> cooler full of pop
> sliding down the aisle.
> She loved the high adventure,
> Pancho Villa style.
> I wonder, would I
> have gotten on a small plane
> for her?
> (1996)

To continue a bit more on the personal side, I need to tell you about *The Scarlet Horseman*. When I was a child growing up in Las Vegas, New Mexico, in the days before television and during the Second World War, there were only books, the neighborhood goings-on, and the movies for entertainment. I was a dedicated movie fan, sitting in the Surf Theater through sometimes two or three double-feature showings, until my father would come walking down the aisles to find me and roust me out. Between showings of the features they would always show serials. For those of you who may not have experienced this phenomenon, they were short, exciting episodes of daring deeds. And, of course, just as the action got suspenseful, they would stop the episode, dangling previews of the next week's attractions so you would return to the theater. My favorite was *The Scarlet Horseman;* there were no serials that I can remember with female heroes, but it was amazing how I was able to block out the fact that the Scarlet Horseman was a man and put myself in his place. Recently my daughter gave me all thirteen episodes of *The Scarlet Horseman* because I talk about it incessantly. I now believe I could put myself in his place because the person who played the Scarlet Horseman was not a handsome superhero and, moreover, like me, he was muy chaparito (short). In any event, this is the plot: the Scarlet Horseman is, in reality, a rancher who pretends he is in a wheelchair. He is a fighter for social justice in the Southwest and carries on against smugglers and other bad guys who want to steal Indian lands, evict poor widows and children from their homes, and put innocent people in jail. He lives in a house that is built above a mineshaft. In this house he has a secret trapdoor, covered by a beautiful Navajo rug, that leads to the mine cave. In fact, when he pulls back the rug, he is able to drop directly onto his horse, white of course, which is always waiting for him under the trapdoor. He then rides out to right evils and serve social justice. Against this background of good versus evil and with the backdrop of the Second World War, where we knew very well that we were good and the Nazis were evil, I grew up always wanting to be the Scarlet Horseman. Moreover, I learned many rope tricks and other fancy maneuvers so that my role would be more convincing. I wanted to serve social justice. This feeling was augmented by the fact that my father was a convinced socialist, but he also believed in Franklin D. Roosevelt, the Federal Works Program, free universities, and Harry Truman. This leads me to the Chronicles of Panchita Villa.

Many years ago, at a MALCS presentation, I created the figure of Panchita Villa and her Chronicles, a paper that, after various metamorphoses, became "The Chronicles of Panchita Villa, a Chicana Guerrillera Literary Critic" (which has become the first essay in this collection). Between 1938 and 1944 a Mexican author, Martín Luis Guzmán, wrote *The Chronicles of Pancho Villa,* a four-volume description of the life and accomplishments (always good, of course) of that revolutionary hero. At the time I was the director of the Women Studies Program at the University of New Mexico (the only Chicana then in the country to serve in such capacity) and envisioned myself in the middle of a revolution. The apocryphal writer of "The Chronicles of Panchita Villa" was Conchita Galindo, an author I imbued with the name of my grandmother and with some characteristics of my own. To make a long story short, in this paper I went after university administrations and mainstream scholars in general for not paying attention to minority scholars and to minority women scholars in particular. I spoke about the exclusion of Chicana writers and critics from the literary canon. In 1985 my talk was mainly against the narrow-mindedness of male-centered academic life and intellectual inquiry. It also sharply criticized white feminists for the exclusion of minority women and for wanting to see only themselves represented. After ten pages of relentless criticism, and feeling that Chicanas had been excluded from many canons, these are the conclusions I reached, and I quote myself (see Chapter 1 of this book):

> Many Chicanas feel that we need to concentrate on our own research, our own classes, our own agendas. We need to finish our dissertations, our articles, our books. We need to be clear on our perspective and to look to other Chicanas as a source of support. When we are invited to be speakers, present papers, or collaborate on books, we must ask who the organizers are, who the planners are. Have they had input from minority women, are they asking for ours? Are we invited at the beginning of the project so that we may take a role in shaping it? If the answers to our questions are not satisfactory, we might perhaps refuse to participate, particularly if we are being used as tokens. . . . Please do not misunderstand me: I am for working together to integrate works by women of color into the canon. But I am tired of being marginalized, matronized, and colonized. I want the texts to be fully integrated from the beginning in a meaningful way, texts that talk to each other in both the minority and traditional canon . . . texts that are selected from a perspective of women of color and not the other way around.

Of course, in that talk I was trying to convince white feminists that they needed to reach a level of consciousness about women of color, but I still believe what I said, and I ended by saying the following: "I would like to acknowledge all my revolutionary co-troublemakers who function on the Theory of Bad Conduct, who resist tradition and easy answers, who want to revolutionize the world to make it more just for all its people, who desire a system of knowledge and learning that is truly egalitarian and who support teachers, texts, and critics who represent the other" (12).

Well, so much for that written ten years or so ago. What do I see in 1997 at this millennium moment? It is a mixed message. I am afraid that Panchita Villa, even through she is getting old and cranky, must get out of her wheelchair, pull aside the Navajo rug, drop onto her ever-waiting white horse and ride through the cave. Clearly some things have changed since the first episode of "The Chronicles." Mainstream publishers have realized that there is a market for Latina writing, and we have a series of new anthologies, new books of criticism. Some of our writers have made it into the really big New York publishing houses and are enjoying seeing their books translated into other languages, finally being able to make a living from their writing. In terms of a growing literature we have made enormous strides in the last few years. And, indeed, some of our writers have even made it into the totally male-centered *New York Review of Books* (at least two) as well as the *Norton Anthology of Literature by Women,* and Sandra Cisneros is no longer "Sandra Who?" (as was reported in one Texas newspaper).

And yet Panchita looks around and sees that not all is well in the West as we are being affected in most egregious ways. Universities are in re-trenchment; the era of Newt Gingrich (hopefully brought to an end by the arrow of stupidity lodged in his heart) and neo-right-wing conservatism has given permission for racism and prejudice to flourish. As history has proven, whenever this country is feeling economic perils, it turns on those it considers "foreign"; the Cold War is no longer around to serve as a target for social and economic restlessness; and so the mainstream culture turns on the Other, and the Other is us.

Mexicans are now even more being portrayed as violent gang members, big-time drug dealers, or impoverished immigrants who live off welfare, have many children (none of whom can speak English, which then places a burden on the school system to "Americanize" them), and suck up any resources that should be going for progressive, not regressive programs, leading to such initiatives as California's Proposition 179. English only should be spoken and taught (in spite of a growing globalization of inter-national life) because, after all, if people are going to live here, they should adapt, ideas that led to Arizona's English Only initiative. Chicano/Latino students don't go on to college because they prefer to go to work to fix up their lowriders, and Chicana/Latinas don't go on because they want to stay home and have children (on welfare, of course). The new 1996 Immigration Bill will, in their minds, control the "flood" of immigrants. I could go on with all the slurs and slanders, misunderstandings, and deliberate misconceptions that you all know about and live with every day.

In 1997 several events occurred in New Mexico that for me mirror the increasing narrowness of vision and outright racism that is spreading in our society. Two Chicana teachers, Patsy and Nadine Cordova, at a high school in Vaughn, New Mexico, formed a MECHA club and taught Chicano studies using Elizabeth Martínez's *500 Years of Chicano History* as a text. This came about after the teachers watched the PBS program on Chicanos and were impressed. Having a large percentage of Chicano students at the school, they wanted to incorporate Chicano consciousness into their classrooms. These teachers were ordered by the principal to disband the MECHA club and to stop teaching Chicano studies. The feeling of some of the members of the school board was that the MECHA Club "is divisive, teaches racial intolerance, promotes a militant attitude in the students" and "we just need to teach our kids the basics and get them on their way" (*Albuquerque Journal,* February 15, 1997). (Funny, I thought Chicano history in the United States was part of the basics.) Some Hispanos in the community agreed with the principal, showing the degree of internalization that occurs in our communities.

On our campus at the University of New Mexico we too have had a recent blatant example of this atmosphere. There is a group called the National Association of Scholars (I call them the Nasties or the NASSES), which for many years has been harassing the ethnic studies and women's studies programs and minority scholars on campus. I myself have often been a target of their harassment. Recently, with a feeling that the contemporary atmosphere was again ripe for the reception of their message, they wrote a letter to the Board of Regents urging the dismantlement of the Student Services Ethnic Centers (they are reluctant to take on the ethnic studies programs, as they have been soundly defeated on those grounds, in particular as ethnic and women's studies have increasingly become accepted disciplines). Their argument is that student services that target specific groups have created a "balkanization" of student services and are superfluous. Clearly having lost the fight on one level, they continue on another. Fortunately, it seems the moment was not right for them yet, although movement toward their position is growing.

The impact of this escalating racism and narrow-mindedness is most

certainly reflected in universities and in attitudes about learning and affirmative action. Unfortunately, it comes at a time when we had begun
to think we were making progress about the incorporation of Chicana/
Chicano faculty into the curriculum, the ever-growing numbers of Chi-
cano/Latino students at the university, the growing numbers of students
in Chicana/Chicano studies classes. Recently a Chicana graduate student
in my class on Chicana literature came to my office to tell me how happy
she was that, for the first time in her life, she had a Chicana professor.
In fact, that she had three Chicana professors. At the University of New
Mexico we have been fortunate to have three Chicanas in the same department. However, you all know the old adage: If you have one Chicana in
a department, the university is liberal and the department can pat itself on
the back for its openness; if you have two Chicanas in the department, the
university is very progressive and on the cutting edge; if you have three
Chicanas, the department is in deep trouble, the program is going to the
perros, and there are no standards left. Moreover, the department has now
become a gynocracy and no white male will ever get a job there again. In
spite of this, our department has three Chicana professors. But as I look
around, I see disaster. (And I want you to understand that in what I have
to say I am not talking about myself.) My senior colleague has recently
been lured away to a university in Oregon, two junior colleagues in other
departments have not made it through their third-year and tenure-review
processes, and a third, having received ambivalent third-year reviews, is
leaving for another college. Junior Chicana colleagues in other universities have not received tenure (I know of at least three). I do not see these
scholars being replaced on any level. I fervently hope there are younger
scholars making their way up the ladder. And I hope that there is an up-
coming generation of Chicana intellectuals who will survive. As we all
know, the demands on Chicana faculty members are very intense. It is
well known that in addition to publishing and research, we are expected
to be active in our communities, mentor students and each other, work on
Chicano and/or feminist agendas, and serve as token members of committees. We would also (how dare we!) like to have a personal life. Some of us
are single mothers, trying to raise young children on our own; others opt
to have children; others make choices in the face of reality—we know we
must and should publish, but we don't. The Cenicienta Syndrome? The
community asks us why, as academics and role models, we don't do more
for the community, not understanding that the university and its students
is also a community, an extremely demanding one. We try to satisfy on

all fronts. And sometimes we fail. Sometimes we are called elitists, *que qué nos creemos* (who do we think we are)? And still, sometimes we do what is expected of us . . . everything, and it is not enough.

In 1990 sociologist Mary Romero interviewed twenty-one Chicana faculty members about their academic jobs, and what she discovered was depressing. I am briefly going to share her findings with you. The late 1980s, the era of affirmative action and multicultural change, was when many Chicanas were hired, but often life for our academics has been difficult. In her study Romero found that Chicana academics face an uphill struggle. First there is an internalized stereotype on the part of the university that women of color are unable to be professionals. This comes about when those who have been in control feel threatened and undermined, along with the notion that an "affirmative action" hire is not as good as everyone else. The women are at times forced into male models of behavior and may be asked to sever ties between the collective self and become a "university" person, or are given contrasting and discrepant messages. Because there is lack of diversity, often the academic is the only Chicana. There is a feeling of loneliness and exclusion, and our academics are not incorporated into existing support networks. This was particularly true among the women if they were perceived as an affirmative-action hire. In addition, the women felt the burden of being on display as the ethnic person. As one Chicana stated, "Too often we're railroaded into not only servicing everything but reforming everything. Everyone comes to us. When you're hired as a minority faculty member you become the representative of the University, so you're usually brought out at every function on display. Even just to parade you in front of the parents and visiting administrators. That's one level. At another level you're inundated with students" (Romero, 151). Often we don't know whether we are agents of social change or whether we are maintaining the status quo. We are hired to teach the curriculum of tomorrow in traditional and conservative departments, so the canon wars start. Moreover, when students get our perspective for the first time, they think it is militant and radical: they don't see it as a viable alternative; they see it as a minority perspective. Chicana/Chicano faculty are asked to do *all* the tasks in a department or program, many of which would be the traditional role of a faculty member, but not all of them together at the same time. And finally there is the feeling that the institutions are only creating the illusion of change, but not real change itself.

Last but not least, by any means, the university is still an "old boys'" club. We know this about general university politics, but we believe—naively so, I think—that our Chicano colleagues don't behave that way. After

all, NACCS is now the National Association for Chicana/Chicano Studies, isn't it? Nevertheless, habits of the past are hard to break, and movidas,
entretenimientos, y dinero still pass from bato to bato. Often it is still las
mujeres who do all the work and los hombres who get all the credit.

At the same time, our Chicana/Latina students are very demanding.
And they have a right to be. Often at the university for the first time, they
want their money's worth—and they expect time and energy from their
Chicana/o professors that they wouldn't dream of asking from others. I
believe it is our duty as role models and mentors to try to fulfill those
demands.

The ride on this caballo blanco is getting lumpier and lumpier. Let
me share with you some ideas of what we need to do to continue our
revolution. I have seen transformation and progress in the twenty or so
years I have been participating in NACCS. In the early years when just a
few Chicana graduate students were in school, we looked for support and
mentors, and there were none. No models, no guides to help us though
the mazes of power. Few women writers were taught in courses, and there
was no such thing as Chicano literature. Yet we looked around and saw
each other: our abuelitas and our mothers, although perhaps not formally
educated women, were women of great strength. They were survivors.
One such woman, for me, has been the poet and writer Margarita Cota-
Cárdenas, whom I met when we were students in graduate school. She
was also my guide into Chicana literature, as I published my first article
on Chicana literature on her poetry. This lack of mentors and guides has
changed: there are Chicanas in academia and in classroom texts (although
not as many as I would like). Yet I still hear tales that make me shudder:
that a prominent Chicana professor asks payment to write a letter for pro-
motion for a Chicana colleague (who wrote the prominent professor her
letters?), that another will not write a letter of support for a younger colleague, that another disparages the other Chicanas at her university. But
because I, Panchita Villa, am a revolutionary (an aging one, it is true), I
refuse to give in to despair and cynicism and so I issue El Plan Revolucionario de la Chicana!

First of all, and once again I say, we need to do our work: research and
writing. And let's follow through. We research the paper, we write the
paper (pues, no 'sta tan malo!), and then it sits in the cajón. No, rework it
and send it out to be published. Finish our dissertations within a reason-
able period of time. Publish our books, be kind to ourselves and others,
without letting go of standards.

Next, let's give ourselves a break! We are imperfect creatures, not supermujer. If our Chicana role models occasionally don't have time to be role models, let's not say, behind their backs, "Híjole, she never has time to talk to me," or worse, "She doesn't support Chicanas at all." (I have heard both said about Chicana colleagues.) Let's be open-minded to other Chicanas, after all *we* are not el enemigo—just because someone doesn't agree with you, it doesn't mean that she may not have her own experiences or her own perspectives on an issue. I have heard some Chicanas make judgments about others that they are vendidas because they don't work in the community or because they are not in agreement on an issue. We are not an essentialist, monolithic entity; we are Chicanas/Latinas with varying experiences, varying perspectives, varying backgrounds, and problems. We should show our respeto for each other, for there is more than enough work to do and we all have our abilities, our own special talents. Don't let us pick each other apart.

As a student, don't tune out, not go to class, not turn in assignments. Instead rededicate yourselves with focus and energy. Challenge: learn to be diplomatic and persistent. Tell your role models how much you appreciate them, let them know they have been important to you, keep them posted on your éxitos as well as los fracasos.

To faculty, don't forget who you are, that your community is the university as well as the community; take time out if you need to, but when you are there, focus. Remember the ones who come after you as well as the ones who came before. Hold everyone accountable, even yourself.

As for those outside the Chicana community, hold our male colleagues responsible for responsible action. Our Anglo colleagues, too (don't always be the one to speak out against injustice; make them responsible). Form coalitions.

Even the Scarlet Horseman was not able to do it by herself. We need to treat each other with respect for varying positions, maintain our mutual obligations, and to rededicate ourselves with energy to all the different tasks we need to do, recognizing that some of us are better at community involvement, others at writing, others at mentoring students. We need to continue to bond with each other and look to each other for support, be true comadres, recognizing that we can't do everything. We need to support our writers, our activists, our role models in every way that we can. We need to make sure that our women scholars also get the nourishment they need. We must buy the bilingual children's books of Gloria Anzaldúa, Pat Mora, Carmen Lomas Garza, and Lucha Corpi and give them to the children we know instead of candy and toys.

In all of the struggle and chaos, there are some hopeful signs.

1. I am encouraged when I see more Chicana students than ever before taking Spanish, Chicana literature, history, and sociology courses, going into education as well as business, trying their hands at creative work. I see Chicana art historians, museum curators, and young women in many fields exploring their heritage and trying their wings. If as just one teacher I have had one thousand students, can the flood be far behind?

2. Many old boys and girls will be retiring from colleges and universities in the next few years, so it is a good time to be an intellectual. There might be a glut of academics, but there is no glut of Chicana/o academics.

3. There is a sense of excitement for all the creative energy that has developed.

4. Our cultural, social, and political critics are also rising to the occasion with an outpouring of creative and analytic material.

We need, however, to have the courage to persist and maintain lines of inquiry that are not mainstream, and we must continue to theorize from within, not forgetting from where we come. And, above all, we must remember that Panchita Villa continues to ride; she is there on the top of the monte, on her caballo blanco, beckoning us on to follow her, and her scarlet cape is gently blowing in the wind.

THREE

Women Writers, New Disciplines, and the Canon (2000)

I started late.[1] I was forty-two when I received my Ph.D. in 1979. I had had many lives before I went back to school as a graduate student to study Latin American literature. Actually, going back to graduate school was one of the better things I have done in my life. Not only did I come in contact with exciting ideas and intellectual challenges, the world had changed since I had been in college. Or perhaps I hadn't started so late. Even in college I was struggling against disciplines and against established canons. When I was a senior at Connecticut College for Women in 1959, majoring in Spanish, I decided to write an honors thesis, one of the options the department allowed. The head of the department was a Spaniard, a peninsular specialist whose name shall remain anonymous. He was fond of spending class time talking about how he would drink wine in the cafés of Madrid with such notable writers as Federico García Lorca, Ramón Valle Inclán, and others. You know the type. Of the other two professors in the department, one was an instructor who taught basic languages because she had never finished her Ph.D., and the other was a Latin Americanist. In his classes we studied the prominent and often boring writers of the nineteenth and early twentieth centuries (this was before the great boom in Latin American literature), and so I read novels by male writers who are virtually unread today. The only women we read were the so-called great "poetesses" (heaven forbid they would be called poets): one poem, "Hombres Necios," by the great seventeenth-century Mexican nun Sor Juana Inés de la Cruz, in which she chastises men for their infidelities and double standards, and one poem by the early twentieth-century Argentine poet Alfonsina Storni, in which she criticizes men for their infidelities and double standards. Oh, and a great novel, *Doña Bárbara,* written by Rómulo Gallegos, where the central character is seen as the devourer of men and dies in the end. In college in the 1950s, I never understood why she was so angry at men because a crucial scene, where she is raped, had been edited out of the student edition we read. I guess young women at a genteel girls' school should not have known about those things.

Well, because it was an option, I decided to write a thesis, not about women writers (at the time that would not even have occurred to me) but about two Latin American male poets I considered interesting: José Santos Chocano, a mestizo poet from Peru who sang about the Indians, their culture, and civilization as the founding discourse of the Peruvian nation, and Nicolás Guillén, a mulatto poet from Cuba who wrote about the struggles of blacks. I did research, wrote my thesis, and was denied honors. Perhaps my thesis was not very good. But the official reason given to me was that Latin American literature was not on the same level as peninsular literature and thus not deserving of study.

Time went on. I was back in graduate school, and one of my first classes at the University of Arizona in 1973 (after the civil rights movement, the Chicano movement, and the feminist movement) was a course, the first of its kind, on Latin American women writers. What a revelation! These women were strong and powerful; they wrote poems about things other than men and their infidelities, and they spoke to me. I wrote my dissertation on one of the women, Rosario Castellanos, a fabulous Mexican poet who, as we say in Spanish, "no tenía pelos en la lengua" (she had no hairs on her tongue), meaning that she was forthright and said whatever she needed to say. Beyond this revelation in this class, one of my classmates was the Chicana poet Margarita Cota-Cárdenas. It was Margarita who invited me to a student poetry reading where she was reading her poems. I had never conceived of such a thing as Chicano literature, but in 1973 this new discipline was fermenting, passionate, revolutionary. And of course, my interest was piqued and has never waned. Clearly, once Latin American literature became accepted, women writers had to struggle to establish their place in it. Then the minority literatures, such as Chicano literature, had to struggle to find their place within American literature. And the women, then, had to struggle to claim their rightful place within Chicano literature. At the beginning, this was very difficult, as the Chicano movement was dominated by men. It was the men who were planning the Revolution in the living room while the women did the work. As a poem from Margarita states:

> he's very much aware now
> and makes fervent Revolution
> so his children
> and the masses
> will be free

but his woman
    in every language
    has only begun to ask
    —y yo querido   viejo
    and ME?
    (*Marchitas,* 42)

But I was intrigued by the writing done by women. It was compelling, it was passionate, it was a search for voice. However, among the first important Chicano publications published by Quinto Sol Press, only one woman was included, Estela Portillo Trambley. But just as Margarita was publishing her poetry in chapbooks, paid for by herself, other women, students at universities, were doing the same. I began collecting material. When I began, I didn't mean to create an anthology. In some senses I do think anthologies create canons, what you choose ratifies certain writers and leaves others out. If I had thought that far ahead, with all its implications, I might have been so intimidated that I never would have started. No, at the beginning I was just collecting things I liked.

In 1978 Eliana Rivero of the University of Arizona, who had been my professor in that first Latin American Women Writers class, and later my dissertation director, got together a group of scholars to solicit funds to write a book of literary criticism on Chicana literature. Although our grant application to NEH was initially turned down, Eliana and I continued working on the project. My job was to collect material, which was a challenge in itself. In 1978 there were not many women published; as I mentioned, Estela Portillo Trambley was the exception. Other writers such as Sandra Cisneros, Pat Mora, and Denise Chávez were just beginning to publish, with Arte Público Press, although they had been writing for some time. With a grant from the University of Nevada, Reno, where I was teaching, I was able to spend a summer going to the main libraries where I thought I might find materials. I returned that summer in a state of shock, having discovered that only a few libraries, such as UC–Berkeley, were collecting Chicano/a literature. As I stated, at that time, most of the material was to be found in small publications: self-published chapbooks, small press distribution, and a few Chicano literary journals. The ephemeral materials published by the authors themselves, or with help from friends, often numbered one hundred copies, were given away to family and friends, and were in danger of disappearing. I collected whatever I could, made photocopies of the rest, and began diligently to buy first books of whatever Chicana writers I could find. I collected texts for about five years (by this time the project had dwindled to just Eliana and myself), and, as we read texts and separated them into themes and subject matter, it became clear that there were certain themes and representations that occurred time and time again in the texts. We therefore divided the texts into sections, hoping to find some coherence in them. At this point we were still thinking of using the texts as the basis for a book of literary criticism.

As we proceeded, it became clear to me that no book of literary criticism would be useful if the texts were not available to read and compare. Since we were proceeding very slowly on the critical book, we decided to go ahead on some sort of anthology. We divided the texts into sections: foremothers, self and identity, self and others, spaces, myths and archetypes, writers on language and writing, growing up, and celebrations. What we wanted was to give the texts in these different sections some sort of coherence. We hoped that texts on the same themes—for example, myths and archetypes—not only would show the wide variety of representation on such topics but also would talk to each other. Thus, in *Infinite Divisions,* the anthology, there are seven texts on Malinche, almost all of which subvert the traditional representations of her. Malinche is the native Mexicana who became Hernán Cortés's translator and later his mistress. Although the voice of the historical Malinche does not exist, in these texts she speaks in her own voice, she is sarcastic toward Cortés, and she questions the role traditional society has given her. Margarita Cota-Cárdenas says of her, "Are you Malinche a malinche? Who are you (who am I malinche)? Seller or buyer? Sold or bought and at what price? What is it to be what so many shout say sold-out malinche who is who are/are we what? At what price without having been there" (*Infinite,* 103). What became clear in this literature was that the myths and archetypes became the representations that Chicanas wanted to see for themselves.

In addition to the sections, we needed to write headings to explain the texts. Neither Eliana nor I wanted them to exist in a "New Criticism" vacuum without a context. And finally there was the greatest task of all: I had to write the introduction for the book, an introduction that would firmly place the writings of Chicanas in a historical and cultural context. This was an enormous problem because such a history had never been written before. I started working with traditional literary texts and history books, which featured men and which in one small paragraph would mention a woman's name, or something that women had done. In the introduction I talked about being a literary archeologist, but in fact I was inventing a tradition, dismantling/deconstructing the stories I was reading, and reconstructing and inserting the names and activities of the writers known to us. We started with the oral narratives of Hispanas housed in the Bancroft Library and stories from the Hispanic New Mexican WPA tradition. By the time I reached the 1960s, I felt I was on firmer ground: there was a lot of material to talk about; it just had to be organized, and we had done most of that by creating the anthology. At this point in 1991 there was not yet much literary or historical analysis on Chicana literature, and I did a lot of talking about the emerging literature. But finally it was done. I had asked a lot of questions, skirted a lot of issues, and hoped that eventually scholarship would fill in the lacunae. I know now that the anthology filled a great need and established Chicana literature, in fact created sort of a canon.

Just as critical books have some sort of ideology behind them, Eliana and I too had an ideology that we wanted to express in the anthology. First we wanted to show that there was a strong if emerging tradition of Chicana writing and that these texts were not only innovative but also powerful. Second we wanted to demonstrate how Chicana writers were seizing their voices and creating their own subjectivities. Third we wanted to insert this writing into the canons of not only American literature but Chicano literature as well. And finally I, in particular, wanted to illustrate how the Mexican tradition of women writing and women as role models had inscribed itself so strongly onto what we could now call the Chicana tradition. I am not sure that this ideology was evident when we started the project, but it certainly was clear when we finished. Once the anthology was finished and published, I went on to write a critical book based on the material collected, *Women Singing in the Snow: A Cultural Analysis of Chicana Literature.*

What has been the effect of *Infinite Divisions* on Chicano and American literature? Have we created a canon? I think that the anthology strongly demonstrated that there was an exciting, powerful, and creative tradition that had connections and a common base, even if the individual textual creations were different. As I look at other Chicana/Latina anthologies recently published, I recognize that many of those editors did not have the same access to the primary materials as I had. They, of course, have access to different materials, but I am often surprised to see the same five or six pieces that were originally chosen by Eliana and myself reappear again and again in anthologies, often with my English translations of the original Spanish. So unwittingly we did create some sort of canon by the mere selections of texts. But beyond that, I hope the anthology has enabled students and scholars to find a place in which to start, to fill in the missing and invented spaces, to discover new writers and texts, and to recognize the inventive writing worlds that they inhabit.

What would I do over? I would double the size of the anthology to include more writers, or perhaps issue a second volume. I would put dates next to the pieces so they could be placed in their proper historical context. And I would rewrite my introduction in order to see whether, in the intervening years, many of my questions have been answered.

And so you see, my professor did me a favor when he denied me honors in Spanish because I was writing about a literature that was not worthy. He made me so mad that I have been struggling against "traditional" disciplines ever since. (And I too often sit in cafés, restaurants, and bars and drink wine with famous authors: Margarita Cota-Cárdenas, Norma Cantú, Denise Chávez, Demetria Martínez, Helena María Viramontes, Pat Mora, and others. Las hermanas de mi corazón.)

FOUR   *The Politics of Poetics*

OR, WHAT AM I, A CRITIC,
DOING IN THIS TEXT ANYHOW? (1987)

In the essay "Retrieving Our Past, Determining Our Future," poet Pat Mora chose to begin with a pre-Columbian poem:

> Also they grow cotton
> of many colors:
> red, yellow, pink,
> purple, green, bluish-green,
> blue, light green,
> orange, brown and dark gold.
> These were the colors of the cotton itself.
> It grew that way from the earth,
> no one colored it.
> And also they raised these
> fowl of rare plumage:
> small birds the color of turquoise,
> some with green feathers,
> with yellow, with flame-colored breasts.
> Every kind of fowl
> that sang beautifully,
> like those that warble in the mountains.
> (LEÓN-PORTILLA, 41)

Mora chose this poem because she liked the images of music, color, and nature. But then she is a poet. I would like to underscore Mora's choice and begin with some definitions.[1]

Politics: intrigue or maneuvering within a group; one's position or attitude on political subjects. *Poetics*: literary criticism dealing with the nature, form, and laws of poetry; a study of or treatise on poetry or aesthetics. *Criticism*: the art, skill, or profession of making discriminating judgments, especially of literary or artistic works; detailed investigation of the origin and history of literary documents. *Discourse*: to run about; to speak at length; the process or power of reasoning.

My understanding several months ago was that this symposium, "Chicana Creativity and Criticism: Charting New Frontiers in American Literature," would undertake a dialogue between Chicana creative writers and Chicana literary critics with regard to several topics: Are Chicana critics friends or foes to the writers? What function do or can we Chicana critics play in relationship to our literature? And, what the heck are we doing in and to these texts anyway? As Chicanas we are all in this *revoltura* and explosion of literature and poetics together. It is time, perhaps, to take a step back and analyze where we are and where we might be going.

I do not mean the remarks I am about to make to be anti-intellectual, anti-theoretical, or anti-aesthetic. Nor do I mean to assume the position of any critic other than myself. Nor am I criticizing the work of any particular literary critic. Nevertheless, I am commenting on what I see as a general phenomenon, one that we need to take stock of and one that affects Chicano male critics as well as the females. Juan Bruce-Novoa, in his article "Canonical and Noncanonical Texts," thinks that there is now a "body of work" that constitutes Chicano literature and is recognized as such. He recognizes that previously "any mention of canon was clearly understood as a reference to mainstream literature." He adds, "To state we were excluded from the canon was to utter the obvious. Moreover, there was an ironic sense of worth associated with being outside the canon, almost a feeling of purity, because beyond the exclusionary ethnocentrism implied by *The Canon,* Chicanos infused the term with a criticism of the very existence of a privileged body of texts" (Bruce-Novoa, *Retropace,* 132).

It seems to me that in spite of the explosion of creative and critical activity on the part of both critics and writers, Chicana writers and critics are still within a framework of marginality among Chicano writing as well as in mainstream writing. Some of this may be attributed to time—that is, time for the maturing of our literature as well as of our criticism. In addition to the creation of new insights and perspectives, we are also at a moment of rupture in which we are just beginning to look back to uncover our traditions, whether they be written or oral, and to talk back—to unsay what had been said and frozen in time and place. We are at the moment of questioning everything, even ourselves. Only when it is accomplished can we, with clear conscience, proceed toward some understanding of critical difference.

At a 1987 Chicano studies conference in Salt Lake City it became clear
that, for the past several years, social scientists and literary critics alike
have been engaged in a desperate search for a theoretical/critical discourse
in which to situate what is happening to us. There have been discourses
and counter-discourses. We talk about historical/materialist perspectives,
transformative perspectives, pluralism (which some called a pre-prostituted
dominant discourse)—and the word "hegemony" was used in one session
alone thirty-two times. Some of the talks began with a few of the questions to be asked, then discussed the methods used to answer those questions, mostly the methods used. I would say a typical talk could be summarized in the following way. The speaker begins, "This paper will focus
on the ideology of cultural practice and its modes of signifying." S/he
then spends twenty minutes discussing how the works of whatever theoretical great s/he selects will define, inform, and privilege the work s/he
is doing. Such names as Jameson, Said, Williams, Hall, Burke, and other
contemporary *meros meros* (mostly male) will be invoked over and over.
The speaker is then sent a note by the chair of the panel that there is no
time left. And whatever the Chicano/a writing or phenomena that were
to be discussed are quickly summarized in two minutes. The talk is over.
We have talked so much about theory that we never get to our conclusion
or focus on the texts. By appropriating mainstream theoreticians and critics we have become so involved in intellectualizing that we lose our sense
of our literature and therefore our vitality. This priority of placing our
literature in a theoretical framework to "legitimize" it, if the theory over-
shadows it, in effect undermines our literature or even places it, once again,
in a state of oblivion. Privileging the theoretical discourse de-privileges
ourselves.

In puzzling over this scenario, which in fact occurred many times in
Salt Lake, one would be left with various insights about what is happening
to us:

1. We have so internalized the dominant ideology that only by talking
theory (construed as a superior form of logic) can we make our literature
and our cultural practices intellectually viable—that is, acceptable within
the traditional academic canon as "legitimate."

2. We are trying to impress ourselves and others with our ability to
manipulate theoretical discourse, to use buzzwords such as "hegemony,"
"signifying," and even the word "discourse." Someone once said to me,
"You are so articulate. You are able to talk in *their* language." I am not sure
what this means. On the one hand, they may be telling me that I am totally
assimilated, or they may, in reality, be saying that no Chicana can truly be

articulate. (I myself often feel that it is only our baroque *conceptismo* that has been transferred into English.)

3. We have entered into the "Age of Criticism," which could be defined as a preoccupation with theoretical structures often not internalized: we feel that theory is power.

4. We have a genuine desire to look beyond the elements (the texts) to the conditions that structured them. We are truly in search of a theoretical framework that yet eludes us, or at least some of us (and I count myself among those eludees).

I would like to outline some of the problems that I think we Chicana critics face, or that at least I, as a critic in training, think about from time to time. They often as not deal with the question, what *am I* doing in this text anyhow?

1. First of all, I am a reader. But I am not just a reader. My job, as a university professor, is to bring the attention of my students to the text itself. How can I do this if the text is not included in the general course curriculum and the anthologies, or is not in any way accessible to the student or to the population at large? Perhaps my primary responsibility, therefore, is the promulgation of the works of these writers, to make the writers known. We all know that the material production of Chicana writers is often limited to chapbooks, journals, and the few that are accepted as books by Arte Público Press and Bilingual Press. It is limited even to the Chicano reading audience and from one region to the next, from one big city to the next; we may not know what is happening. The work being done by Juan Rodríguez (Relámpago Press), Third Woman Press, and the Centro de Escritores de Aztlán, for example, helps, but as these texts go out of print the production becomes more difficult to find. At Salt Lake City a copy of the first printing of Quinto Sol's *El Grito* was proudly held up as the rarity it has become. Of the chapbooks that were produced in the sixties, seventies, and eighties, many will end up in a rare-book room in a library if we are fortunate. Fortunate because they will be preserved as artifacts—the same phenomenon that will make the books even more inaccessible.

If this product is inaccessible to those who are its targets, in terms of interest, it is virtually unavailable to a larger audience. The role of the Chicana critics then becomes one of facilitator: reproducing and making known the texts of our authors. In itself this may not be an insignificant task since, for example, in a recent struggle with some of my coauthors (not the editors) of a book published by Yale University Press, I was told that my method of writing—that is, including entire poems written by Chicanas instead of dissecting them by including between slashes "pertinent" quotes from the text—made my article "hard to read" and "jumpy." While this may be true of my *own* writing, it certainly was not true of those texts of the authors I had included. I was very troubled by the inadequacies of a vision that presumed to have me speak for all Chicanas when they were perfectly able to speak for themselves. My arguments for entire text inclusion were the following: (a) these texts were unknown and therefore needed to be reproduced in their entirety; (b) these writers were more passionate, forceful, and graphic than I; and (c) I did not want to do to these writers what others have been doing to all of us for centuries—that is, to appropriate their discourse through my discourse. I commented that I had no problem with my strategy and if they were not happy with publishing my chapter as it was, I did not wish it to be included in the volume. Fortunately the article will be published in its jumpy entirety in *The Desert Is No Lady,* whose title poem is by Pat Mora (Rebolledo, 96–124).

2. The second function of a critic may be to analyze the content of the literary production—stepping back from the product in order to see what may be the dominant concern and themes. I myself have indulged in this type of descriptive thematic analysis (adding, I hope, some analysis in depth as to cultural context and history). One example is a paper I wrote on *abuelitas,* noting the scope and complexity of this recurring figure and offering an explanation as to why this figure was approaching what I considered to be mythic proportions. This article has brought mixed reviews. My secretary, who was typing it, asked to take it home to read to her children, and many others have used it in their classrooms for teaching. Recently a contemporary writer remarked to me about critics writing descriptively about things that "everyone already knew about," such as abuelitas. Yet descriptive thematic analysis serves its purpose, too, particularly as it grows in sophistication and as historical and cultural analyses are linked to it. I hope that as I have grown as a scholar since my abuelitas article was published, my analysis has, too.

3. Another important current function for us as critics is to remember our literary history. While contemporary writers may feel that they are seeing the world anew, those of us who are searching out our literary roots are finding women writers who were raising many of the same concerns women voice today—written in a different tone and style and conforming to a different mode; nevertheless, contemporary writers have not arisen from a complete void. If the written word did not survive in enough texts to be known today, nonetheless the oral forms of women's concerns, of

women's images have lived in the tradition from one generation, from one century to another. Thus the critic as literary historian is able to fill in the lacunae and to connect the past and the present.

4. Chicana literary discourse, like most feminist discourse, is a troubled one. It is always searching, questioning, and fraught with tensions and contradictions, just as is the creative writing arising from the same creative context. A truly Chicana literary theory would result from the attempt to resolve these things, to mend the rift between doers and thinkers. I think we would all agree that Chicana criticism and theory are still in a state of flux, looking for a theoretical, critical framework that is our own, whatever the perspective. I personally find it difficult to have theory (male oriented, French feminist, poststructural, or whatever is the current fad) dictate what we find in our literature. I prefer to have the literature speak for itself and, as a critic, try to organize and understand it. Perhaps from a more open perspective our own theoretical, critical analysis will arise, rather than finding the theory first and imposing it upon the literature.

Recently several Chicana critics have taken up the issue of a theoretical approach to our literature. Norma Cantú in "The Chicana Poet and Her Audience: Notes Towards a Chicana Feminist Aesthetic" acknowledges the lack of a methodological approach in our work but feels that it is a sense of place and world as embedded in particular language use that the Chicana poet communicated to her Chicana audience. For Cantú it is the special relationship between writer and listener, the shared cultural referents that make the poems work. Norma Alarcón, in her perceptive study on the image of La Malinche, reevaluates and reconstructs the symbolic and figurative meaning this figure holds for us as Chicana writers and critics, dealing with the significance of language and silence within our literature (Alarcón, 356–369). She also sees significant evolution of the Chicana as "speaking subject," one who brings within herself her race, class, and gender, expressing them from a self-conscious point of view. Both of these critics, it seems to me, in addition to being theoretically well grounded, look at the literature from within, in an integrative sense.

5. It is very difficult to work on living authors: authors who read what you write and agree or don't agree. But it is just as difficult to work on authors no longer living. In the practice of literary criticism one (or perhaps I speak for myself only) must practice sound and honorable as well as rigorous criticism. That is, facts must be checked, scholarship must be sound. There is always the danger that the critic, immersed in perusing some essential point, will become overenthusiastic and confuse the autho-

rial voice with that of the narrative or poetic voice. If structuralism has taught us anything at all, it is that the lyric/narrative speaker is just that. As critics we must be careful not to confuse author with speaker.

When dealing with a vigorously living author we must also not be too timid to analyze symbolically what we, as critics, may see in the text—that which the author may not consciously have intended. We know that there are many levels of symbolic discourse that we may not be aware of at any given moment. When the text is published, when the author gives it up to the public domain, it is released and opened up to interpretation by the reader. It exists on its own, separate from the author. The textual interpretation, therefore, is one of integration between the authorial intent, and the text itself, *and* the third (and separate) interpretation or grasping of those two aspects by the reader.

6. We must, as critics, also be careful in our criticism to be honest. I think Chicana critics are often too benign. Our close network between writers and critics makes it difficult to have caustic criticism (which might ruin friendships), but at the same time we may hesitate to be as critical as we should be. One way I know I cope with this, and I imagine others have the same problem, is simply to ignore those texts I don't like, of writers that I do like, or to ignore those writers who say nothing to me. This seems to me to be a function of human nature. What is important, however, is that the critic be conscious of her biases. And while we women may be benign to each other, there are still many Chicano critics who refuse to recognize their own biases and misogyny. Raymond Paredes, in a recent review article, is only able to see Chicana literature through a particularly phallocentric focus. If we were to accept his views, we would see that "if there is one quality that runs consistently through *their* [emphasis mine] stories, plays and novels, it is the conviction that men know and care very little about women and that everyone is the worse for it" (Paredes, 126). His review continues with the assumption that men are the focus of Chicana literature as he assails Beverly Silva, Cherríe Moraga, and Ana Castillo as extremely flawed writers. Their work, he says, is more interesting "ideologically" than aesthetically. Back to the old notion of "Are They Any Good?" Those writers whose perspectives Paredes does not agree with he considers superficial, and Denise Chávez, with whom he is more in agreement, is merely "flawed" (128).

7. Perhaps more dangerous than ignoring texts we dislike is excluding the works of authors whose perspective we do not share or whose perspective we might feel uncomfortable with. Here I mean specifically the perspective of sexual preference. There are some fine lesbian writers such

as Cherríe Moraga, Gloria Anzaldúa, and Veronica Cunningham whose works are often excluded (although less so recently) from our critical thinking. Certainly if critics are serious about historical, cultural, and gender context, then all writers need to be included within the general cultural framework. Then too some critics feel more comfortable with socially conscious literature and exclude that coming from the middle class. As the complexities and shades of our literature grows, we must be careful not to canonize a certain few to the exclusion of other equally fine writers.

8. While some scholars see the need for some resolution of dichotomies—for example, of Chicana and feminist, Chicana and poet, as if they were mutually exclusive—others examine the relationship between dominant and ethnic communities. The dominant discourse, if we internalize it, would have us believe that we function under such labels, and to some extent we do. I believe, however, as Bernice Zamora so succinctly expressed it, that our complexities are infinite: that we have grown up and survived along the edges, along the borders of so many languages, worlds, cultures, and social systems that we constantly fix and focus on the spaces in between, Nepantla, as Sor Juana would have seen it. Categories that try to define and limit this incredibly complex process at once become diminished for their inability to capture and contain. Those of us who try to categorize these complexities inevitably fail.

Margarita Cota-Cárdenas in her novel *Puppet* examines the way in which this dichotomous ideology is imposed. She sees this in part as arising from a single vision of what being Chicana should be: "Are you Malinche a malinchi? Who are you (who am I malinchi)? seller or buyer? sold or bought and at what price? What is it to be what so many shout say sold-out malinchi who is who are/are we what? at what price without having been there naming putting labels tags what who have bought sold malinchismo what other-ismos invented shouted with hate reacting striking like vipers like snakes THEIR EYES like snakes what who what" (Cota-Cárdenas, 93). Her Malinche breaks the silence of centuries, and she does not do so quietly: "yes yes I went yelling loud too why why and they said tie her up she's too forward too flighty she thinks she's a princess thinks she's her father's daughter thinks she's hot stuff that's it doesn't know her place a real threat to the tribe take her away haul her off she's a menace to our cause that's it only learned to say crazy things to say accuse with HER EYES and they didn't want then troublemakers in their country" (86). These labels, specific here to La Malinche but clearly extended to all Chicanas, are of course the very labels culture uses to restrict and limit women's activity, socially as well as intellectually. Women are so silenced that they are only left to speak with "their eyes." In a country defined as "their" country, one that does not belong to her, Cota-Cárdenas makes the connection between Mexico and the United States: "The country, well I suppose Mexico, Aztlán . . . ? Well, it could have been a little more to the north or a little more to the south, it makes no difference now, what I was telling you was my version, that's it, **my version as** . . . as a woman, that's right, and they can establish the famous dialectic with the other versions that you already know very well" (95). Cota-Cárdenas thus introduces the complexities, the ambiguities in our lives, and while she does not deny the legitimacy of the other versions (acknowledging them for what they are), she overlays another perspective that is hers alone.

These remarks I have made may seem to be arising from some simplistic assumptions. I myself was trained as a structuralist, semiotic critic. But increasingly I have become suspicious and yes, even bored, by a criticism that seems alien to the text about which it purports to talk, by a theoretical basis of patriarchal norms or a theory that does not take the particular concerns of minority writers and culture into account. I am suspicious of criticism that ignores the texts of our writers and turns the vitality and the passion of those texts into an empty and meaningless set of letters. This sort of criticism, it seems to me, might as well be analyzing a menu or a telephone directory, and would perhaps be better directed in doing so. As Sor Juana criticized Aristotle—he would have been a better philosopher had he studied cooking—I believe that our critical discourse should come from within, within our cultural and historical perspective. This is not to say that I am advocating limited, regional, small-minded descriptive literary analysis. But I think we should internalize and revolutionize theoretical discourse that comes from outside ourselves, accepting that which is useful and discarding that which is merely meant to impress. In the search for our own aesthetic, for our own analytical direction, we need to look to each other, to recognize that our literature and our cultural production does not need legitimization from the academy, that it already is legitimate in itself. Above all, we must not forget that the most important aspect of our analysis are the texts themselves. As we ask ourselves where are we, what are we doing, we must never appropriate into our own discourse the discourse of the writer herself. If we are to diffuse, support, promote, analyze, and understand the work of our writers, we must let them speak for themselves. As a critic I desire the same as poet Pat Mora: I want to see the cotton of many colors, the small birds the color of turquoise, and hear the birds that warble in the mountains.

FIVE

"Sprinkling Wildflower Seeds"

A PLÁTICA ABOUT CRITICAL PERSPECTIVES IN
CHICANA/LATINA LITERATURE (1998)

I begin with a quote from Pat Mora's *House of Houses*:

> The sensuality of gardeners and cooks. Women who but-
> ton their blouses to the neck, avert their eyes at bare curves
> and cleavage across a room or on canvas; such women in their
> kitchens and gardens release their senses to play. With firm
> hands, they knead bread dough and smell the drunk steam
> from cranberries simmering in port, with a tasting spoon sip
> the crimson concoction. They spread their fingers deep into
> warm beds they mulch on their knees outside, sprinkle wild-
> flower seeds and their headstrong surprises into the garden,
> bend into the honeysuckle's gold buzz and place the clear
> drop of nectar on their proper tongues, watch snails lazily
> revealing their skin.
>
> Such sensuality is sanctioned, even sacred when performed
> in the service of others, self-sacrifice a noble path for women,
> certainly in both Mexican and Church culture. But don't the
> physical pleasures themselves—tasting the wild orange wind,
> peering into the hibiscus' open mouth, hearing the tongued
> trees, smelling the heat of rising dough, stroking the plums'
> red curves—the private body pleasures also lure women to
> those kitchens and gardens?
>
> Sexual loves, poetry and song remind us, simmer in kitch-
> ens and gardens too, of course, two bodies with eyes, hands,
> mouths feasting on one another.
>
> These summer months women are intoxicated by the
> senses, by honeysuckle and loves real and imagined; old and
> new loves, unrequited.
>
> (MORA, *House,* 158–159)

Since the Chicana/Chicano movimiento of the 1960s there has been enormous activity in the creative area: poetry, essays, novels, cuentos, teatro, paintings, sculpture, and other endeavors (including conferences) have sprung forth as if from Athena's head or from Coatlicue's skirt, almost fully clothed like Huitlipochtli, the Sun God, reaching to race across the sky. This outpouring has, in turn, necessitated new critical perspectives and approaches to these outbursts of creativity. The writers and artists are forging ahead, sending out their antennae and radar and capturing their *medioambiente,* their *cultura,* their *sensualidad* in their work. As always they are the *delanteras,* the pathfinders, *las clarividentes,* the clairvoyants, the ones who truly see and who are able to articulate the sensuality, joys and ills, politics, and social problems of culture, society, and their own lives. We, as critics and *estudiosas,* are of necessity behind and justifiably so. After all, we are the *atrasaderas,* the ones who come after to compile, historicize, analyze, and debate the meaning and significance of those delanteras. As an atrasadera who tries to make meaning of the wonder of it all, I would like to briefly outline for you some of the directions and contemporary trends I see happening today in the analysis and criticism of Chicana literature, and also some of the problematic areas. I see myself as having been in this field a long time, perhaps I am getting *chocha* and cranky, but I would like to *platicar* a bit about what has been done, what we need to do, and about some *vacíos* I see.

First of all, I am elated that there is such a thing as Chicana literature, and so much of it, and so much of it is wonderful. Many years ago, in the ice ages when I was in graduate school at the University of Arizona, I never dreamed that there was writing that in so many ways reflected my life, my family, my food, my images, my stories. The first Chicana writing I was aware of was the poetry of my fellow student, Margarita Cota-Cárdenas, who invited me to a poetry reading. Most of those reading their creative work were graduate students. Now daily I turn around and there is another new and enticing adventure awaiting me. My reading here is Pat Mora's *House of Houses* (1997), a house in which ghosts, saints, Pat's family, and yes, even Pat herself, talk to each other, a house in which past and present merge in a skillful blending of poetry, family history and myths, and narration. The complexity and richness of Chicana literature is simply amazing.

In addition to the writers themselves, I see many new, young critics coming to the fore with wonderful seminar and conference papers and articles that leave me astounded by their insight and understanding. Several years ago I worried that all of us in the old guard, those who had trained in Peninsular and Latin American literature and in old-style English departments, but who had enthusiastically redirected and retrained ourselves to look at our amazing literature with new and fresh eyes, this old guard was getting tired, ready to take to our rocking chairs. Looking around, I didn't see new, young and energetic readers and critics (in particular, women) jockeying to take our places. I despaired of having a generation to follow us. No longer. I see more and more younger scholars writing creative, innovative articles and papers, more and more students both graduate and undergraduate in our classes and going to conferences. And I see our literature being mainstreamed into American literature, Spanish literature, ethnic studies, and even women's studies classes. Our literature is now included in major anthologies and collections such as, finally, *To Speak or Be Silent* (1993), *The Woman That I Am* (1994), *Through the Kitchen Window: Women Explore the Intimate Meanings of Food and Cooking* (1997), as well as in major publications of our own such as my *Infinite Divisions* (with Eliana Rivero; 1993) and *Goddess of the Americas/La Diosa de las Americas* (1996), edited by Ana Castillo. Sometimes we are included with other Latina writers such as in the *Hijas del Quinto Sol* anthology. Critics like Claire Joysmith, who edited *Las Formas de Nuestras Voces: Chicana and Mexicana Writers in Mexico* (1995), are introducing Chicana writers in Mexico. Our writers are written about, read, known. So for all this activity I am enthused and happy. Let me outline some directions in which I see critical perspectives going.

1. We continue our recuperation work. All over the country students and professors are working in the field doing oral interviews, in libraries, and in the archives to put together our literary histories. Stimulated by the Recovering the U.S. Hispanic Literary Heritage Project at the University of Houston, the recent publication of previously unpublished texts, fugitive texts (those published in small numbers and not reprinted until recently), and out-of-print texts has clarified what we suspected all along, that ephemeral materials previously thought lost or nonexistent do indeed exist and in abundance, that older, out-of-print texts have a market. Magnon's *The Rebel,* edited by Clara Lomas; the California Testimonials; two novels by María Amparo Ruiz de Burton, *Who Would Have Thought It?* and *The Squatter and the Don,* edited by Rosaura Sánchez and Beatrice Pita; *Mexican Village* by Josephine Niggli; and the work of Texas, Arizona, and New Mexico writers such as Fabiola Cabeza de Baca, Cleofas Jaramillo, and Jovita Gonzales are being reedited, recuperated, and studied by scholars. Oral histories, stories of immigration, the frontier and its multiple meanings, its hybridity, are being studied through ever-expanding

multiple lenses and with multiple perspectives. The sheer volume of this material is amazing.

2. Much of the older work as well as the contemporary work is being contextualized within its historical and cultural framework; thus we are better able to understand the environment and struggles out of which it grew. And as scholars continue this archaeological work, we begin to understand the cumulative trajectory of our literary and cultural history. Literary historians as well as students of popular culture are adding to our understanding of issues contemporary to their times.

3. Many of these older works are being studied from the viewpoint of the discursive strategies our writers have used to be able to insert themselves into narratives from which they had been marginalized, outcast, erased, forbidden, or otherwise forgotten. We are able to see, for example, how these women use, and used, their narrative power to insert themselves into culture and into history, in spite of being denied representation by mainstream and patriarchal culture.

4. We are studying how contemporary writers gain subjectivity and agency by using women's knowledge. Instead of a Herman Melville telling us tales of the sea, the ship, the instruments and maneuvers of the ship, the animals in the sea, how the men live on the ship, and how they know the weather—in sum a man's knowledge of science, a man's knowledge of the world—we see Norma Cantú in *Canícula* setting up her knowledge of the beauty parlor, the chemistry that a beautician needs to know, the precise maneuvers, knowledge, and experience she needs to have to get the job done; she gains authority precisely from her ability to articulate this precision. And in Denise Chávez's *Face of an Angel,* we see the waitress as a team player in a fugue, as a precise musician who coordinates the food-serving symphony. Our study of the domestic—food, recipes, quilt making, sewing, and makeup—also functions as an authoritative representation of the working side of a woman's life as well as her pleasures, giving value and authority to those women who do such work. This writing and study of the domestic and the workers' world and agency has opened a new, creative and vital world for our writers, our critics, and our students.

5. Our critics are adapting new theories with which to look at our literature and are creating new theories by which to analyze it. Two books that attempt to do this are Alvina Quintana's *Home Girls* (1996) and Annie O. Eysturoy's *Daughters of Self-Creation* (1996). Quintana has been, for some years now, articulating a theory for the representation of Chicana aesthetics. In *Home Girls* Quintana positions herself with personal anecdotes as a "home girl," thus becoming an "inside" ethnographer and at the

same time an informant to the literature. Quintana articulates what she considers to be four modes of Chicana literature: apology; rage; opposition, struggle, and identification; and finally new vision (39). Eysturoy focuses on the study of the novel of self-development, which she determines is both utilized in its traditional form and changed by Chicana writers. She demonstrates how Chicana writers subvert and revise the traditional *bildungsroman* in order to create space and authority for their heroines. For Eysturoy the Chicana creation of self can never be an individual one but must also connect with family, community, and traditions; this development she calls a *bildungsheld* or liberating self-creation. Both books are good examples of critics trying to define and create new ways to look at Chicana literature.

6. Interest in children's literature. As we understand the importance of libraries and books on and for children, our writers finally have the space to create such literature. Books by Gloria Anzaldúa, Pat Mora, Rudy Anaya, Sandra Cisneros, and Carmen Lomas Garza are filling the void we have had in children's literature. *Tomás and the Library Lady* by Pat Mora is a book that takes up the issue of the impact of libraries and books on children, the child being Tomás Rivera in Mora's story. Our authors have always understood the value of children seeing themselves reflected in the literature, and as more and more Latinas write children's books, we scholars and critics need to analyze and comment on them. Moreover, we need to support our writers in this effort by buying the books and giving them to all the children we know.

7. Finally, I see our students and critics doing new and radical readings of texts: they link the personal with the political; they study the impact of immigration, violence, and politics on our literature. They are folklorists and ethnographers; they study testimonials. Our critics disseminate and propagate our literature. They see how our writers write their sexuality, their language, their textuality. We are, I hope, creating reciprocal spaces where we will all feel safe to be, centered and vitalized. The study of hybridity, mestizaje, whiteness, brownness—all can only contribute to an elaboration of the richness of our literature and, it is my hope, to the richness, profundity, and complexity of our analysis. We are placing that clear drop of nectar on our tongues.

Okay, now to the problematic parts.

8. The problem with publishing, or how to cure my boredom. As part of the academic world in which we live, we all know the routine: we find something we enjoy, we find a theory by which to analyze it, we spend two or three or perhaps more years writing the dissertation (*pues ya merito*

merito acabo), we rewrite the dissertation, perhaps adding a few interesting things to it so it won't sound like a dissertation. We submit it to a press, it takes six months for readers to read it (if we're lucky). The press says they will publish it but you need to rewrite it (this takes six more months to a year). Another year goes by, and the book is out! How many years have gone by? Is it still vital? Fresh? Interesting? Or is it *ya pasadita*? I must confess I am somewhat bored by academic books, certainly including my own. I want criticism that is vital, provocative, insightful. As presses close down, as publishing venues dry up, where and how are we going to get our information? I think we need to have a publication on the order of the *New York Review of Books,* but not incestuous, male, and stuffy, where we could ease our intellectual isolation, read hot new reviews of hot new books, publish provocative articles and profound and scandalous poems, argue with each other (*pero con respeto, claro*). We need to communicate and dialogue in new ways. *Lo merecemos, verdad?*

9. Why don't we take risks? As Cherríe Moraga said to me during an Hijas del Quinto Sol conference, we don't get rewarded for taking risks. If we critics and writers write strong and visionary stuff, the likelihood is we'll get fired, criticized, and/or have no friends at all. We need to go out on a limb in our writing, in our analysis, in our criticism. How do we do this? How do we do this in a way that is supportive to our goals and not destructive? How do we do this in a way that is also visionary?

10. Many Chicana scholars and writers feel isolated. How can we diminish our sense of isolation? During the conference and at our evening "Tequilazos," I looked at all the strong and powerful women around us—writers, critics, scholars, and students. I felt a sense of communication. But the truth of the matter is, when we are back in our universities and in our communities, many of us feel alone and isolated, lone voices struggling to survive. Over and over our writers tell me they feel their work is not given value, that no one is listening. And the irony is that it is precisely this writing that is supposed to provide the communication. What can we do about this? For one thing, I think we need to write to our writers to let them know that we appreciate what they are doing, the risks that they are taking. We need to let them know that we are engaged and we are listening, that we *are* lured to their kitchens and gardens.

11. Have we been able to create a theory of our own? We continue to use theory that is useful, and certainly Gloria Anzaldúas's *Borderlands* has been an important model, but is it enough? As our writers themselves slip back and forth between writing and criticism, perhaps new models will

emerge, and as critics themselves become more adelateras and claravidentes, we may have homegrown models of our own.

I certainly have no answers to these problematics. I believe that we have made some gains in our cultural trajectories, but there is so much more ahead. I do know for sure, however, that "these summer months women are intoxicated by the senses, by honeysuckle and loves real and imagined; old and new loves, unrequited" (Mora, *House,* 159). But as Mora says, "Poetry and song remind us . . . they release our senses to play, to create, and to imagine." I will leave it to you, the present generation, to release your wildflower seeds to their widest and wildest potential and possibilities—I hope to see the results of their bloomings.

SIX

Reconstructing Sor Juana's Library

TWENTY YEARS OF CHICANA LITERARY
REPRESENTATION (1999)

$\int$or Juana Inés de la Cruz, Mexico's brilliant and intellectual seventeenth-century nun, loved books. She loved reading and thinking. One of the reasons she entered the convent, as she tells us in her
Respuesta (Letter of Response), is that she had no "inclination" toward
marriage and in the convent she would have time to read and study. Over
the years, as was allowed to nuns if they were so inclined, she had acquired
an extensive library; in fact it was one of the premier libraries in colonial
Mexico, rivaled perhaps only by that of Carlos Siguenza y Góngora, also
a philosopher and thinker. At one time the abbess of Sor Juana's convent,
who "believed that study was a thing of the Inquisition," commanded her
not to study, and Sor Juana obeyed, as she tells us: "I did not take up a
book; but that I did study not at all is not within my power to achieve, and
this I could not obey, for though I did not study in books, I studied all the
things that God had wrought, reading in them, as in writing and in books,
all the workings of the universe" (Peden, 58). Books for Sor Juana were
very important, however, in particular books by and for women, although
in her time there could not have been many. She says,

> I confess, too, that though it is true, as I have stated, that I
> had no need of books, it is nonetheless also true that they
> have been no little inspiration, in divine as in human letters.
> Because I find a Debbora administering the law, both military
> and political, and governing a people among whom there
> were many learned men . . . I see adored as a goddess of the
> sciences a woman like Minerva . . . An Aspasia Milesia, who
> taught philosophy and rhetoric, and who was a teacher of
> the philosopher Pericles, . . . a Jucia, a Corinna, a Cornelia;
> and, finally, a great throng of women deserving to be named,
> some as Greeks, some as muses, some as seers; . . . for all were

nothing more than learned women, held, and celebrated as
such by antiquity.
(PEDEN, 64–66)

Although Sor Juana survived the order to curtail her intellectual activities, at the end of her life she turned more to her religious duties and
dispersed her library. Her translator, Margaret Sayers Peden, says,

> Parting with her beloved books must have been the most
> painful act of Sor Juana's life. Some have speculated that the
> number of volumes contained in her library may have been
> as high as four thousand. This seems unlikely, since this is
> almost the total number of books imported into New Spain
> during Sor Juana's lifetime. But it was a famous collection.
> We can see some of the titles in one of the best-known of her
> portraits. . . . A few of the books were retained in the con-
> vent for the use of her sisters, but most were sold, along with
> her collection of musical and mathematical instruments. The
> proceeds were distributed among the poor.
> (12–13)

Given Sor Juana's predilection for creative endeavors and her great de-
fense of women and women's knowledge, I would like to think that if
today she were to reconstruct her library, it would contain the works I will
discuss here, for Chicana writers of Mexican American descent are truly
Sor Juana's intellectual heirs. They look to her as a role model, they write
about her. For them she embodies all that is great as a thinker, a creator,
and a questioner: she too suffered erasure, oppression, and neglect.

The critic Homi Bhabha, unpacking books after his move from London to the University of Chicago, speculates on what the accumulation
of books "in disorder and in unlikely pairings" tells about the history of
oneself and one's times (Bhabha, 199). As he continues to unpack, Bhabha
philosophizes about "temporalities that articulate transition" or those un-
canny moments in social transformations as illustrated in the books he
has bought. Among the many problematics raised in Bhabha's essay is the
sense of "double consciousness"—that is, the inheritance of the postcolo-
nial subject, the culturally hybrid identity that is mediatory, one of class,
community, equity, access, race, and sexuality (207).

Now I have not unpacked and repacked my own library lately, pausing
to appreciate, as did Bhabha, books packed away and then emerging in

chaotic yet meaningful fashion. But in 1998 I was on sabbatical, working on several extensive projects at once, and before I can begin to ponder (having been trained by my sometimes meticulous Mexican mother), I often have to clean up my study, rearrange my library into some semblance of order, giving me the illusion that I can exist in a rational, coherent world—at least temporarily. And in so straightening my books (and after reading Bhabha's essay) I was struck by the historical moments I have lived through and participated in—the establishment of Chicana literature as a serious and complex subject of study, a moment that is still evolving. As I pulled the books off my shelves, I was also profoundly astonished by what I saw happening in the presentation of these books and what I call both the politics and the poetics of Chicana literary production. Because how these books are presented tells a discursive and aesthetic narrative, I decided to show the artistic text (and its subtext) evolving in the political and cultural production of Chicana literature. These also raise all the mediatory questions articulated by Bhabha on ethnicity, community, gender, class, equity, and access.

To begin, in the contemporary moment known as the Chicano Renaissance (1968 on) many Chicanas were writing, but they were not published. Mainstream presses were not interested in what they considered to be "regional, minor, minority literature" that did not speak to "universal" interests and which they did not consider very cosmopolitan. The publication of mainstream women's writing on a large scale was just evolving, and many of these presses and editors did not consider Chicana writers worthy of inclusion. The few minority Chicano/Latino presses that existed, such as Tonatiuh/Quinto Sol, were interested in establishing a nationalist agenda, and when they published, in the main they published the male writers who were writing the sort of founding narratives espoused by the editors. Thus, mythic narratives such as *Bless Me, Ultima* by Rudy Anaya, Aztec/Aztlán myth poetry by Alurista, migrant/working-class narratives, *And the Earth Did Not Swallow Him* by Tomás Rivera, and Klail City, Texas, narratives by Rolando Hinojosa were published. It helped that many of these writers were established academics at mainstream universities. The only woman's narrative to be published by Quinto Sol was Estela Portillo Trambley's *Rain of Scorpions* (1975). Yet the women writers were not overly discouraged and began to publish themselves. Many, many self-publishing and small presses sprang up, with such innovative names as Descalzo Press (Barefoot), M and A (the initials of the publishers), Scorpion Press (the birth signs of the editors,) Grilled Flowers, Maize (established by Lorna Dee Cervantes), Caracol (Snail), Oyez (Hear Ye), Relámpago (Lightning), and Capirotada (a Mexican desert). After Bilingual Review Press, Arte Público Press, and Third Woman Press were founded by Chicana/o intellectuals and supported by their respective universities, more and more creative literature began to be published. At the beginning these were labors of love with much volunteer effort. Small magazines and university department publications (often with contributions by graduate students) started up and died, giving us ephemeral glimpses of Chicana creativity. In these early days, for the women the presentation of the chapbooks and books involved a significant relationship between Chicana writers, their editors, and Chicana artists. Because all felt they were engaged in significant acts of cultural production, the presentations of the books went beyond the mere selling of the book (often only several hundred copies could be printed for lack of money), although the sales and distribution were part of the ideology of making the work known. The artist's work would enhance the poetics of the writing in question—and the creative work would make the work of the artist (also largely unknown) more widespread. It was a mutual symbiosis. The money for the production would be raised by the writer, or by the editors, by writing grants to arts organizations, or by appealing to academic resources or family and friends. I remember once Ana Castillo writing to all the people she knew for donations to publish *The Invitation,* and at Academia/El Norte, a small press with which I am involved, all the money we make from selling books goes back into the publishing of the next book.

Along with the symbiosis between writer, artist, and publisher (sometimes all rolled into one) was the fact that the production was a community venture; we had the feeling that we were accomplishing something and it was fun. Because we had been primarily an oral culture, to have the actual written artifact to hold and to pass on was very important to us and to the community. I will never forget the day that photographer Miguel Gandert and I went down to the press to check on the colors for the duotones of the photography for *Nuestras Mujeres: Hispanas of New Mexico.* As those photographs rolled off the presses, we felt that we were giving birth to a baby. (Something of what I think Virginia and Leonard Woolf felt as they hand-produced their books).

Thus of great importance in the production of these early books, and before Latina writers were taken up by New York presses, was the depiction on the covers of the hybridity, that double consciousness of the past and present, tradition and change, multiple subjectivities, and the slipping translations and transitions of the modern moment that Gloria Anzaldúa and Bhabha are so fond of discussing. In other writings I (and others) have commented on the translativeness and multiplicities of Chicana writing and how the speaking subject struggled to insert herself into subjectivity. This is no simplistic identity narrative, but rather a complex historical and cultural struggle based on a social reality that continues to this day. This is not identity in the sense of mythical origins, although that too is present, but a sense of perception as to where we came from and the struggle that brought us here, what we owe to the community that supported us.

In addition to the women and men who self-published and established presses, others who have helped continue the relationship between authors and artists have been our very real advocates, the feminist editors of university presses: advocates such as Theresa May, Andrea Otáñez, and Joanne O'Hare.

The representations by Chicana artists on the covers of books extend beyond each individual cover—often to the body of the artist's work. Therefore, although the cover of a book might be an individual portrait, those who are knowledgeable about Chicana art would also connect to the artists' other political and social representations, as we will see in the work of Yolanda López, Carmen Lomas Garza, and Pola López.

As an addendum I want to emphasize that when they have the opportunity, Chicana writers continue to participate in this cultural production; yet as you will see, often when the big publishing houses agree to publish Latina/Chicana writers, they are so thrilled just to be published (and perhaps if they have an agent) that they are pushed farther away from the production process, they lose control over the input, and they become once again the object of the literary production rather than the controlling subjects. Please do not misunderstand me: I am not against fame and fortune for our writers, I can only wish it for them. Thus said, I want to take you on a brief pictorial and descriptive journey to illustrate what I have just talked about.

1. Poster for "Reconstructing the Canon," 1986. In preparing this poster for our conference we tried to graphically represent what Bhabha was talking about, the commentaries and reflections one can make looking at books (although here not haphazardly put together), and to show what an integrated curriculum in American literature might look like. Also we interpolated titles that commented ironically on Chicana/o literature.

2. Fabiola Cabeza de Baca, *We Fed Them Cactus,* University of New Mexico Press, 1954. Cabeza de Baca was an early New Mexico writer who wrote a hybrid text—part testimony, part memoir, part family and community history. The water windmill, pictured on this cover, was a staple on the desert landscape well into the 1960s, representing for Cabeza de Baca

Poster for "Reconstructing the Canon: Chicano Writers and Critics" Conference, University of New Mexico, 1986.

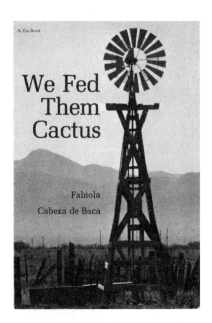

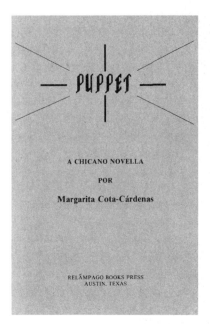

Cover of Fabiola Cabeza de Baca, We Fed Them Cactus. *Albuquerque: University of New Mexico Press, 1954. Cover of Margarita Cota-Cárdenas,* Puppet. *Austin: Relámpago Press, 1986.*

the loss of Hispano land to Anglos due in part to lack of water. The representation conjures up drought, nostalgia, and a sense of the depression.

3. Margarita Cota-Cárdenas, *Siete Poetas,* Scorpion Press, 1978. This was one of the early self-published chapbooks and was self-distributed. The cover is plain, but on the inner pages where the work of each poet is introduced, there is the outline of flowers. For the poets it was important to have something visual to connect to their poems. Here is an image of the corsage that Cota-Cárdenas's daughter had saved from her junior-high prom.

4. Margarita Cota-Cárdenas, *Puppet,* Relámpago Press, 1986. The novel is about a young pachuco mistakenly killed by the police, who then try to cover up his murder. On the cover we have a depiction of the *crucesita,* the cross that the Pachucos (and now gang members) tattoo on the inside skin between the thumb and the index finger, and the cover is textured to look like skin.

5. Margarita Cota-Cárdenas, *Marchitas de Mayo,* Relámpago Press, 1989. Here the cover, in red and black, duplicates the colors used by César Chávez's United Farm Workers in their banner; the red also symbolizes the rage and anger felt by the author. It links the author with the farm work-

Inside page of Siete Poetas. *Tucson: Scorpion Press, 1978.*

ers' struggle, which she at one time in her life rejected and then embraced. It is part of her journey in the process-of-becoming.

6. Evangelina Vigil, *Thirty an' Seen a Lot,* Arte Público Press, 1982. Here Vigil takes up the question of equity and access for women. A young Vigil looks at us fetchingly as she beckons, with thumb out, and invites us into the bar (in Chicano/Mexicano culture traditionally a male space). However, this bar sign says "Ladies Welcome." This book of poems is filled with strong language as Vigil appropriates not only the space in the cantina but male language as well.

7. Evangelina Vigil, back of *Thirty an' Seen a Lot.* On the back of the book Vigil has accessed the cantina and is seated comfortably. Elizabeth Ordóñez writes in the introduction, "In many ways Vigil has tapped the uncertainty many have felt at the twilight of the seventies, and by expressing those doubts in the vernacular of the majority, she speaks not as a single, alienated intellectual, but as a spokesperson of a community now embarking on a new decade, into still uncharted—and often even frightening—directions."

Photographs were one inexpensive way to represent on the covers of these books, but it seems to me that the use of the photography is more complex; it inserts our subjectivity into cultural history, refuting that traditional erasure of Chicanas/Latinas. In the real world we are there, aren't we? The photograph proves it. It documents our space in the symbolic

Cover of Evangelina Vigil, Thirty an' Seen a Lot. *Houston: Arte Público Press, 1984. Back cover of* Thirty an' Seen a Lot.

and in the aesthetic. It suggests tradition and place at the same time that it inserts itself into artistic subversion, as I will explain later.

8. Ana Castillo, *Women Are Not Roses,* Arte Público Press, 1984. The cover of this book has several long-stemmed red roses, out of water. One rose, about to bloom, is broken. The rose symbol is very important to Chicana writers because of its connection with the Virgin of Guadalupe and the rose as mandala in the Christian Church, but the connection of women to flowers is also problematic. As Cota-Cárdenas says,

> it's very hard   being a flower
>   sometimes
>   when we're all alone
>   and on our way
> we concentrate real hard   like this
>   and wrinkle up our brow
>   so that we'll wither up beforehand
> and when we get to the market   hee hee
>   they can't sell us.
> (IN REBOLLEDO, "WALKING THE THIN LINE," 100)

9. Sandra Cisneros, *My Wicked Wicked Ways,* Third Woman Press, 1987. In this picture of Cisneros herself, the editor plays with the tinted photos of our families that were so popular in the early twentieth century. I myself have a tinted photo of my grandmother and her three sisters as well as one of my mother and myself as a child. However, this photograph goes beyond those staid pictures, as Cisneros mischievously and suggestively looks at us, her cowboy boots neatly tucked under her dress with her lips, earrings, and wine in the glass crimson tinted. It is in this book where Cisneros explains her transgression, that of wanting to be a writer, to have access:

> I was born under a crooked star.
> So says my father.
> . . .
> You see.
> An unlucky fate is mine
> to be born woman in a family of men.
>
> Six sons, my father groans,
> all home.
> And one female,
> gone.
> (36–37)

10. Sandra Cisneros, *My Wicked Wicked Ways,* Random House, 1992. The cover is illustrated by Cisneros's friend Terry Ibáñez, "one of las girlfriends," a raucous accomplice in wicked ways, as Cisneros writes,

> last week in this same bar,
> kicked a cowboy in the butt
> who made a grab for Terry's ass . . .

she is a "black lace bra kind of woman" (Cisneros, *Loose,* 78). The figure painted by Ibáñez is a naked woman, playing an acordión (part of Texas conjunto music) with the catrina calavera, dancing death, by her side. Here Random House did a nice combination of author and artist, but for me the cover is not as compelling as the original published by Third Woman Press.

11. Ana Castillo, *My Father Was a Toltec,* West End Press, 1988. Again we have a photograph inscribing cultural history, as Ana too is in the

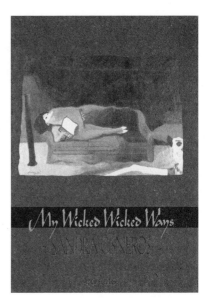

Cover of Sandra Cisneros, My Wicked Wicked Ways. *Berkeley: Third Woman Press, 1987. Cover of Sandra Cisneros,* My Wicked Wicked Ways. *New York: Turtle Bay Books, 1992.*

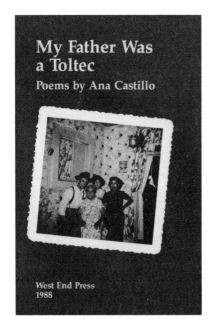
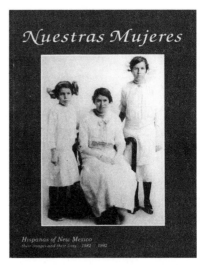

Cover of Ana Castillo, My Father Was a Toltec. *Novato, Calif.: West End Press, 1988. Cover of Tey Diana Rebolledo,* Nuestras Mujeres. *Albuquerque: Academia/El Norte Publications, 1992.*

photograph. The blurb reads, "Castillo invokes her origin as the daughter of a street warrior, a member of the Toltec gang in Chicago, and carries her own fight from memories of schoolyard battles into adulthood." The book is also a tribute to the strong women in the Chicana community, where women survive rape, poverty, exclusion.

12. Tey Diana Rebolledo, *Nuestras Mujeres,* Academia/El Norte Publications, 1992. In this cover picture, there is a photograph of what at first glance may seem like upper-class women. Upon closer examination the working-class origins of the women may be seen. The lace on the dresses is crochet and the dresses homemade, the stockings the girls are wearing are black everyday stockings, not elegant white ones, and the shoes on the younger girl look like hand-me-downs. We were trying to convey the simple elegance of hardworking families.

13. Tey Diana Rebolledo, *Nuestras Mujeres*. This picture of five Mexican midwives is the picture that I would have liked for the cover of the book. However, after we put it on a publicity poster for the photographic show that grew out of the book project, it was fairly controversial. We were told that the women (who are actually *curanderas*) looked like *brujas* (witches) and that they were smoking. If you look carefully at this historical photograph, you can see that two of the women are smoking.

14. Vera Norwood and Janice Monk, *The Desert Is No Lady,* University of Arizon Press, 1997. On this cover the Taos Gorge is made to look like a woman's body. This painting by Pola López is much more representative of the contents than the original cover published by Yale University Press. The title of the book is from a poem by Pat Mora.

15. Erlinda Gonzales-Berry, *Paletitas de guayaba,* Academia/El Norte Publications, 1991. Again we have a play on a tinted photograph, this time one of those tourist pictures taken on the border. We gave the original to artist Soledad Marjon, thinking she would tint only parts of it, but Soledad went crazy.

16. Tey Diana Rebolledo and Eliana S. Rivero, eds., *Infinite Divisions,* University of Arizona Press, 1993. This painting by Cecilia Alvarez of her mother and aunt, who were twins, was part of the CARA show. We felt that twins exemplified divisions, multiples, and complex units we were representing in the anthology.

17. Carmen Lomas Garza, *Family Pictures,* Children's Book Press, 1990. In these pictures from the book Lomas Garza turns around stereotypes about the family and about women. In "Beds for Dreaming," we see two children on the roof looking at the moon. The mother is inside making

"Five Mexican Midwives," Taos, 1940s. Photo by J. Valentine, Farm Security Administration Archives, Library of Congress. In Rebolledo, Nuestras Mujeres.

the bed. Lomas Garza says, "My sister and I used to go up on the roof on summer nights and just stay there and talk about the stars and the constellations. We also talked about the future. I knew since I was 13 years old that I wanted to be an artist, and all those things that I dreamed of doing as an artist, I'm finally doing now. My mother was the one who inspired me to be an artist. She made up our beds to sleep in and have regular

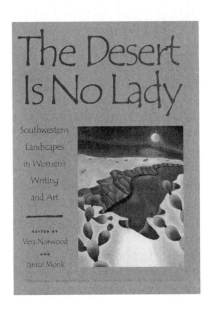

Cover of Vera Norwood and Janice Monk, eds., The Desert Is No Lady.
Tucson: University of Arizona Press, 1997. Painting by Pola López.
Cover of Erlinda Gonzales-Berry, Paletitas de guayaba. Albuquerque:
Academia/El Norte Publications, 1991.

dreams, but she also laid out the bed for our dreams of the future" (Lomas
Garza, 30).

18. Carmen Lomas Garza, *Family Pictures.* About "Making Tamales"
Lomas Garza writes, "This is a scene from my parents' kitchen. Everybody
is making tamales. My grandfather is wearing blue overalls and a blue shirt.
I'm right next to him with my sister Margie. We're helping to soak the
dried leaves from the corn. My mother is spreading the cornmeal dough
on the leaves and my aunt and uncle are spreading meat on the dough. My
grandmother is lining up the rolled and folded tamales ready for cooking.
In some families just the women make tamales, but in our family everybody helps" (22).

19. Tey Diana Rebolledo, *Women Singing in the Snow,* University of Arizona Press, 1995. The cover is Ester Hernández's lithograph of the famous
Texas conjunto singer Lydia Mendoza, who was well known regionally
and for her song "Mal Hombre." While the cover of the book is "pretty,"

Cover of Tey Diana Rebolledo and Eliana S. Rivero, eds., Infinite Divisions: An Anthology of Chicana Literature. *Tucson: University of Arizona Press, 1993. Cover art:* Las Cuatas Diego, *by Cecilia Concepción Alvarez. Cover of Tey Diana Rebolledo,* Women Singing in the Snow. *Tucson: University of Arizona Press, 1995. Cover art: "Lydia Mendoza circa 1930," by Ester Hernandez,* ©1987.

the subtext for Chicanos in the know would be the political representation and commentaries of Hernández's art. Other paintings state her representation of farm workers as guerilla fighters, as in "Luna Llena" (1990); her outrage about the disappeared, "Tejido de los desaparecidos" (1984); and her parody of the evil of pesticides, "Sun Mad" (1981).

20. Norma Cantú, *Canícula,* University of New Mexico Press, 1995. Again we see a collage of photographs and symbolic jewels. The story itself has photographs that document the invented and real autobiography.

21. María Herrera-Sobek and Helena María Viramontes, *Chicana (W)rites: On Word and Film,* Third Woman Press, 1998. Portrait of the Artist as the Virgen of Guadalupe is part of Yolanda López's well-known series of representations of ordinary women as the powerful Virgin of Guadalupe. Others in the series include her grandmother, Victoria F. Franco, as *Her Lady of Guadalupe,* and her mother, Margaret F. Stewart, as *Our Lady of Guada-*

Cover of Norma Cantú, Canícula. *Albuquerque: University of New Mexico Press, 1995. Cover of María Herrera-Sobek and Helena María Viramontes,* Chicana (W)rites: On Word and Film. *Berkeley: Third Woman Press, 1998. Cover art: Portrait of the Artist as the Virgin of Guadalupe, by Yolanda López (oil pastel on paper, 1978).*

lupe. Other commentaries by López include the powerful *Who's the Illegal Alien, Pilgrim?*

22. Sandra Cisneros, *Loose Woman,* Alfred A. Knopf, 1994. This book illustrates what happens when the big publishers take over and the writers and artists are no longer intimately connected with the presses. This cover is not, for me, a successful one, nor does it have much connection with the content of the poetry itself.

From the beginning Chicana literature has opened up that profound yet ever amorphous space-in-between ("retro-space," as Juan Bruce-Novoa called it in 1988), which is constantly exploring and changing its representations, especially as a subject in progress, at times unified and mythic, at times fragmented and chaotic. As we have seen in this journey through creative production, Chicana writers and artists have worked together to insert Chicanas into subjectivity and to explore a Chicana aesthetic. The contemporary Chicana subject remains in a pondering, contemplative,

Yolanda López, Victoria F. Franco: Our Lady of Guadalupe *(oil pastel on paper, 1978). Yolanda López*, Margaret F. Stewart: Our Lady of Guadalupe *(oil pastel on paper, 1978).*

Cover of Sandra Cisneros, Loose Woman. *New York: Knopf, 1984. A great-aunt on the Galindo side of the family, 1920.*

ironic, questioning mode. It is certainly a mode of which Sor Juana would have approved. For myself I have to have this photograph as the cover of a book I am writing titled *Family Secrets*. Renata (reborn) Galindo, my heroine, is emerging from the giant egg, just as Jorge Luis Borge's endless plain of mirrors reflect onto themselves. This photograph is of an aunt in 1920, endlessly reflecting me.

Part Two

On Chicana Literature

SEVEN

Who Killed Presiliano Ulibarrí?
Or, the Case of the Missing Women

CLUES FOR CULTURAL STUDIES (1993)

The women are missing, the women are missing! What cry is this that springs forth from history books, chronicles, biographies of Hispanos in the Colonial Southwest from the 1600s to the beginning of the twentieth century? Have the women been abducted? Have they, in contemporary terminology, been "disappeared"? The phenomenon is simple to explain. They are missing because they were not put in these records in the first place. They are missing because the lives and achievements of Hispanas in the early history and literature of the Southwest were not considered memorable, not important enough to put into the history record. We literary historians, social historians, and cultural historians must adopt a new profession: that of detective. I was a fan of Nancy Drew when I was young (even if Ned did have to intervene from time to time to save her and her girlfriend George, as they got themselves into one scrape after another). But Nancy was always alert in her search for clues and in her ability to solve the mystery. As an adult I continue to be seduced by detective novels, especially by academic mysteries; an example here would be *Murder at the MLA*. But my new heroine is a Chicana detective named Panchita Villa; or she could be Asian American, Native American, African American. In any event, Panchita is an academic who is interested in cultural studies and in the mysteries not revealed in standard texts. Her case? Where are the women? Her detecting spaces bounce back and forth from what could be called the locked room mystery (in this case the dusty venue of the special collections in basements of libraries) or the more public space of finding papers in old trunks, clues in old photographs, recipes, and scary tales told by the neighborhood viejas. One of the cases she is currently investigating is "Who killed Presiliano Ulibarrí?" a murder that occurred in the nineteenth century and is still unsolved today. Only tantalizing clues, vague and dusty accounts of what happened, who was accused and what the outcome was drift in to us from that time so long ago; but Panchita is

María Inez Trujillo and her son, Elías, Lumberton, New Mexico.

on the case. Let me give you some details, although I must warn you that what little we know cannot be verified.

María Inez Trujillo, known locally as "La Trujilla," lived in La Puente, New Mexico. Now we know that unless someone was well known in a community, I mean very well known, they would not have the article "la" placed before their name. In any event, María Inez was married to Presiliano Ulibarrí, a gambler, and had two daughters by him. In 1897 Presiliano was found beaten to death in his house. La Trujilla was accused and found guilty of his murder. Was this a domestic-violence situation? Was Presiliano cheating on her? Did she have the strength to beat him to death? Were there accomplices? María Inez was pregnant at the time— whose child was it? Family history has it that Sheriff Agapito Archuleta of Rio Arriba kept her under house arrest until her child was born, telling her that if she had a boy, he would let her go free, but if she had a girl, she would go to prison. (I guess the sheriff reasoned that if she already had had two girls, chances were pretty good that she would have another one.) Fortunately for La Trujilla, she had a son, Elías, pictured in this photograph with her. To this day we still don't know who killed Presiliano Ulibarrí.

Let me tell you how the case of the missing women began. It was the photograph in the National Archives in Washington, D.C., that did it (see p. 68). Those five women all dressed in black, staring, staring at the camera. The picture is blurred, as if the photographer had jiggled just a little bit. Five women, four old, one young, all dressed in black. One has a cigarette dangling on the edge of her mouth. They look cold. They aren't smiling. I guess no one smiled for photographs in those days. The picture is labeled "Five Mexican Midwives" and was taken by a photographer named Valentine in Taos in the 1940s. But even in the 1940s they are all wearing long black dresses.

It was that photograph and the red petticoats; no, these women aren't wearing red petticoats (at least we can't see if they are). No, I mean the red petticoats listed in the muster rolls of the Oñate expedition of 1598, indicating that although we are told soldiers, priests, and horses explored the Southwest, there were also women and servants who accompanied them. And it was the tale of Bersabé Gonzales pouring water on the snakes that lingered under the board floor of the house, and of the nun who couldn't teach but when put in maintenance discovered she loved tools, and of her sister, also a nun, who wore lavender pink pantsuits after Vatican II, much to the distress of her family, and, of course, the tale of La Trujilla. All of these stories express the culture and community of Hispanas in the Southwest. But I am getting ahead of myself. Back to the five women dressed in black in the photograph in the National Archives.

The women are unidentified, as most archival photographs of minority group members are; the labels say "unidentified Hispanics," "unidentified Indians," "unidentified Asians." One of our goals in the Nuestras Mujeres project was to put together the names and stories of as many people in the photographs as possible. As we were talking about the project on television and showing the photo of the five midwives, a niece of one of the women saw the photograph and wrote to tell us she could identify all, who were indeed parteras from Talpa, a small community near Taos. They were respected and important women in that community. We have also been able to identify other women in the book.

Nuestras Mujeres was a collaborative project between researchers at the University of New Mexico and people in the community. Working together, we collected stories and photographs and have begun the documentation of the incredible contributions of these often unsung and unnoticed workers. We have documented their struggles, their survival, and their successes. We have also seen their resistance to oppression and injustice, their tenacity when they needed something for their families and their communities.

I am not a historian. Years ago I studied history at the University of New Mexico, but dates and great men held little fascination for me. What I liked was scandal, the secrets people hold close to their chests, the romance, the silences. I liked the stories I have already told you, and that of the woman in colonial New Mexico who fled with her lover, the governor, to Mexico to have their child because he was already married. So I became a literary critic. As our detractors say, we always put our imaginations to use anyway. But reading between and underneath the lines, being a detective in cultural studies, is something literary critics do very well; in academic talk we call it "deconstruction."

Seven years ago I was invited to give a keynote address at the University of California-Irvine on the topic of Hispanas in colonial U.S. literature. I accepted with some trepidation because there was little documentation and scarce research on the place of Hispanas in the early history and literature of the colonial West and Southwest. What I discovered is that social historians such as Salomé Hernández and Deena Gonzáles, researching Hispanas in the seventeenth and nineteenth centuries, had uncovered much information in unexpected sources. Using muster rolls, baptism certificates, marriage declarations, wills, inquisition records, judgments, and other creative ways of exploring history, they have been able to circumvent the "traditional" canon to research the ways in which women participated in the exploration, colonization, and settlement of the Southwest. These exploratory investigations are bringing life and vitality into an area little known and almost forgotten.

If traditional history is the history of power narratives, defined as primarily political, economic, and military, how do we come to an understanding of the consciousness of a people, and of ordinary life? Where conventional documentary evidence is not available, we must turn to evidence of a different kind: folklore, ritual, religious ceremonies, and even food preparation. As yet no official "literary" texts written by women in New Mexico during the colonial period have been found; nevertheless, we see glimpses and hints of their lives in songs and plays, *dichos, cuentos,* and *memorate,* popular chronicles of local origin in which people tell their own history.

I want to take you on an adventure of detection of women and community in the Southwest, a journey from the colonial period to the present. We will explore the mysteries, the clues of oral and material culture that will tell us about their lives, their hardships, their struggles, their triumphs. We will examine how women created and enriched community and how they have been empowered by the process, even in the face of incredible difficulties.

The accounts of expeditions, *crónicas* of exploration, letters to the viceroy, and other documents ascertain the place of the Spanish / Mexicanos on the frontier of the New World: all of these accounts were written by men;

their readers, the men in power. While certainly the discoveries were led by military men and priests, shortly after the first expeditions to the north the areas were settled by colonists: families that included a good number of women.

Indeed, in the early expedition of Espejo to New Mexico in 1582, there was at least one woman who accompanied the soldiers. Miguel Sánchez Valenciano was accompanied by his wife, Casilda de Amaya, and three young sons. In Diego Pérez de Luxán's account of this expedition there is little mention of this woman; nothing is revealed about how she endured the arduous journey across the desert or how she fared in the end. We are told she became pregnant during the journey. Discouraged by the little progress that had been made searching for mines, some wanted to return to Mexico. One of the soldiers declared that he meant to take the priest, Father Beltrán, and Miguel Sánchez's wife to the land of peace (Hammond and Rey, 198). After some discussion Miguel Sánchez Valenciano, four other men, and the priest go with him. Did Casilda de Amaya and her children also return with the men? We are not told and must leave it for future detectives to discover.

Many colonial texts contain highly descriptive and creative passages that highlight the sense of adventure and discovery these soldiers had. And while they take for granted the women who accompanied them, they display great interest in the Indian peoples they come across. We therefore often know more about the indigenous women than we do about the Spanish/Mexicanas. From the Juan de Oñate expedition in 1598 we know more about the number of carts and wagons (and their contents), the quantity and quality of the horses and armor, than we do about the women and children who accompanied them. For example, we know that a quantity of paper (forty-one reams) made the journey as well as stuff for women's clothing (this is where the petticoats come in). One wonders who were the petticoats for? Why were they red? Documents mention the presence of forty-seven wives and Doña Inez, an Indian. Only the names of a few of these women are known (Hernández, 21). What they experienced, except for a few heartrending scenes, is lost.

In addition to their historical presence on the colonial frontier, women also exerted influence through myth and popular belief. One incident, the miraculous conversion of the Xumana nation, is attributed to a female, the Lady in Blue. In his *Memorial* (1634) Fray Alonso de Benavides, a Franciscan, tells of a tribe of pious Indians who continually requested a priest live among them. When asked why they wanted to be baptized, they told of seeing a woman dressed in blue who talked to them in their language.

Upon seeing a portrait of a nun, Mother Luisa, in the convent, they said that the woman they saw was younger and prettier than the one in the portrait. This apparition was further complicated when some newly arrived friars declared that it "was common news in Spain that a nun named María de Jesús de la Concepción, . . . residing in the town of Agreda in the providence of Burgos, was miraculously transported to New Mexico to preach our holy Catholic faith to those . . . Indians" (Hodge, Hammond, and Rey, 93). When Benavides traveled to Spain in 1630, he visited with this nun and wrote, "She convinced me absolutely by describing to me all the things in New Mexico as I have seen them myself, as well as by other details which I shall keep within my soul. Consequently, I have no doubts in this matter whatsoever" (95).

María de Agreda in 1630 was twenty-nine years old (although she had started her bilocations to New Mexico in 1620 when she was nineteen), and for some years she had been experiencing ecstasies. In 1627 she wrote a book, *The Mystical City of God,* detailing the life of the Virgin Mary, particularly the nine months she spent in her mother's womb. The book was condemned by the church for indecent language, and she was ordered to burn it, along with the daily dairies she had kept of her bilocation to New Mexico. As a result of her fame as a bilocator, she met King Philip IV of Spain and they became good friends, corresponding with each other for over thirty years. The story of her miraculous apparitions profoundly affected the consciousness of Hispanos in the Southwest and constantly reappears in later folk literature. How did María de Agreda know about the Southwest? How could she describe this region to Fray Benavides? Did she read descriptions from other Franciscans? Did she really bilocate? It will be up to you to decide.

The frontier was a place of great hardship. In 1680, after ninety years of settlement, the Indians rebelled against the often harsh treatment and injustices by the Spaniards. The rebellion was well planned and affected the lives of the 2,400 settlers living in the area. Four hundred Hispanos died; surviving were 2,000, mostly women and children (Hernández, 55). Ultimately everyone retreated to El Paso, the women and children walking since there were only twenty carts (57).

Many women were killed during the Pueblo Revolt. Some of the women were captured. These and subsequent captivities are important to the literature because even though they did not produce a form of literature known in Anglo-America as captivity narratives, they resulted in the telling of the tales of these women in songs known as "cautiva Inditas."

These Inditas are often passed down from mother to daughter and honor and record the experiences of women during their captivity. They may be one of the few creative forms that record these experiences of both Hispanic and Indian women of this time.

With the Vargas resettlement effort in 1692, many women and children returned to their homes in New Mexico; many new settlers were also recruited. Among these women there were widows and single female heads of household. They included Hispanas, Mexican Indians, New Mexican Indians, blacks, multatas, lobas, coyotes, and Mestizas (Hernández, 87). These women were strong and independent. They ran households, worked in the fields, and managed ranches in addition to bearing, raising, and educating children. They came from all social classes. Their lives continued to be difficult, concerned with survival. There were few doctors in the region, and knowledge of medicinal herbs and curing techniques were highly prized skills. As towns grew, life around the church became important for women. They cleaned the church, plastered its walls, cared for the priests, and gave religious instruction to their children. Communal and community life were essential to their well-being.

Important also are the legal rights that women enjoyed under the Spanish system of law. Women were entitled to own and inherit property under their own names and separately from their husbands. They made wills; they had the right to litigate in court and often did. For example, Ramón Gutiérrez studied a 1702 court case on seduction that illuminates for us not only the relationship between the sexes, but also important social issues of the time. In this case we hear the voice of a young woman, Juana Luján. She had been seduced by Bentura de Esquibel, and he promised to marry her. But Juana was not of the same social class and Bentura's father wished to stop the marriage. Bentura soon became betrothed to another. Juana Luján, who was pregnant, asked to court to stop the marriage since she already had a claim. Bentura claimed that Juana was not a virgin when he seduced her, but Juana defended herself, moreover recognizing the real issues in the case: "that Bentura has had a change of heart and now wants to marry Bernardina Lucero saying that she is honorable and Spanish, I can only say that I cannot dispute that Bernardina is indeed from a very honorable family; but that she is better than me in racial status is disputable, for I am as good as she" (Gutiérrez, 454–455).

Juana, however, gave up her claim because she had been threatened by Bentura's family. She also recognized that she could not live happily with someone forced to marry her. How did she find the independent resolve to stand up for herself and her family name? Although we will never know the answer to that question, the court decided that Juana was entitled to the sum of two hundred pesos for her "dishonor."

If we accept the gloomy perspective of conventional historians, we determine that women during this time are more creatures of procreation than of creation. This is still held to be generally true as we have not yet discovered the letters written to families left behind or who have moved away, the diaries, the journals. Did these women never seek to capture and narrate their experiences? We know the women shared their lives, their gossip, their needs. We know that from mother to daughter entire generations transmitted their recipes, the rituals of food, and special occasions on which it was served. With the scarcity of medical personnel, it was essential that they pass on their knowledge of herbs and cures. Sometimes they told stories about personal events that were picked up in the oral literature. Often they were "supernatural things" that might happen to ordinary women and men. Through these stories they have transmitted to us their consciousness and their fears. Through these stories we see often a glimmer of what might have been recorded if there had been leisure to learn and time to write.

During 1880–1911 voices of women from territorial and pre-statehood New Mexico begin to merge. Their stories are to be found in the oral folklore collected in the Federal Writers Project and in the oral histories told in our families. Some of the stories can be verified, some comprise the realm of "family scandals and secrets." In the 1930s and 1940s there was a great deal of interest in the Southwest region, sparked by the Federal Writers Project. The Federal Writers Project was a part of Franklin D. Roosevelt's New Deal program in the 1930s. There were guidebooks to the forty-eight states. This project in New Mexico, Arizona, and Texas gathered oral histories, trying to preserve the history and culture of the "old-timers." Because Hispanas (many of them older women) were included in the project, valuable information about their lives, education, and traditions as well as important folktales about women and their roles have been preserved. In New Mexico the Federal Writers Project is important because it yielded a source central to the preservation of Hispana culture: a collection of the *cuentos* and the *memorate*. Some of these texts are variants on European tales and have been studied by scholars eager to show European influence. Fortunately, however, many of the texts are very local and chronicle the lives of people living in remote areas. Even if they could not read nor write, women could nevertheless tell stories, stories fired with imagination and symbols that were subsequently passed down from generation to generation. Many contemporary Chicanas are "first generation" writers who are telling the cuentos of their mothers and grandmothers, thus preserving this oral tradition. The stories contain humor, along with careful descriptions of people and places as the storytellers strive to recollect the images long gone.

Stories and beliefs about witches abound in New Mexico. The earliest written history contains accusations of witchcraft and mentions the beliefs and participation in heathen rites, hexing, mal de ojos, and miraculous apparitions. It may be that witch stories prevail more than others because of the merging of multiple cultures. One of the Placitas witch stories was told by Rumaldita Gurulé about her grandmother, Quiteria, who would have been born around the early 1800s, and another woman, Doña Tomasa, who was probably born around 1750. The story deals with generational change, the young replacing the old; its moral, however, is that in order to function, the new system must learn the ways of the old. Doña Tomasa is seen continually outwitting her young rival.

"Quiteria is the best nurse and she is young," the people said, and it made Doña Tomasa, the witch nurse, very jealous. So Quiteria was afraid of her and she tried to keep out of her way. The witch nurse might play an evil trick on her. Then one day somebody whispered to Quiteria that if she stood on Tomasa's shadow, Tomasa could not move and she would have Tomasa in her power. At noon one day Doña Tomasa came to visit Quiteria. Ah, thought Quiteria to herself, I must keep her until her shadow grows a little. So she invited the witch nurse to eat dinner with her. The woman was hungry so she stayed and drank the good atole and she ate the tortillas. But she was in a hurry and soon she was leaving. Quiteria picked up her new reboso and followed Tomasa out the door. "See how fine my new reboso is. Touch it," and Quiteria came very close to the witch nurse and stood on her shadow. The witch nurse tried to move. She could not. So she acted very natural as if she did not wish to go. She talked of the people to Quiteria. She talked of the crops. She rolled many cigarettes and smoked them. She must get away. She cried out, "I am sick. Run quick. Get me some water!" Quiteria saw that she looked pale, so she ran into the house for the water. When she returned Doña Tomasa was gone.
(REBOLLEDO AND RIVERO, 46)

Once we arrive at the end of the nineteenth century, we begin to study the images of women seen through the photographers' eye and their representation of themselves in their own words. Women such as Nina Otero Warren, Fabiola Cabeza de Baca, and Cleofas Jaramillo are just beginning to be seriously studied. As more contemporary writers come onto the scene, New Mexico is richly represented by Erlinda Gonzales-Berry, Demetria Martínez, Denise Chávez, and Rosalía Otero, among others. But these women did not spring out of the blue; it was their Abuelas, Mamás, Tías, and Primas that inspired, sustained, and supported them.

In a photograph Carlota Gonzales stands in front of an adobe house. There is a young man in a cap walking behind her. Carlota has short hair; her left arm is placed on her hip. Her dress is elaborate, with delicate scallops on the ends, and around the collar and sleeves; small buttons form a vertical pattern. She has a direct gaze as she looks at the camera. She is not smiling. The photo, taken around 1925, when she was fifteen, signals a serious, independent young woman. Another picture shows her standing behind her rural school class in Cerro, New Mexico, in 1928. Carlota was born on a ranch near Roy. Her father died when she was seven, and her mother, Bersabé, cleaned houses and took in laundry to support her seven children. Their home had wooden planks through which the children could spy on the snakes that lived beneath the floor. Erlinda Gonzales-Berry tells us, "In order to discourage the unwelcome tenants, Bersabé poured boiling water between the cracks" (Gonzales-Berry, "Carlota," 35). When Carlota went to school, the nuns changed her name to Carlida, so she went through life, as did many Hispanos, with two names: her private Spanish name and her public English name.

Carlota was one of the first Hispanas to graduate from high school in Roy, New Mexico, and she became a rural schoolteacher at a young age. "She didn't know that being a teacher in a 'one-room' schoolhouse also meant being the janitor and the coach. The latter role she loved. Her experience on her high school basketball team had prepared her for softball. Few of her students, including the fifteen-year-old farmer boys, could pitch as mean a ball as she could" (Gonzales-Berry, "Carlota," 36). Carlota's sense of responsibility to her family was so strong that not only did she send her mother most of her salary but she vowed not to marry until her brothers and sisters were on their own. At twenty-eight she married her childhood sweetheart, had a family, and then returned to teaching. "Extreme conditions of poverty did not keep her from realizing her dreams; raising a family did not keep her from having a career. Her life is unusual if we consider that she came from a traditional culture whose values sup-

Carlota Gonzales, circa 1925. Photo courtesy Erlinda Gonzales-Berry.

posedly proscribed dependency of women on their husbands, restricting them to the home and to the family. . . . It is truly amazing how *nuestras mujeres,* through sheer will and hard work, were able to develop strategies that allowed them to go beyond cultural constraints and, at the same time, to conform to cultural expectations" (36).

Another photograph is that of Josephine Córdova of Taos, taken by Miguel Gandert when she was eighty-five. Her lined face shows her

Josephine M. Córdova. Photo by Miguel Gandert, 1992.

experiences, her hand lies gently over her heart. Córdova was born in Arroyo Seco and was, like Carlota, a schoolteacher. When she was young, she didn't want to get married because she, too, felt she had to support her mother. In 1976 she wrote *No lloro pero me acuerdo,* a book in which she describes her life, her family, dichos, stories about Taos, remedios, and creative work. She said, "My idea in publishing this book was to leave this generation a glimpse of what life was like long before they came. Having lived a long life I was here to see the covered wagon, and the beginning and outcome of the First World War. I enjoyed reading with the use of candles and kerosene lamps. I went to school when we had to carry our own table and bench" (Córdova, 4). When she was teaching in a northern village in 1932, she was told by her landlord not to visit certain homes in the village because she would be bewitched. "The people believed that there was a *larga* who appeared at night and scared the wanderers away. They also mentioned La Llorona, who came out at night wailing and scaring people off the roads." After Josephine had met the people in the village, she could not believe that there were any witches there. And although she tells of the stories about witches that she had heard, she comments: "Every couple who had children in that school became my friends. They invited me to their homes and treated me with love and respect. I enjoyed their hospitality, and while I was there I never saw a witch" (10).

Hispanas have been central to the construction of the fabric of family and community life. They have built and supported schools, churches, and community centers. They have written books, created poems, used their imagination. They have been successful in the domestic sphere as well as the public. And the stories continue. As a result of the project, several young Chicana journalists became enthusiastic and re-interviewed some of the women involved in the book, elaborating on their stories. Emiliana Sandoval interviewed María Jaramillo Mascarenas, an eighty-two-year-old sobadora/curandera from Taos. The headline reads "María Margarita Jaramillo y Mascarenas can mend fences, chop wood, drive a team of horses 18 miles and take care of cows, calves, pigs and chickens." Mascarenas said, "I've worked very hard in my life, mostly on my feet. I'm strong as an ox and very healthy, except I move very fast and last year I tripped and fell on a rock and broke my kneecap. It healed in two weeks, though. I'm tough. I only weigh about eighty, eighty-two pounds, sometimes ninety and I'm thin but I'm strong. I have to keep going, keep moving" (Sandoval, 29). Mascarenas became a *sobadora* (masseuse), a profession she still practices. She said, "I'm very interested in the welfare of my patients. I treat them kindly, let them relax, I talk to them and tell them jokes to keep their minds away from the pain. I try to keep them entertained. I sing to them in both Spanish and English while I work" (Sandoval, 30). Sandoval wrote, "Mascarenas has no intentions of slowing down, brushing aside curious visitors who want to talk to her about her methods. 'People came and asked questions and it was a big bother. I'm too busy to stop and talk to people. They ask me to teach them and I'm not qualified to teach—I tell them to go to a school. I've been very fortunate. My hands are blessed, a gift of the Holy Spirit. You can go to all the massage schools you want, but if you don't have it in you, you aren't going to make it'" (Sandoval, 30).

The photograph of Mascarenas shows a thin woman, hands outstretched on the massage table as if to beckon to her patients. She is smiling. Her certificates and images of the sacred heart are on the wall behind her. How does this woman find the strength to continue to treat patients?

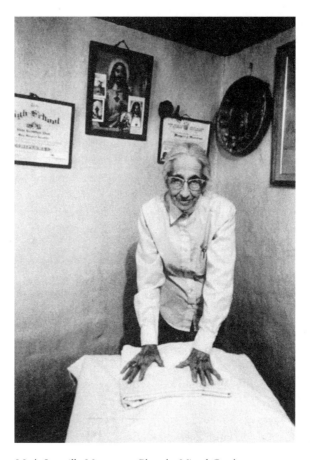

María Jaramillo Mascarenas. Photo by Miguel Gandert, 1992.

As can be seen by this brief essay, the images of Hispanas are many and varied both in the history and in the literature. And although until the 1920s we have no formal literature, we are able to approach their lives through a reading of the underside of history and the underside of story-telling. Cultural studies allow us to study material culture such as paintings and photographs, inquisition records, letters, and recipes, look at women's work in terms of embroidery, songs, weaving, and dress. Cultural studies encourage us to be detectives as we look at women's makeup and beauty secrets, health resolutions, religious and folk ritual. A good detective uses all of her analytical, logical, and intuitive skills to solve the mystery. We need to do the same. With Panchita Villa, our detective, we have much work to do, we need to storm the archives and reread the documents, we need to rethink the statistics in a positive way, we need to search our family trunks and our neighbor's family trunks. As we document women's lives and women's culture through community projects, I believe we will begin to find some of that formal literature to substantiate what we already know, that women's culture was a rich and essential component of community.

EIGHT

Las Mujeres Hablan

CREATIVITY AS POLITICS (1996)

*L*as mujeres hablan. Las mujeres pintan, cantan, escriben, crean
(Women speak. Women paint, sing, write, create).[1] The subject of the symposium and exhibition "Las Mujeres Hablan" was the presence of women
in all their creative aspects: in particular, the presence of Chicanas as
they make a place for themselves within a dominant culture that has often
silenced and erased them. As they speak and write, paint and sing, and
create, they become empowered not only within the creative sphere but
also within the cultural and social sphere. The symposium was also a seminar on the politics of creativity and of creativity as politics. As Demetria
Martínez put it, the poet and activist are one.

Chicanas in the creative arts met in Lubbock, Texas, in 1993 in a symposium that brought together artists and musicians, writers and critics,
teachers and students, and community. The featured artists and writers
were musicians Ivón Ulibarrí and Jean LeGrand; artists Barbara Carrasco,
Celia Alvarez Muñoz, and Tina Fuentes; writers Demetria Martínez,
Helena María Viramontes, and myself. This interdisciplinary and inter-
artistic approach combined analytical, critical thinking and speaking
with the creative spirit in a conversation and dialogue about the nature
of empowerment and the ways in which creativity, broadly defined, can
represent strength, spirituality, and subjectivity. It demonstrated how the
women project ethnicity and gender in a world that would deny them. It
was a dialogue about speaking and silence, activism and passivity, tradition
and innovation, and also about taking power into your own hands to turn
it into something other: a book, a poem, an artwork, a piece of music.
Beyond those material things, creativity was viewed as an instrument of
change. The conference addressed the presence of Chicanas and their attempt to represent for themselves. It showed how Chicanas have struggled
to create their art and say their words in a world that would prefer to
silence their creations. It has been a struggle against erasure and disappear-

ance. Nonetheless, the absence would always remain an echo of what was, and what would have been.

As I listened to the various speakers, I heard certain themes and survival strategies raised time and time again: the importance of listening to yourself ("listening to your rhythms," Alvarez) and to your culture, how one must be aware of one's own history, how stereotypes can be dissolved through action, how being bicultural has brought enrichment, and how they have, through their various approaches to creativity, taken on these difficult issues. These women have learned that words, music, and art are powerful tools of representation that can create change.

Many of the speakers, artists and writers alike, told stories of their childhood and how these stories came to represent an examination of critical moments in their young lives that shaped them. Thus Celia Alvarez Muñoz declared that understanding chickens and learning to speak English were the hardest things for her in the primary grades. These two ideas became powerful icons in her art as she explored the subtle relationship between the birth of an egg and the birth of language. Communication and its (mis)representation was the focus of these explorations. Helena María Viramontes explored early childhood in terms of domestic violence and a child's coming to terms with death. Searching for a way to articulate these difficult events, Viramontes said she was forced to come to an understanding of the social and cultural forces that made her father behave as he did: the racism and prejudice that migrant workers in the United States face. These childhood explorations are not nostalgic; rather they are basic to finding out who and what we are today.

And today's Chicana? Expect the unexpected. She can be a lawyer turned rock/salsa/mariachi musician because she loves her Mexican musical heritage (Jean LeGrand). She can be a writer turned community activist trying to save the library in a poor neighborhood because she grew up in a bookless home (Helena María Viramontes). She can be a musician working with gangs (Ivón Ulibarrí) or a mural painter incorporating the history of racism into her art (Barbara Carrasco). Thus, for these Chicanas, social activism and cultural continuity are intimately bound to an innovative creative process, and it is through the creative process that activism can be communicated.

For Demetria Martínez the importance of the process of memory (collective as well as individual) was paramount. For her, memory is the only protection against tyranny and erasure. She likened the process of remembering the "disappeared" in Latin America, those people who have simply ceased to exist under the tyranny of dictatorships and political repression, to the process of survival. In her work she deals not only with issues central to the Chicana experience but issues of violence against women and against human rights that cross boundaries. The act of remembering is a strategy for survival that echoes across borders and across countries. For her this role of memory is integral to healing. This healing is linked to the grandmother, a *curandera* (healer) who uses traditional herbs to begin the curing process. For by returning to that to which we are grounded, by heeding the creative process and articulating the wounds as well as the cure, writers can use their words to change society.

The idea of *las mujeres hablan* was linked in a parallel fashion to Martínez's idea of the mother tongue, the sense that women's language and women's words arise powerfully from listening to culture and to tradition. There is an old *dicho* in Spanish that is often used to control children (and women): *En bocas cerradas no entran moscas* (Flies don't enter closed mouths). As Ivón Ulibarrí stated, *bocas cerradas* don't bring about change. Thus the sense that women should be quiet and should remain in the house and out of sight was dispelled by all: indeed it was a sense of adventure, a sense of women taking on difficult issues of social evils and of erasing the erasure that permeated the conference. These women have done so through their art, their music, and their writing. Thus they have found a voice through various and compelling media.

While outsiders may view Chicana creators as being on the margins of American culture, it seems clear that although they may have been marginalized by their gender and ethnicity, the Chicanas themselves feel grounded in their culture and the traditions from which they create. This creativity was exemplified by various approaches and perspectives. As Ulibarrí said, "Art just is," and Barbara Carrasco epitomized the struggle against male artists who tried, but in no way succeeded, to marginalize her. Ulibarrí personified this creative spirit when she talked about wanting to take plastic underwear tubes and fill them with BB's to make a musical instrument.

The scholars attending the conference analyzed the relationship of Chicana and women's creativity to culture and to living on various borders. There is no monolith of what this creativity is—it appears in such multiple facets that it cannot be pinned down and dissected. And, of course, that is also its source of energy. The multiplicity of seeing, of interpretation, and of articulation enriches not only Chicana/o culture but all of us.

NINE

"No More Cookies, Please!"

CHICANA FEMINISM THROUGH LITERATURE

(1997)

In the early days of the Chicano Renaissance, Chicana feminism burst through its latent confines and began to manifest itself on the streets, in kitchens, in bedrooms, and in essays, poems, and narratives. In its inception there were at least two fronts of the attack as the women prepared to do battle against the forces they saw as restricting, defining, and objectifying them. At the same time they had to prepare and fortify their own defenses: this they did by beginning to define for themselves who and what they were as well as to come to consciousness as women, as Chicanas, and as the subjects of their own stories.

I want to outline the historical trajectory of feminist evolution and define the directions that I see Chicana feminism taking in our contemporary world, as seen in Chicana literature.

1. Rejection of white Anglo/Euro–centered feminism.
2. Consciousness of the treatment of Chicanas by Chicano males, the enemy within.
3. An understanding that we define ourselves by our special circumstances.
4. The recuperation of the women around us.
5. Recognition of class differences and power differences that forged an alliance between academics and the working class.
6. The separatist movement in the struggle for lesbian acknowledgment.
7. Pan/Latina feminism, always with an eye to Third World women's struggles.

1. At the beginning of the 1970s, when Anglo American feminism was making its mark, it was mainly a middle-class movement. While women

were beginning to give voice to their concerns about inequality in the home, in the workplace, and in society, it was a movement focused on white women. In truth, women of color were of little concern to the movement, and the opinions and values of minority women, at times different from those of Anglo American women, were not taken into account. It was as if the feminist movement was speaking for all of us, although it often did not speak for any of us. For many women of color, the feminist movement appeared to be extremely elitist. As an example, one of the standards for white feminist writers was that set forward by Virginia Woolf as having a "Room of One's Own." This was an ideal impossible for writers of color who were writing on buses, in the bathroom, and at the kitchen table, since they were not in an economic position to have a room separate from family. Another ideal of the Anglo feminist movement was that of separatism, creating a space for women only, feeling that the only way to overcome patriarchy was to create a space where women by themselves could reinforce and empower each other. While by itself this may not have been an altogether bad idea, women of color saw it differently. They realized that their men were also oppressed by the dominant powers in the United States, that their men also suffered economic, ethnic, and racial discrimination. Thus they did not feel, at the beginning of the feminist movement, that their cause could be separated from that of their men, or from their families. This also was their reaction to the Marxism that was prevalent at the time: gender concerns should not necessarily be put before those of class. It is true that Chicanas felt that they were triply oppressed—because they were women, because they were Chicanas, and because of their largely poor, working-class status.

This is the background, then, for the poem by Marcela Christine Lucero-Trujillo, which gave this paper its title, "No More Cookies, Please." This poem, published in 1977, is addressed to a "WASP" liberationist who has approached the lyric speaker "over cookies and tea," saying, "Sisterhood is powerful." The first objection the Chicana speaker has to the feminist is the fight at the forefront over women's right to choice. The speaker sees that, for women of color, the push for abortion rights is a way to do away with more "brown babies."

> "No more cookies, please."
> You differentiate between the two,
> but can you really separate
> your sex from your color.

No? Then see, it won't do.
And, by the way
have you offered the campesina
a piece of the American pie?
Did I hear you say?—
"She can be the baker
in this 'land of opportunity.'"
See?—Only the rich are free—
free to dictate the right
of their to be
and our not to be
in this, quote, land of liberty.
See?
"No more cookies, please."
(IN FISHER, 403)

Thus Lucero-Trujillo takes on the issues of class and ethnicity as well as family values that the Anglo feminist does not understand.

2. The struggle for Chicana rights continued and still continues, with many writers speaking out for economic and social equality. They recognize what a struggle it has been for the many women impoverished by a system that not only limited their opportunities and their possibilities, but also, in effect, silenced them. Chicanas realized that they were oppressed not only by patriarchal mainstream culture but also by white women. Moreover, Chicanas were oppressed by their own men. At the beginning of the Movimiento of the 1960s it was important to maintain an image of solidarity: thus the movement was fairly nationalist and single-minded. However, Chicanas also participated in different phases of the movement: in the student movement, in the United Farm Workers movement, and in other areas. Often, however, they were relegated to secondary, even tertiary positions of leadership (if they were considered leaders at all); they were delegated to support the men by typing the manifestos and cooking in the kitchen. As the women became more dissatisfied with these roles, an acute awareness of the machismo in the movement grew. Although machismo was always recognized, the Chicano movement made the lack of concern over women's interests even more evident. Frustrated, the women began to write about these matters. In Lorna Dee Cervantes' "Para un revolucionario," the lyric speaker describes her man as someone who has power with words, who is lyrical and philosophical. He speaks of "a new

way of life," and she states, "When you speak like this/I could listen forever." However, the reality of the situation is this:

> *Pero* your voice is lost to me, *carnal,*
> in the wail of *tus hijos,*
> in the clatter of dishes
> and the pucker of beans upon the stove.
> Your conversations come to me
> *de la sala* where you sit,
> spreading your dream, to brothers
> . . . when I stand here reaching
> . . . (for I too am Raza).
> (IN FISHER, 382)

Margarita Cota-Cárdenas will echo this sentiment, saying:

> . . . he's very much aware now
>   and makes fervent Revolution
>   so his children
>   and the masses
>   will be free
> but his woman
>   in every language
>   has only begun to ask
>   —y yo querido   viejo
>   and ME?—
> (COTA-CÁRDENAS, *Marchitas,* 42)

Although these writers were calling attention to the plight of women,
these poems were not aggressive in their language. They still maintained an
attitude of affection for their men: Cervantes calls her man *carnal* (brother,
companion, of my flesh), and Cota-Cárdenas calls the man *querido viejo*
(beloved old man). Yet these women would later be called Malinchistas, or
traitors, by the militant men in the movement, who felt that group solidarity was too important to be deflected by women's issues. La Malinche
is the name of an Indian woman who was given to Hernán Cortés during
the conquest of Mexico and who served as the translator for the Spaniards.
The term *malinchista* refers to anyone who sells out, but especially to for-
eigners. Chicana lesbians, who were also considered traitors, were likewise
called Malinchistas.

What did the women do about this negative attitude? Both heterosexual women and lesbians embraced the image of Malinche, incorporating it into their literature and making her their heroine. In fact, overcoming these negative connotations around the image of Malinche led to an enormous amount of creativity in treating the subject.

3. There was a recognition that Chicanas were defined by their own special circumstances, such as language, family, and cultural surroundings. These circumstances had to be defined for and by ourselves if we were to understand our stories, our myths, our traditions. Thus in the early days of Chicana feminism there were many poems and stories about developing an identity of our own, about growing up, and the coming into Chicana consciousness. Our spaces were articulated by Gloria Anzaldúa, in a much-quoted book, as being that of mestiza consciousness—that is, a consciousness aware of being able to choose from the ethnic groups of our heritage and slip back and forth in multiple ways, all of which often overlap. This mestiza consciousness is awareness of being American, Mexican, Indian, and all the spaces in between. It is an awareness that allows Chicana writers to utilize the richness of language and cultural icons that float within that mestiza consciousness. As Anzaldúa states: "I will no longer be made to feel ashamed of existing. I will have my voice: Indian, Spanish, white. I will have my serpent's tongue—my woman's voice, my sexual voice, my poet's voice. I will overcome the tradition of silence" (Anzaldúa, *Borderlands,* 59).

4. Early on, it became important that we begin to recover the tradition of women in our culture, finding strength in numbers. When in the academic and writers world we looked for guides and mentors, there were none. In the professions there were no models, no teachers to guide us through the world of power. Yet we looked around and saw each other, and we saw our abuelitas, our mothers, who were women of great strength, who were survivors. We converted our cultural images into images of power: Sandra Cisneros sexes the Virgin of Guadalupe, the curanderas become our guides. Coatlicue, that fearsome and terrible Aztec goddess—creator and destroyer at the same time—becomes a talk show hostess, giving pertinent advice, and La Llorona's moans, that wailing woman mistakenly seen to be searching for lost children, are, all along, the moans of pleasure as she sneaks off to the river to find rapture in the arms of her lover. Malinche, la lengua, becomes the mediator. As an example of this empowerment, Pat Mora takes the negative images of snakes, attributed to La Malinche, Eve, and Medusa, and turns them around, thus intertwining notions about language, rewriting of myths, and

the identification of ourselves with strong cultural icons. As her Llorona tells us,

> Don't think I wail every night.
> I'm a mother, not a martyr.
> But try it. I wear a gown, white,
>   flowing for effect
> and walk by water. Desert women
>   know about survival.
> Join me sometime
>   for there's much to bewail,
> everywhere frail, lost souls
>   We'll cry, ay, ay ay.
> Oye: never underestimate the power of the voice.
> (MORA, *Agua Santa*, 77)

5. In Chicana feminism there is continued recognition of class and power differences. Lorna Dee Cervantes, for example, always states that she came from a struggling female-headed household in the "welfare" class and this has infused her work. Working-class women are especially valued in Chicana writing. The plight of the migrant workers is addressed in many creative pieces, as, for example, by Helena María Viramontes in her novel *Under the Feet of Jesus,* dedicated to her parents, "who met in Button-willow, picking cotton." In this powerful novel a young girl overcomes her fear and timidity confronting authority in order to help her young friend who has been seriously injured. In the last stunning image of this novel, we see Estrella's hope for the future:

> Estrella stood bathed in a flood of gray light. The light broke through and the cool evening air pierced the stifling heat of the loft.
>   She was stunned by the diamonds. The sparkle of stars cut the night—almost violently. . . . The birds pumped their wings in the skies furiously like debris whirling in a tornado, and it amazed her that they never once collided with one another . . . nothing has ever seemed as pleasing to her as this. Some of the birds began descending. . . . Estrella remained as immobile as an angel standing on the verge of faith. Like the chiming bells of the great cathedrals, she be-

lieved her heart powerful enough to summon home all those
who strayed.
(VIRAMONTES, 175–176)

There is also active support for those abused by violence and rape. The earliest Chicana writers talked openly about incest and rape in an effort to bring these evils to consciousness, evils so suppressed in our culture. An early poem, "A Woman Was Raped," by Veronica Cunningham, states:

> a woman
> was raped
> by her father
> and she was only
> thirteen
> and
> I never laugh
> at rape jokes
> another woman
> was raped
> on her first date
> and
> I kant laugh
> at rape
> I just kant laugh
> (IN REBOLLEDO AND RIVERO, 152)

While today it might be difficult to remember that rape jokes were told, and it might be difficult to believe that ethnic and sexist jokes were told, the truth is that they were and they are. The concern for the struggle for women's dignity and rights continues in contemporary Chicana literature. As María Saucedo wrote in the 1970s, when the Chicana overcame her oppression, "se puso a hacer tortillas y Revolución" (she went to work making tortillas and revolution; 112).

6. Just as Chicanas struggled against the macho oppression from within, Chicana lesbians struggled against heterosexual oppression. While lesbian Chicana writers were often at the forefront of radical change in the movement, their voices were marginalized. The Chicana lesbian movement found its voice in several volumes, such as *Chicana Lesbians: The Girls Our Mothers Warned Us About* and *Latina Sexuality,* as well as in the writings of Gloria

Anzaldúa and Cherríe Moraga. They were also included in many anthologies published by Third Woman Press. Chicana lesbians have had to struggle to obtain a public space and voice in such organizations as NACCS.

7. Through the evolution of the last twenty-five years of Chicana feminism, it is clear that Chicana writers are strongly motivated to expand their personal worlds of human understanding. Chicana feminism and Third World feminists can know no borders. Chicanas actively support the struggles of their Latina sisters in the United States: Cubanas and Puerto Riqueñas. Moreover, in today's contemporary atmosphere, with its power struggle against people of color and against immigrants of color, in Chicana feminism we find a sympathy for the plight of the immigrant, in particular, immigrant women and their children. Pat Mora in her early books was always deeply aware of the power and class differences between middle-class Chicanas and Anglos on the border and their Mexican maids. She is sensitive to and plays on the nuances of what makes a person "legal" on the border. In her poem "La Migra" Mora ironically pits the powerful Immigration Service against the mexicana.

1.
Let's play La Migra.
I'll be the Border Patrol.
You be the Mexican maid.
I get the badge and sunglasses.
You can hide and run,
but you can't get away
because I have a jeep.
I can take you wherever
I want, but don't ask
questions because
I don't speak Spanish.
I can touch you wherever
I want but don't complain
too much because I've got
boots and kick—if I have to,
and I have handcuffs.
Oh, and a gun.
Get ready, get set, run.
2.
Let's play La Migra.
You be the Border Patrol.

I'll be the Mexican woman.
Your jeep has a flat,
and you have been spotted
by the sun.
All you have is heavy: hat,
glasses, badge, shoes, gun.
I know this desert,
where to rest,
where to drink.
Oh, I am not alone.
You hear us singing
and laughing with the wind.
Agua dulce brota aquí, aquí, aquí,
but since you can't speak Spanish
you do not understand.
Get ready.
(MORA, *Agua Santa,* 104–105)

Certainly, because of cultural and language alliances, there has been a particular emphasis on support for women who are oppressed in Mexico, in particular, for the plight of the women in the Zapatista movement. As Demetria Martínez says,

in a world where Wall Street memos
have obliterated the memory of corn
and a Brazilian tribe
that has no word for war . . .
hauling faxes, press releases
to a land where la virgen de Guadalupe
wears a Zapatista ski mask
and makes her appearance on laptops in the Lacondón
(MARTÍNEZ, 41)

And Sandra Cisneros writes to the *New York Times* about the plight of women in Sarajevo and holds weekly rallies against the terror and massacre there.

The truth is, if we are to gain liberation and social justice, it cannot be just for a few of us. For writers, then, the task is to continue to write our "hisssssstories," to struggle for dignity, respect, and choice. For many writers, the new image is to be a *malcriada,* a troublemaker, or a loose woman, for only by creating new spaces and new rules will we be free. Sandra Cisneros aptly expresses what may be the feminist manifesto for today's Chicana:

> I'm an aim-well,
> shoot-sharp
> sharp-tongued
> sharp-thinking
> fast-speaking,
> foot-loose,
> loose-tongued,
> let-loose,
> woman-on-the-loose
> loose woman.
> Beware, honey . . .
> ¡Wáchale!
> (CISNEROS, *Loose Woman*, 114–115)

The cautionary "Wáchale" (Watch out for her) indicates that this new role model is a woman conscious of her power and of the world around her. She has lost her naiveté; she is a worldly, wise, transgressive woman. She is a woman to be watched. And her voice is a voice to be heard.

TEN   *"Jugando a la vida con poemas"*

CONTEMPORARY CHICANA POETRY IN SPANISH
(1998)

In this essay I analyze the poetry of some Chicana poets who write in Spanish, tracing their political development from 1970 until today in relation to their themes, their challenge to the language and their struggle with it, their sociopolitical vision, and their place within the realm of Chicano literature given the fact that they write in Spanish. Among the poets I include Angela de Hoyos, Margarita Cota-Cárdenas, and Raquel Valle Sentíes.

Sociopolitical fermentation and developments from 1968 on in the United States with the advent of the protests against the Vietnam War, the feminist movement, civil rights movement, and what we now call the Chicano Renaissance, a movement that embodied the struggle for social and political justice but that was, at the same time, a literary and artistic revival. This revolution, in part, began when the voices of ethnic minorities and women clamored to be heard. Within a nationalistic ideology that wanted to reclaim or construct a unique national cultural/ethnic identity, the fact of being a Mexican American man or a Chicano was important. Part of this identity was the construction of a homeland (patria) that was to be called Aztlán, and to create around that homeland a mythology and set of symbols that would be heroic and at the same time represent the ideas of a separate cultural nationhood. The creative voices that came from the narrative were principally those writers linked to the publisher and editorial house Tonatihuh/Quinto Sol, whose principal writers were Rudolfo Anaya, Rolando Hinojosa, Tomás Rivera, and the only woman to be published at that time, Estela Portillo Trambley. Among the poets were Alurista, who featured prominently in his poetry figures of Aztec heroes and Aztec symbols; José Montoya, who elevated the figure of the Pachuco and of common people; and Corky González, with his heroic poem *Yo soy Joaquín*. But in general, except for a few writers such as Miguel Méndez and Sabine Ulibarrí, who wrote in Spanish, the majority of the Chicano writers wrote in English, at times mixed with a little bit of Spanish, or in Caló, a slang mixture of the two. At the beginning of the Chicano movement the primary focus was on these male writers, but many women at the time were also writing, although it was not as easy for them to be published by the few existing editorial houses. In spite of that, they began to publish through other means, many times in small publishing houses, at times publishing venues that they themselves established.

Many of the Chicana writers who published (or published themselves) during these years of the Chicano movement wrote in Spanish. They wrote in Spanish because it was their native language, or their childhood language, or because they felt much more comfortable writing in Spanish. For example, Margarita Cota-Cárdenas has stated that there are many concepts that she cannot adequately express in English. Or they wrote in Spanish for ideological reasons: the readers they wanted to reach were those whose primary language was Spanish. In addition, they felt that Spanish was better able to represent their Mexicanness and it retained, as well as signaled, their cultural expression of that Mexicanness. Thus, among the writers who wrote and published in Spanish were Angela de Hoyos, Lucha Corpi, Margarita Cota-Cárdenas, and Evangelina Vigil. De Hoyos and Vigil also published bilingual editions of their work. Although Angela de Hoyos translated (or had translated) all her work, Vigil published some poems only in Spanish and others only in English, or English poems with some words in Spanish, but she never translated them. Corpi and Cota-Cárdenas published in Spanish with a few words in English included. Those poets who published in English—Sandra Cisneros, Lorna Dee Cervantes, Ana Castillo, and Pat Mora—did so because they felt more comfortable writing in English, they had been educated in English-speaking schools, and they wanted to reach a more ample audience within the United States. For these writers it was easier to find a publishing house for their works, although even for them the publishers were, in the main, small Chicano presses such as Bilingual Press, Third Woman Press, or Arte Público Press. These presses published more often those writers who wrote in English. Nonetheless, if we examine that poetry published in English, we see the same phenomenon as that published in Spanish, words in Spanish or Caló included. Like Cota-Cárdenas, they too felt that there were certain concepts or words that could only be expressed in Spanish or in slang. Often those poets writing in English were not completely adept in Spanish, because for one reason or another they had become distanced from or were forbidden their mother tongue, but they retain enough cultural signs or culture that gave a certain flavor to their poetry. At times they included cultural concepts translated from Spanish to English, thus giving a sense of "ethnicity" to their poetry, which also marked it as Chicano.

The title of this paper, "Jugando a la vida con poemas" (Playing at life with poetry), comes from a poem by Miriam Bornstein-Somoza. However, it is a line that could be applied to any of the poets I am going to discuss here.

One of the first poets who published during the Chicano Renaissance was Angela de Hoyos. De Hoyos was born in Mexico but grew up in San Antonio, Texas. She began to publish in 1975 and she continues to publish. She and her husband, Manuel, established a small press, M & A Editions, which published not only Angela's work but also that of many other Chicano writers. To date, the books of Angela de Hoyos include *Arise, Chicano! and Other Poems* (1975), *Chicano Poems for the Barrio* (1976), *Selected Poems/Selecciones* (1979), and *Woman, Woman* (1989), as well as many poster poems, broadsides, and poems published in anthologies. Angela's first poems were written in English and then translated into Spanish by Mireya Robles. But as the years went by, Angela began to interchange English with Spanish in code switching and later to write in Spanish. Her poetry is strongly social-political in content, commenting on the struggle of Chicanos in the United States and also the struggle for equality between women and men in their interpersonal relations. The feminist voice of Angela de Hoyos is an ironic one, commenting with dark humor how Chicanos try to control the lives of their women and how, little by little, the women have been able to find their own voice. Evangelina Vigil wrote the following about Angela de Hoyos, and in these words you can see the play and playfulness of language that de Hoyos utilizes.

> Angela de Hoyos is a poet with a paintbrush for a pen. Like a real artist, she transforms her perception of life into una obra de arte, each poem an exquisite masterpiece for us to hang in the galleries of our minds. . . . With ungiving ánimo y determinación, the poet confronts life's natural preocupación—la muerte. But death, not in its ultimate end, for what she speaks of is what that end holds—que's la vida. Angela struggles with life's forces and this she does with artistry. She stands maciza y llena de fuerza and energia. . . .
>
> What these poems shade and shape is the soul—el alma, el espíritu. In them we find love, cariño, ternura—these nour-

ishing the soul and nurturing life. We see un alma coming
to terms with life, thus death. Y de este entendimiento es de
donde nace el juicio que Angela nos regala con sus poemas.
El juicio de una mente, corazón y alma keenly in tune with
the rhythm and color of the world.

    O y es Chicana.

    Evangelina Vigil C/S

    (INTRODUCTION TO DE HOYOS, *Selected Poems*, 7)

    One of Angela's most important poems is "Levántate, Chicano/Arise,
Chicano." Written in 1975, the poem is a revolutionary call to Chicano
farmworkers, a call for them to assume their own voice and power.

En tu mundo migratorio arrastrando días,
tus hijos hambrientos de sonrisas habitan
    la fría cama;
las paredes desnudas arrullan la misma
        canción amarga,
una raída endecha, fina como el aire . . .
Te he visto descender
bajo el agudo tacón de la hazaña,
tus largos soles de sudor brutal,
de innoble ración coronado.

. . . .

De aquí la amargura en tu vida:
donde buscas paz
está el embargo.
Cómo expresar tu angustia
cuando ni aun tus quemantes palabras
te pertenecen, son prestadas
de los purulentos barrios de pobreza,
y la tristeza en tus ojos
refleja sólo el dolor silencioso de tu pueblo.

Levántate, Chicano!—te dicta
la divina chispa íntima—lava tus heridas
y venda tu agonía.
Nadie te redimirá.
Eres tu propio mesías.

(DE HOYOS, *Arise*, 13–15)

In this text, then, de Hoyos exhorts the Chicano to be his own Christ/ savior and admonishes him that he will have to do it by himself. In another text, "La gran ciudad," the poet expresses her disillusion with ideals that for Chicanos are unrealized. These are ideals articulated within the ideology of the United States, which boasts of being the land of opportunity.

1
No one told me.
So how was I to know
that in the paradise
        of crisp white cities
snakes still walk
                upright?

Una mujer de tantas
sola
        divorciada
        separada
        largada
        —what does it matter?—
llegué a la gran ciudad
con mi niño en los brazos
por sembrar su camino trigueño
con las blancas flores
        de la esperanza

(. . . but how quickly they wilted
beneath the scorching
breath of evil.)

2
El barrio, indefenso:
the pit of the poor.
Mi raza: el *ay* por todas partes.

When I couldn't pay the rent
the landlord came to see me.
Y la pregunta, que ofende:
        Ain't you Meskin?
        How come you speak
        such good English?

Y yo le contesto:
Because I'm Spanglo, that's why.
. . . Pero se cobró
el muy pinche
a su modo.

3
And every day the price of hope goes up.
Every day in the bleak pit
the sun casts a thinner shadow
(algún día nos olvidará por completo.)

Hijito, nos comemos hoy
esta fiesta de pan
o lo dejamos para mañana?

4
So where is the paradise?
In the land of the mighty
where is the shining
—THE EQUAL—opportunity?
Can I skin with my bare teeth
The hungry hounds of night

. . . lárgense con su cuento
a otra parte!
I know better.
(DE HOYOS, *Chicano Poems*, 21–22)

As can be seen, the code switching in these poems by de Hoyos is not a superficial poetic technique, but one that establishes a cultural linguistic tension that illuminates not only everyday Chicano speech but also a linguistic response to lived social repression. The irony expressed in the poem also plays on the "whiteness" of the dream in the "white" city, dreams that cannot be realized by the Mexican/Spanglo brown person. The resulting contrasts further emphasize how unattainable the "American dream" is for Chicanos, particularly for women.

Another important early poet is Margarita Cota-Cárdenas. Cota-Cárdenas began to publish poetry shortly after Angela de Hoyos. She published her poetry in *Siete Poetas* (1978), *Noches despertando inConciencias* (1977), and *Marchitas de mayo (sones pa'l pueblo)* (1989). Cota-Cárdenas also has a novel, *Puppet* (1985), and a forthcoming novel, *Sanctuaries of the Heart.*

In a certain sense, Cota-Cárdenas and de Hoyos have many of the same thematic preoccupations, arising from the revolutionary period in which they began to write: the struggle for equality and justice for Chicanos and the special concern for equality for Chicanas. They are also similar in their invocation of the ironic voice that permeates their poetry. Cota-Cárdenas stands out for her sense of humor and the verbal and mental games within her use of language. This does not mean that the content of her poetry is not serious, because it is, but rather that at times it is easier to express difficult things by playing at life with words. Cota-Cárdenas was born in Heber, California, and as it says in the introduction to her poetry in *Siete Poetas,* "Her poetry, constructed as it is from the full taste of life and dialogue, has truly opened consciousness in the lyric work of contemporary Chicanas, and it discovers an experimental purpose which plays coherently with themes that question personal and societal myths" (59, translation mine). Her poem "Creidísimas" is a good illustration of this.

> qué paciente
>   qué insólita
>   tejes tus paisajes
>   Penélope
> él allá circeándose
>   tomándose la buena gana
>   tú trabajando tan bonito
>   símbolo ahora de la paciencia
>   despacito despacito despacito
>   por tantos años   muy lindo ejemplo
>   haciendo   deshaciendo
>   años frustrados
>   o
>   te saciaba por egoística telepatía
>   o
>   tú tenías amante
> (COTA-CÁRDENAS, *Siete Poetas,* 65)

In "Nostalgia" Cota-Cárdenas also plays with those myths and ideals that we had when we were children:

> creía entonces
> que me gustaría ser monja de
> velo largo blanco en el viento

montada a caballo como María Félix
cabalgaba cabalgaba hacia
un bello oriente cinematográfico
en el Convento del Buen Pastor
comíamos cornflakes oscuros
el mois con café y no leche y así
llegaríamos pobres y puras
a ser monjas instantáneas
como creía yo que se podía todo
como en las películas de los años '40
del Motor-Vu
(COTA-CÁRDENAS, *Siete Poetas,* 69)

In this poem Cota-Cárdenas merges childhood dreams of being a nun
with the sexual image of María Felix, a sultry Mexican movie star of the
thirties and forties.

Her latest book of poetry, *Marchitas de mayo,* reveals a mature voice, one
that is reflective but playful at the same time. In this book she considers the
consequences of the massacre at the Plaza de Tlatelolco in Mexico City
in 1968, the betrayal of the Chicano movement by some Chicanos, the
political climate within the United States, and the vital but stagnant relationships between men and women. The book is marked throughout by
a sense of lack of true brotherhood among Chicanos/Chicanas, especially
clearly seen in "Series Compraventa" (The Bought and Sold Series):

V
Mira
No solamente
son ELLOS
los que nos están matando.
Somos nosotros mismos
que *no sabemos*
lo que es Hermano
que *no* reconocemos
nuestra misma propia
matachista historia.
Y muchos critican muy bajo
y otros hablan muy alto
pero como te digo manito

entre nosotros   mismos
    los hay.
(COTA-CÁRDENAS, *Marchitas,* 13)

This book contains strong sentiments and language, for example, in
the poem "Símbolo," which begins "Envidio / a los hombres / el pene"
(I envy men their penis), but the sharp sense of humor in which they are
couched makes us laugh at even harsh themes; at the same time the reader
recognizes the truths that lie loosely beneath the laughter. Playing with
the ideas of Sor Juana as found in her "Redondillas" (Roundelays), Cota-
Cárdenas constructs a modern reality based on Sor Juana's articulation of
hypocritical morality, where she recognizes that there is one sexual standard for men, another for women. In "Todavía es así, Sor Juana" (Things
Are Still the Same, Sor Juana), she says:

> Que fácil burlarse
> de la que se entrega
> y él que más se ríe
> fue él que más rogaba.
> (No creo que todas
> hicimos caso.)
> Y eso pues
> más rabia les da.
> (COTA-CÁRDENAS, *Marchitas,* 35)

Playing in this way with well-known texts and with language, by making us laugh, she also brings recognition to the social situation that tries to
take advantage of women. For Cota-Cárdenas, language—whether it be
Spanish, English, Caló, or code switching—is what carries culture, emotion, and protest. In recognizing this she comments on the difficulty on
being raised in one language and having to express yourself in another:

> Lo que siento,
> lo siento en español.
> Pero en el Valle allá
> las monjas mexicanas
> nos enseñaron a rezar
>   en inglés.
> (COTA-CÁRDENAS, *Marchitas,* 17)

This questioning of language has its counterpart in the questioning of identity: of that feeling Chicanos/as have that they do not fit within either Mexican life and culture nor life and culture in the United States. Who Am I? is a problematic examined in early Chicana literature and one that continues today. In her book *Soy como soy, y qué?* (1996), which won the José Fuentes Mares Prize for Chicano literature, Raquel Valle Sentíes continues the questioning of that problematic. Rejected by Mexicans who deny her her Mexicanness, and by Americans (United States) who say she is not American, Sentíes feels she is neither here nor there. This is a sentiment expressed over and over by Chicana writers, such as Gloria Anzaldúa, Pat Mora, and Erlinda Gonzales-Berry. Sentiés comes to the conclusion, one already comprehended by many Chicana writers, including de Hoyos and Cota-Cárdenas, that she has to occupy a different space, a special space that is separate from the mainstream, but one that is biliminal, complex, and transcultural. The space is that of a border where cultures exist separated and intertwined at the same time, just as the language is. She says:

> "Soy de la frontera,
>   de Laredo,
> de un mundo extraño
> ni mexicano, ni americano
> . . . .
> donde en el cumpleaños lo mismo cantamos
> el *Happy Birthday* que Las Mañanitas,
> . . . .
> donde en muchos lugares
> la bandera verde, blanco y colorada
> vuela orgullosamente al lado de la *red,*
> *white and blue.*"

> Soy como el Río Grande,
> una vez parte de México,
> desplazada.
> Soy como un títere
> jalado por los hilos
> de dos culturas que chocan entre sí.
> Soy la mestiza, la pocha, la Tex-Mex,
> la Mexican-American, la *hyphenated,*
> la que sufre por no tener identidad propia
> y lucha por encontrarla,

. . . .
la que en Veracruz defendía a Estados Unidos
con uñas y dientes,
la que en Laredo defiende a México
con uñas y dientes.

Soy la contradicción andando.
 En fin como Laredo,
  soy como soy, y qué?
(SENTÍES, *Soy*, 91–92)

 This walking contradiction is the mestiza consciousness articulated by Gloria Anzaldúa, and it is depicted as a fluidity, at once nurturing and dry, like the Río Grande. Sentíes is the most recent in a long line of border women.

 Thus it can be seen that Chicana poets struggle with the transculturation of ideology, transnational identities, and multilingual/polyvalent languages and that they do so "jugando a la vida con poemas." Nonetheless, these poems are serious—serious as life itself.

ELEVEN

"Mi Vida Loca"

SYMBOLIC SPACES IN THE CONSTRUCTION
OF IDENTITY IN CHICANA LITERATURE (1998)

In this essay I want to briefly sketch out the cultural and
societal boundaries perceived in the figure of La Loca, the mad heroine
so often seen in Chicana literature, how her symbolic space is constructed
by Chicana writers, and to examine how Chicana writers seize upon this
figure as a representation of how women may function within societal
boundaries that wants to limit their activities and their lives. Within the
purview of this paper I will not be talking about actual mental illness as
reality, but about the perceptions of the behaviors of women who function
outside traditional cultural norms of how women should behave. Moreover, I want to examine how this symbolic space that La Loca inhabits becomes an icon of cultural identity as an ethnically marked site. I will outline how La Loca is seen as "Other" in "La Loca de la Raza Cósmica" by
La Chrisx, as a character in *So Far from God* by Ana Castillo, and as a loose
woman in Sandra Cisneros's book of poems by the same name. These are
only a few of the many representations of *locas;* we could also include, for
example, "La Llorona Loca: The Other Side" by Monica Palacios and the
figure of Petra in Margarita Cota-Cárdenas's *Puppet.*

What does it mean to be a loca? How are locas represented and stereotyped by the society in which they are formed? How do they function? Why are they used as a cultural icon by Chicana writers? We know
that throughout the ages society has tried to control women's minds and
bodies by setting limits on sexuality and on their power. When women
do not function within the norms set by society, they are considered to
be outside those limits, out of control, *fuera de sí* (outside of themselves).
When a woman seems to be out of control, people say, *Pues, qúe le pasa?*
'sta loca (what's wrong with her? she's crazy), usually accompanied by a
spiral gesture pointing at the head. In many ways, this 'sta loca provides
an explanation for behavior that deviates from the standard. Quickly, let
us review the imprints of language that emphasize this behavior. Crazy

women in particular talk too much, often aimlessly; they are loquacious, they are lunatics (coming from "moon," also connected to women and their menstrual flow), they are loony. The word "hysteric" comes from the Greek *hyster,* meaning "uterus." In the nineteenth century the womb was considered to be the cause of emotional illness. As women try to survive in societies that do not allow them the full range of their possibilities and the full expression of their potential, it is not unusual to see many women considered maladjusted and hysterical.

In Chicano/Mexican society there are fairly strong traditions as to how women should behave. Women should be good, like La Virgen María; they should be strong and silent; they should fulfill their responsibilities to family. They could, however, be like Eva, the first temptress, a sexual woman. It has been an either/or proposition. If they are not good, then they must be bad. And bad women are evil, loose, *escandalosas* and *malcriadas.* I have spoken of this phenomenon elsewhere.[1] Often locas are women who have tried to conform to familial religious and societal rules and pressure, but have been unable to. In order to survive, the self splits, fragments, and becomes Other. The Other then can turn to anger (especially against oneself, as in depression) or to unacceptable behavior whereby La Loca is seen as a menace to others. She has gone crazy. She is marginalized because she is out of control and out of touch with "reality."

As menacing as this loca state seems, it is embraced over and over by Chicana writers. Why? Why does this out-of-control woman have so much appeal? Certainly it cannot be because these locas are victimized by their madness and powerlessness; on the contrary, it is precisely because once the anger and condition of being Other is understood and assimilated by La Loca, this symbolic state of *locura* creates and appropriates a transcendent space for new ways of seeing and thinking, a space where anything is possible. Often spaces of locura are original, unique, unpredictable. Often locas show a rare courage. Moreover, even the creative state is seen as one of a temporary *locura.* Throughout literature it is the locas who see the truth, who arrive at new understandings. They are the ones who are clairvoyant, unfettered by old ways of knowing; they are the women who are unhampered by rules and tradition.

In the poem "Malinche's Tips: Pique from Mexico's Mother," Pat Mora writes:

> My reputación
> precedes me. I come
> from a long line of women

much maligned,
hija de Eva,
rumors of gardens,
crushed flowery scent
. . .
velvetmoist with petals,
piel, fruitflesh, ripe
tempting tongue,
sweet juice of
words, plural hiss
of languagessssss
. . .
Women. Snakes.
Snakes and tongues. Snake-haired
women. Loose-haired women. Loose-tongued
women. Open-mouthed women. Open
women. Whores. Mothersssss.
Virgin mothers.
Women of closed
uterus. Women
of closed
mouths. Women
of covered
hair. Women
of cloaked
bodies. Women
who crush
víboras. Women
who crush their
own tongues.
Silent women.
Altared women.

Tip 4: Alter
the altared women.

I became bilingual,
learned to roll
palabras in my mouth
just to taste them,

chew, swallow,
fruta dulce.
(MORA, *Agua Santa,* 64–66)

In this poem Mora plays on images that reconnect women to ancient myths and to language. While the lyric speaker is Malinche, the Indian woman who gave birth to a child by Hernán Cortés, a child symbolically viewed as the first mestizo, Mora nevertheless connects the image of Malinche to that of Eve, as well as to that of Coatlicue, the all-powerful Aztec goddess, both life giver and destroyer. Medusa is also connected in this symbolic circle back to Eve because of the snake images. These multiple images carry the lyric speaker onto sexuality and onto language. Because Malinche was the female translator, she is spoken across her body and across her tongue. It is through her body that she creates the first mestizo child, and across her tongue that she creates a mestizo identity, a bilingual identity. As Eve is condemned in biblical history as a traitor, Malinche is condemned in Mexican history; like Eve, she is cast out into the world as a seductress, prostitute, puta, hooker, bitch. Malinche was feared and reviled because she controlled language and destiny; Coatlicue was feared because she is the powerful all-knowing and destructive goddess; Medusa is feared because, with her snakelike hair, she had the ability to turn people into stone. The space, or identity, that all these females share is that of the angry woman, the mad heroine, La Loca, living a space outside, the space of "Mi vida loca." Moreover, a facet that Medusa, Coatlicue, and Malinche share with woman writers is that most of the characteristics essential to any kind of creative or artistic achievement are valued in men but are considered negative and unnatural in women. Some of these are initiative, assertiveness, strength, aggressiveness, and physical or intellectual superiority. As Susan Kilgore points out in "Through Medusa's Eyes," these same traits are often the outstanding characteristics of the mad heroine.

Through the Locas portrayed in Chicana literature, Chicana writers challenge the cultural stereotypes about women and through their voices reflect their tensions as women "living and working in a male world" (Kilgore, 3). The "mad heroine stands . . . as a metaphor for female experience in a fragmented world" (4). Kilgore asserts that often women writers do not write autobiographically about themselves as artists, but instead "create female lunatics and cloak in illness what is in essence the fury, fear, conflict, artistic selfishness and self assertiveness intrinsic to artistic accomplishment, but antithetical to traditional conceptions of femininity"

(6). Indeed, often the lunacy is directed precisely against those who want the heroine to be a "good girl," against the tyranny of niceness. Because the mad heroine is outside the norms, she explores new ways of thinking and escapes the "female" code. She can emphasize the dissonance in women's lives. "Her power to turn life into stone is the threatening power, to the writer, of inflicting silence . . . ," says Kilgore. "She represents the threatened revenge of a male world . . . the intellectual and thinking head severed from the female body" (16). For all of these reasons, Mora links the loose-haired women to the loose-tongued women.

Thus this vida loca, this crazy space, is deeply and profoundly linked to woman, womb, and word. Moreover, Kilgore goes on to assert that the mad heroine symbolizes women's sense of fragmentation and monstrousness in a society where they are designated as "the Other." She sees this as tragic because American women writers are often seen as lonely and powerless. They represent not only the grotesque images of the female self but also analyze the circumstances that teach women to see themselves as such. Beyond this, however, the madwoman "frequently reveals the creative women" behind Medusa's mask.

I agree with Kilgore's preliminary analysis, but I believe that contemporary Chicana writers go beyond this mere representation of the madwoman and turn the symbolic space created by "Mi vida loca" into a powerful and transformative space, using Greco-Roman myths and hybridizing/syncretizing them with Aztec-Mayan myths to create an identity that is truly their own, both in myth and in language. In an early poem, "La Loca de la Raza Cósmica" by La Chrisx, the lyric speaker dedicates the poem to "las mujeres Chicanas. Está dedicado a las Locas/a las Reinas de la Raza Cósmica" (All Chicanas. It is dedicated to the Crazy Women/the Queens of the Cosmic Race). Here *loca* is equated to *reina* (queen). Moreover, the poem is intended to outline the various complex roles that women have as the speaker juxtaposes all the contradictions and fragmentations that Chicanas live as they try to survive the limitations and the possibilities offered by society. As has been pointed out by many critics, "La Loca de la Raza Cósmica" is one of many "yo soy" (I am) contestations to the epic sweep of Corky Gonzales's "Yo soy Joaquín." However, instead of having heroes of mythic proportions, as in "Joaquín," La Loca sees heroism in the common work, contradictions, and lives of women in the community. Why is she a loca? Because she is creating and seeing outside of masculinist society.

In *So Far from God,* by Ana Castillo, one of the main characters is La Loca Santa, a child who was thought to have died when she was three but who then "woke up." Diagnosed as an epileptic, she nevertheless exhibits very peculiar behavior all of her life: "She became known simply as La Loca . . . even La Loca's mother and sisters called her that because her behavior was *so* peculiar. Moreover, La Loca herself responded to that name and by the time she was twenty-one no one remembered her Christian name" (25).

La Loca will not let anyone except her mother and sisters come close to her, and so she is able to live in isolation, untouched by society. Because of this peculiarity she acquires healing powers, and in particular is able to heal those "traumas and injustices" her sisters were dealt by society. La Loca has special abilities: she intuits when someone has died, she senses the needs of people. She is outside of traditional obligations, although she becomes, of her own free will, an excellent cook.

> There was so much Sofi did not know about the whys of Loca, despite the fact that since the age of three when she had died and been "resurrected" at her funeral Mass, Loca had never left home. . . . She had never been to school. She had never been to a dance. She never went to Mass. (At first this, above all, had concerned Sofi due to pressure from el Father Jerome, but no coaxing, no threats about punishment neither here nor in the afterlife bothered Loca, who, when, the priest told her on the phone that if she did not honor the Lord's day in His Home she would surely burn in hell, said, "I've already been there." And then, much to Sofi's embarrassment, certainly having learned this expression from that other malcriada daughter Esperanza, Loca added, "And actually, it's overrated."
>
> . . . To her sisters, the saddest part of all was that Loca had never had a social life. Her limber horse-riding body had never so much as felt the inside of a dress, much less of a bra! No, Loca had done none of the things young ladies did or at least desired to do.
>
> She had become proficient in cooking and sewing but only to help her mother and sisters at home. She was the caretaker of the animals and had done excellent training with the horses since she was barely five or six years old.
>
> And though no one had given her a single lesson, and surely no one in that household could even carry a tune, nobody played the fiddle like Loca—the very one that had

belonged to her abuelo and which she found as a child in her mother's armoire.

So it may be said she had a full life. Maybe not one re-served for a lady, but then, neither had the rest of the women in her family. (220–222)

Loca takes into her very being all the injustices of society, and in the end, because she is such a sensitive creature, she dies of AIDS, "thinking that for a person who had lived her whole life within a mile radius of her home and had only traveled as far as Albuquerque twice, she certainly knew quite a bit about this world, not to mention beyond, too, and that made her smile as she closed her eyes" (245). After her death she becomes venerated as a saint, one of the altared women Pat Mora writes about, but she never feels obligated to answer anyone's prayers.

Finally I want to discuss the loose women so artfully depicted by Sandra Cisneros. In *Loose Woman* we see represented the "bitchy" heroine, a doubling device meant to be read against the eyes of good women. These loose women do not succumb to the tyranny of niceness; rather they are the locas who "break laws, upset the natural order, anguish the Pope and make fathers cry" (12). They are "loose-tongued, let-loose, women-on-the-loose" who are wicked and "break things." Their choices are between being "good" and being powerful, and they choose to be powerful. They join the long line of freewheeling, liberated, angry locas slinging crockery at their men, at the world. These loose women let their minds, their tongues, and their language hurl themselves at control, order, and limitation.

In *Loose Woman,* as Xochitl Shuru points out, Cisneros depicts several degrees and stages of locura, which Shuru delineates as (1) manipulation and self-destructiveness, (2) denial of hysteria, (3) exasperation and lack of self-control, and (4) embrace and acceptance of locura (4). In these poems we see the lyric speaker's lack of control and alienated identity, particularly manifest when in "Pumpkin Eater" she says:

> I'm no trouble.
> Honest to God
> I'm not.
> I'm not
> The kind of woman
> who telephones in the middle of the night . . .

—who told you that?—
splitting the night like machete. . . .
No, no, not me . . .
I swear, I swear, I swear . . .

I'm no hysteric,
terrorist
emotional anarchist.
(170)

The denials won't work, and it is only when the writers are able to understand and define their anger as well as accept the reasons for their fragmentation and their alienation that they will be able to seize the words and their own language. While often the anger of las locas is turned against themselves, in Chicana literature the anger is turned against social injustice. These loose women, malcriada locas, so eloquently captured by Chicana writers, have created a special place, a place of women who live life to the fullest, who talk and scream, who write and create themselves. The space created in "La vida loca" is a useful paradigm that allows the Chicana author to label, articulate, allow, and make conscious her experience in dealing with the dissonance in her life between myth and reality, to express her anger and fury as does Medusa. They finally seize the power of all the powerful women such as La Malinche and Coatlicue in order to redeem the loca as a full, profound, sensitive, and transformative figure. Las locas are not to be feared. To paraphrase Helene Cixous, you only have to look at Medusa (or Coatlicue) straight on to see her. And they are not deadly. They are beautiful and they are laughing.

TWELVE

The Chicana Bandera:
Sandra Cisneros in the Public Press

CONSTRUCTING A CULTURAL ICON (1996–1999)

Sandra Cisneros is one of the few Chicana writers who has "made it" into the mainstream publishing world, and indeed she is internationally recognized as an excellent writer. She has also become a cultural icon in the public press. By icon I mean an image or portrait, a representation of something monumental. Traditionally icons are paintings of saints such as the image of Christ or the Virgin Mary, but in contemporary life an icon can be a representation of a person who has acquired larger-than-life stature—a recent example of a cultural icon would be the Mexican painter Frida Kahlo.

In fact, while preparing this essay and after I had titled it, I found a pertinent interview with Cisneros in which the very subject of iconography is discussed in "An Afternoon with Sandra Cisneros," by Katynka Zazueta Martínez:

> Martínez: At the writing workshop you encouraged us (writers) to turn icons on their head and in your novel, *Caramelo,* you've flipped the icon of the compassionate Mexican abuela on it's [*sic*] head. Was there ever, or is there, an icon or taboo you've been scared to touch? It seems like Frida Kahlo is an icon just screaming to be turned on it's [*sic*] head.

> Cisneros: AAAh! I'm tired of the commercialization and martyrdom of Frida Kahlo! . . . I do like Frida Kahlo's work. But Frida Kahlo as a woman . . . she gets pesada.

> Martínez: Do you think that you yourself could or are turning into an icon for Chicanos?

> Cisneros: I hope not because then someone would have to flip me on my head.

Martínez: How do you think they would do that?

Cisneros: I don't know. . . . I'm very sensitive. . . . I don't like
when writers become bigger than their books. I don't like
when people look at me and they don't see me. . . . Because
what's happening lately is people start looking at me as the
work and they don't see me as the woman who writes. If
you look at the work, all you're seeing is the finished product. You're not seeing the first 17 drafts with all the errors
and cliches and mistakes. . . . The art's always more precise,
more articulate, more distilled, wiser, more powerful than I'll
ever be.
(12)

In this essay I am not going to analyze Cisneros's writing. As you may
know, Cisneros is the author of *Bad Boys* (1980), *The House on Mango Street*
(1983), *My Wicked Wicked Ways* (1987), *Woman Hollering Creek* (1991), and
Loose Woman (1994), as well as many essays and interviews. I very much
admire Cisneros as a writer. When I first read *The House on Mango Street*
many years ago, I found it a fresh and innovative work, a distinct voice.
The works that have followed and her many poems and essays have continued to prove Cisneros an original. But there are many writers, also fresh
and original, who have not been elevated to the same status as Cisneros. I
want to examine why.

To begin, the sales of Cisneros's books have been phenomenal. *The
House on Mango Street* had sold over half a million copies by May of 1996,
and her other books have been equally well received. I want to analyze not
the academic examination of her writing but rather how she is seen in the
popular press, the book reviews in newspapers and book trade journals,
her images in popular magazines such as the *New Yorker, Glamour, Vanity
Fair,* and *Ms.,* and how she is viewed abroad, as her books are increasingly translated into other languages. For much of this information I am
indebted to Sandra herself, as she has sent me much of the material to be
archived.

In addition to her own creative voice, Cisneros has been part of the
tidal wave of interest in women's literature and minority literature. In
the last fifteen years there has been extraordinary interest in Latino/a writing. The sales of books by Laura Esquivel, Julia Alvarez, Isabel Allende, and
Rosario Ferré have been excellent. Indeed one headline in the press says,
"Book publishers say 'hola' to US Hispanic Market" (Campbell, 9). Along

with this interest there is a particular emphasis on the women writing. The group solidarity that the women show for and with each other has made it into the popular press as "Las Girlfriends." Although the designation can encompass any of the Latinas writing today, the picture that was published in *Vanity Fair* in 1994 shows Ana Castillo, Denise Chávez, Julia Alvarez, and Sandra Cisneros. They are attractive, appealing, and eminently photogenic.

From the beginning, as seen in her book *My Wicked Wicked Ways,* Cisneros has written about her rich cultural heritage and traditions, and she has not been afraid to tackle taboo subjects. Moreover, she has maintained a healthy sense of self and of life's ironies. Many of her poems and stories are self-reflexive as well as self-referential. At times her ironic voice is misunderstood, as irony often is. She states,

> I am the woman of myth and bullshit.
> (True. I authored some of it.)
> I built my little house of ill repute.
> Brick by brick. Labored,
> loved and masoned it.
> (*Loose Woman,* 113)

When interviewed by the popular press, Cisneros says what she thinks. Thus she admits that she has self-consciously aided in the creation of her own media image. Because she finds herself in the public eye, what she thinks has an impact. She is often in the thick of things, talking about the problems in Sarajevo, involved in the campaign against AIDS, discussing racism and prejudice, and making controversial statements, such as in the recent documentary on Selena where Cisneros said she did not think Selena was a good role model for young Latinas. She becomes a public spokesperson for Chicana feminists, for Latinos, for women. Often she is treated kindly by the press, at times not. Over the years I am sure she has learned when to speak out, bracing herself for the consequences when others do not agree with her views. Thus she can be seen as the woman and the writer who is effective in raising Chicana/Mexicana consciousness, empowering students, and filling the literary landscape. One critic writes, "Writer Cisneros Lends Power to Chicanas" (Walsh, E4), and another says her "tales speak to the hearts of women" (Nakao, C1). On the other hand, she has been seen as an "intellectual shock jock" (Allen). That she stirs the emotions with her writing and her comments cannot fail to interest us. Caroline Pierce states, "Cisneros scattershoots with wicked wit. Rebel-

lious Mexican-American writer spares no one with her acerbic humor."
Later she adds, "Sandra Cisneros is a wicked, wicked woman [playing off
Cisneros's title]," and ends, "And whatever else you do, never repent. . . .
The world needs you the way you are" (Pierce, E7).

The press in the United States delights in seeing Cisneros as a "bad
girl," and Cisneros images herself as that at times. In a particularly crabby
mood in 1994, facing a long book tour and inane questions from reporters,
Cisneros wrote this poem:

> "It Occurs To Me I Am The Creative/Destructive Goddess
> Coatlicue."
> I deserve stones.
> Better leave me the hell alone.
>
> I am besieged.
> I cannot feed you.
> You may not souvenir my bones,
> knock on my door, camp, come in,
> telephone, take my Polaroid. I'm paranoid.
> I tell you. *Lárgensen.* Scram.
> Go home.
>
> I am anomaly. Rare she who
> can't stand kids and can't stand you.
> No excellent Cordelia cordiality have I.
> No coffee served in tidy cups.
> No groceries in the house.
>
> I sleep to excess,
> smoke cigars,
> drink. Am at my best
> wandering undressed,
> my fingernails dirty,
> my hair a mess.
> Terribly
>
> sorry, Madame isn't
> feeling well today.
> Must
>
> Greta Garbo.
> Pull an Emily D.

Roil like Jean Rhys.
Abiquiu myself.
Throw a Maria Callas.
Shut myself like a shoe.

Stand back. Christ
almighty. I'm warning.
Do not. Keep
out. Beware.
Help! Honey,
this means
you.
(IN ESPADA, 39–40)

Part of the Cisneros mystique is the fact that she is an ethnic woman
of working-class background (her father was an upholsterer, her mother
a factory worker); this mystique allows children to see a model for their
own dreams. Cisneros always credits her mother for teaching her how to
be different and for giving her the space to read. Because of this, one of
her greatest causes has been the support of public libraries. As stated in
Library Journal, "For the writer who grew up feeling that 'being good was
never good enough,' the public library was a special refuge. Now Cisneros
is concerned that libraries are closing down, effectively closing out young-
sters like herself who need that refuge. Chicago may have a sparkling new
central library, but the branch in her mother's neighborhood—which has
been located in a former menswear store—has burned down" ("Sandra
Cisneros: Giving Back," 55).

Cisneros often gets high marks for her work with schoolchildren. In
1992 while in Chicago she was invited to give a talk to a class of eighth-
grade girls at Seward School, where 95 percent of the students are Latino.
Cisneros held up her fifth-grade report card full of C's and D's as proof
that bad grades don't necessarily mean a bad mind. In the public press there
are often stories of how children have been affected by Cisneros's writing,
from *Hairs/Pelitos* to *The House on Mango Street.* Seeing themselves for once
reflected in the literature they read has a positive impact on them.

Moreover, her public call to a friend in war-torn Sarajevo, "Who wants
stories now?" published in the *New York Times,* was a call to remember
the personal elements in those strife-ridden war zones. Cisneros said, "A
woman I know is in there. . . . Something must be done! . . . I don't know
what to do!" (17). This was not merely a dramatic call, abstractly thought

out for Cisneros. She had lived for some time in Sarajevo and has close friends there. The war impacted her personally.

Headlines of articles give us some insight into Cisneros's public persona: "Sandra Cisneros: 'Cuando me pedían que hablara de cisnes, hablaba de ratas'" (When they asked me to write about swans, I wrote about rats) ("Sandra Cisneros: Cuando me pedían," 22); "Municiones envueltas en papel picado" (Arms wrapped in delicate cut paper) (Joysmith, 7), a statement reminiscent of what surrealist André Breton said about Frida Kahlo—that she was a bum dressed as a butterfly; "Sandra Cisneros: 'Beware, Honey'" (Bacharach, 4); and "En mi literatura creo mi Frankestein, donde un personaje es diversos cuerpos" (In my literature I create a Frankenstein where a character is many bodies) (Molina, 26). Over the years Cisneros, born and raised in Chicago, has had a problematic relationship with the press in that town. Though she was at first dismissed as a writer by the press, Chicago's attitude toward her is changing. As one reviewer wrote:

> Sandra Cisneros has come a long way from the loose-limbed
> woman featured on the cover of the very first *Third Woman*
> magazine in 1980. Back then she had a hopeful, girl-next-
> door quality about her. . . . Friday night reading at the
> Duncan YMCA . . . Cisneros was something else entirely.
> First, she came back as an out of towner, wryly noting that
> she gets more support now than when she lived here. Second,
> she came back a hero, with two books of poetry and two of
> fiction under her belt, all of them critically praised and door
> openers for other Latino writers. . . . But more significant on
> Friday night, perhaps, was the change to the highly stylized
> and cool persona Cisneros now shows her public. Dressing
> almost exclusively in vintage Mexican wear, Cisneros seemed
> to banter easily from the stage.
> (OBEJAS, 124)

Another reviewer, Kim Berez, said that night, "Both Sandra and Angela [Jackson] have strong stage personalities befitting entertainers." She went on to say, "If you've read Sandra but never heard her, from the strength of voice in print you might be surprised at how small and high and staid her voice is" (Berez, 8).

The decorative aspect of Cisneros, her striking looks and her beauty as well as her costumes and her voice are very much commented on in the press: "Cisneros in horn-rimmed glasses purchased in a Chicago airport looks like a cross between a 1950s librarian and a go-go dancer, with a punchy delivery and an unerring sense for the 'healthy' lie. She writes and speaks in bilingualese, always from her 'corazón'—of fibers and filaments, abandoned daughters, fathers too late appreciated" (Meyers, B1). When Cisneros read at the Poetry Center, Dina Lee Fisher observed: "In walks Sandra Cisneros, just on time. Cisneros, a fiercely passionate woman, has a lot to be thankful for and a lot to be angry about. Born and raised in Chicago, she writes about the dreams, yearnings and realities of lives lived amongst the tenement houses and streets she grew up in. . . . Standing with a black velvet sash crisscrossing her chest in a giant X, arms akimbo and legs planted firmly apart, Cisneros struck me as a modern day bandit making nighttime raids on a wealthy border town" (Meyers and Fisher, 2).

This image of the Mexican revolutionary bandit Pancho Villa strikes home to Cisneros herself as she proclaims,

> I'm Pancha Villa.
> I break laws,
> upset the natural order
> anguish the Pope and make fathers cry.
> I am beyond the jaw of law.
> I'm *la desperada,* most-wanted public enemy.
> My happy picture grinning from the wall
> (*Loose Woman,* 113–114)

When Cisneros read at San Francisco's Herbst Theater, this is the description: "In a stunning off-the-shoulder black gown, draped by a long yellow scarf, Cisneros charmed the audience with her little girl's voice, which deepened and stretched as she read passages from her books. . . . Earlier that day, Cisneros admitted that costumes are one of her greatest loves. 'I should have been a spy,' she said, dark eyes twinkling, 'I'm kind of chameleon-like. I have a chameleon-like wardrobe. I have all these different selves'" (Nakao, C1, C4). And, in a 1992 article in the *Chicago Tribune,* she is described as "a tiny woman with cropped hair, . . . wearing an ankle-length brown crushed velvet dress and black suede boots, and puffing on a cigar" (shades of nineteenth-century bluestocking feminists). In this same article she has "a voice like Tinker Bell's, smokes Fidel-style cigars and packs a Mexico-sized disdain for Chicago" (in Garza, D1).

In a report from New York, Mary B. W. Tabor writes:

Ms. Cisneros who can be both fiercely feminine and an-
drogynous, idealistic and deeply cynical is herself a study in
contradiction. Before her audience . . . she cuts a sophisti-
cated figure in a long, sleek crushed velvet outfit, boots and
short dark hair. But her expressions are whimsical, her voice
small and childlike.

　　Her writing is lean. Her conversation style is chatty and
rambling. . . . She is a self-described "terrorist," "anarchist,"
and "Chicana feminist." . . . But it is finding the middle
ground between the Latin and the American that has
provided the most creative tension for Ms. Cisneros.

(TABOR, C10)

　　Moreover, Cisneros says, "It's so wacky. I was the girl with the C's and
D's. I was the girl in the corner with the goofy glasses from Sears. I was
the ugly kid in the class with the bad haircut, the one nobody would talk
to" (*Albuquerque Tribune,* February 1, 1993, D1–D3). Thus, in the United
States she is represented as a stylish woman, a terrorist bandit, a nineteenth-
century bluestocking, and an eccentric but diacronic writer. Let us see
how the she is represented abroad and in Latin America.

　　When her books came out in Germany, the German journalistic community focused on her ethnicity: her Mexicanism seemed very exotic to
them. Headlines said things in English like "Cheek to cheek, spell chiqui-
tita" (Schouten, 67). The focus of the Mexican press is on Cisneros's use of
language, which intrigues journalists. One headline says, "Neither English
nor Spanish." They are also interested in the articulation of Chicanos as
marginalized in both U.S. and Mexican culture. In Spain, however, with
her books published in Barcelona, the emphasis is on the fairy-tale aspect
of her life. The title of *Woman Hollering Creek,* translated into Spanish, is
Erase un hombre, érase una mujer roughly translated as "Once upon a time
there was a man, once there was a woman." Seizing upon the mythic
aspect, other critics also present Cisneros herself as myth: "erase una niña
escritora" (once there was a little girl writer) (Carbonell, 1). She is portrayed as "Hija del hambre y la marginación" (the daughter of hunger and
marginalization). The article goes on to say, "Sandra Cisneros creció ley-
endo cómics y fotonovelas, chamullando un inglés macarrónico de color
café con leche que tiene su máximo exponente en el 'spanglish.' Un lío"
(Sandra Cisneros grew up reading comic books and fotonovelas, making a
macaronic like English sort of coffee with milk color, which has its stron-

gest outcome in Spanglish. It's a mess") (Carbonell, 1). Like the Mexicans, the Spaniards are concerned with and fascinated by the language mixtures, conceding that a "new" sort of language is being created.

Cisneros began to get national attention when she won an NEA fellowship in 1982 for poetry as well as in 1987 for fiction and with the publication of her books by Random House. By 1994 the headlines read, "Defiant Sandra Cisneros gains literary acclaim" (McIlvain, 1A). When *Woman Hollering Creek* was published in 1991, the writers couldn't make up their minds whether she is "Hollering Loud," as the *Texas Observer* stated (Littledog, 4), or softly, as suggested in the *Kansas City Star* headline "Whispers from a Brave Author" (Dion, 3). By this time all concede that she has "Rare Talent" (Milner, 10).

In 1995 Cisneros was awarded one of the coveted MacArthur Foundation grants. By now, Cisneros was accepted by San Antonio and Texas as one of theirs. Rick Martínez in the *Houston Chronicle* said, "Genius lives in gawdawful places like Texas, too" (Martínez, 31A), and Elda Silva of the *San Antonio Express-News* wrote: "Local author recipient of valued grant," going on to say, "San Antonio author Sandra Cisneros has been awarded a 'genius grant' . . . from the John D. and Catherine T. MacArthur Foundation. She is the second San Antonian to win the prestigious award. Cisneros, a novelist, poet, short story writer and essayist is one of two Texans in a field of 24 to receive the prestigious fellowship" (Silva, 1A, 7A).

Later, Hilton Kramer on National Public Radio took issue with the selections, implying that Anglo males had been overlooked. While Kramer's remarks were not focused directly on Cisneros, San Antonio journalists, Chicano writers, and women all over took offense at his remarks. As Rick Martínez wrote in the *San Antonio Express-News,* "Had Kramer been on West Martin Street in Cisneros' current hometown of San Antonio the day he made his comments, he no doubt would have gotten his butt kicked because many Cisneros fans took it personally" (Martínez, "Cisneros Scenario," 31A). Martínez goes on to equate the controversy with the growing wave of anger being directed currently at Hispanics and other minorities, and with the class struggle repeated throughout history. For Martínez, "The lesson for Hispanics is to not forget the dynamics of this class struggle and lend a hand to those in their respective fields who come after them." And, as he further comments, "it was no surprise to those who know her that the day after winning her $255,000 MacArthur grant, Cisneros was back in the barrio lecturing to students in San Antonio's Guadalupe Cultural Arts Center" (Martínez, 31A).

Another answer to Kramer came from Barbara Miles, who wrote in the *San Antonio Express-News*: "I was at our beautiful new library the evening of June 1 and heard and enjoyed Sandra Cisneros and the other authors. It was a wonderful experience to hear their words in their own voices. Cisneros has a wonderful way with words, and she is a world class writer and a very classy lady. We are so lucky to have her make her home in San Antonio. I am not an English major, a writer or even a very educated person, just a 50-year-old Anglo woman with a GED. But I can tell when I read and hear something that is true and from the heart. And this is how Cisneros writes, and this is how she is. Who cares what some critic thinks in New York?" (Miles, 4).

Now I want to discuss the King William "color flap," as one newspaper called it. This incident (it started in 1997) in the life of Sandra Cisneros tweaked the linguistic creativity and sense of humor of journalists who, indeed, helped make it a cause célèbre. Here is the story. Several years ago Cisneros bought an old Victorian home in the King William Historic District of San Antonio. The King William Neighborhood Association is keenly interested in historic preservation, and all the houses in the area have to conform to a series of rules; one of them was that the houses should be painted according to "historic guidelines." When Sandra decided to paint her house, she decided on a "periwinkle blue" (a blue that was decidedly purple). This choice of color scheme started a controversy as some of her neighbors complained to the Historic Preservation Office about the color. This of course set off a wave of headlines about the debate: "King William Seeing Red over Purple" (Yerkes); "The Color Purple" (in the *Monitor,* in McAllen—a reference to Alice Walker's novel of the same title); "Purple Politics" (*San Antonio Express-News*); and "Now We Know Why Its Called Purple Passion" (Yerkes). The issue began to escalate when many self-righteous critics complained that the transgression of the color scheme would destroy the historical significance of the neighborhood. Ann McGlone of the Historic Preservation Office notified Cisneros that her color scheme violated city historic district requirements, saying, "It's very appealing. . . . But it's not appropriate to history. This isn't about taste; it's about historical content" (Yerkes, "King William," D1). Many articles in the newspaper set out the reasons why there was such a restriction on the use of color. As David Anthony Richelieu said in the *San Antonio Express-News* on August 12, 1997, "The rules are written to protect and preserve the historic value of all homes and structures in historic districts. They echo rules used all across the country" (B1). He then went on for five paragraphs to explain how the historic district defined color schemes by taking paint samples from old houses in the district.

Other articles in the same newspaper felt that, yes, color in historic districts was important, but that some individuality should also be allowed. Mike Greenberg argued on August 13, 1997: "A little noncomformity is a good thing. Had Cisneros painted her house Longhorn orange and fluorescent green, I'd say throw the book at her. But her color scheme is gorgeous, and it respects and delineates the architectural details of her house. Beyond that, whatever your opinion of Cisneros, she is undeniably a figure of historic significance for San Antonio. Her paint scheme takes on historic significance by association. Thus, the proper course might be to designate Cisneros's house, along with its purple paint, a historic landmark. Neither she nor anyone else would be allow to change the colors. Ever" (B1).

After these strong words, the battle escalated. Cisneros stated that she had painted her house that color because she wanted to reflect the passionate, colorful spirit of South Texas and Mexico. The color was no longer "periwinkle blue" but clearly purple. Shortly thereafter, the battle turned ideological and political. Cisneros researched Victorian houses and was surprised to discover that Victorian houses were often brighter than houses in Mexico. This was validated by a San Antonio architect, Andrew Pérez, who stated that Victorians favored bright colors to offset England's dreary gray weather and added, "It's an interesting use of color, but in a way, I feel it's a little conservative" (in Danini, 7B). At a packed hearing about her colors, Cisneros said that upon doing further research, she discovered that her house was originally built to be a rent house in the Lavaca neighborhood and later moved to its present location. She said, "In 1913 my house was sawed in two like a Houdini magic act and wheeled to its present location" (Cisneros, "Our Tejano History," 5J). Other houses in the Lavaca area were brightly colored. And as Carlos Guerra commented in a column after the hearing, "Worse, she told the Board, is that in her research she found precious little about the particulars of antique Mexican-American homes of San Antonio since local conservationists chose to preserve precious few of them or even write or photograph them." One of her supporters at the meeting even began her commentaries to the commission by singing "America the Beautiful" (B1).

The brouhaha over Cisneros's house then turned into a serious discussion about the erasure of history. Many callers and writers to the newspaper endorsed the idea that Mexican American history is absent from San Antonio, even in the signage about places and events. Others called the newspaper to complain about Cisneros and Mexicans in general. One caller said, "As a U.S. citizen, I'm getting real tired of these people that want to bring Mexico to the United States." And another repeated the trite "If they want to live in Mexico, Why don't they, ah, she, go back where she came from?" (Yerkes, "Now We Know," G1). Once again columnist Yerkes focused on Cisneros, the icon, saying, "The Board never came down to a showdown with the eloquent Cisneros, who argued her points in her riveting, little-girl voice. (She did not wear purple, but a red dress and green shawl, with cactus-decorated cowboy boots.)" ("Purple Passion," B1).

Various letters to the editor were printed on August 12, defending Cisneros. Martha Durke wrote:

> As a designer and lover of antiques and architecture, I appreciate many of the benefits of having our historic buildings protected, especially against demolition or poor renovation, but legislating color choice is absurd. I also appreciate the value of color as a form of self-expression and cultural evolution. The real issue here is tolerance. Most people conform by nature. When one individual attempts to express a different point of view, the city design authorities whip out their big paintbrush and wipe out those poisonous colors before they spread. Scary, isn't it?
> (6B)

And José García de Lara, an architect, wrote:

> If she decides to concede to the pointless macho fantasies of the Hysterical Review Board, let's examine the options. Hmmmm, we want to express our culture. Current colors in the King William Neighborhood area include white, oxblood red and jalapeño green. That's it! Cisneros could repaint the house vivid *"verde, blanco y colorado, la vandera del soldado"* (saluting at attention). This would accentuate the statue of the sleeping Mexican on the side of her yard.
> (B4)

Thus the ideology over house color, which even made the *New York Times,* became an identity marker about race and color in general. It was also a marker about ethnicity, national alliances, erasure of history. Let me briefly give you, in her own words, what Cisneros sees about her color struggle:

> Ay que telenovela mi vida! . . . One day I painted my house Tejano colors, and the next day my house is in all the news, cars swarming by, families having their photos taken in front of my purple casita—as if it was the Alamo. The neighbors put up an ice tea stand and made $10.
>
> All this happened because I choose to live where I do. I live in San Antonio because I'm not a minority here. I live in the King William neighborhood because I love old houses.
>
> Since my neighborhood is historic, there are certain code restrictions that apply. Any house alteration plans have got to be approved by the Historic Design and Review Commission. This is to preserve the neighborhood's historic character, and that's fine by me.
>
> Because I thought I had permission, I gave the go-ahead to have my house painted colors I considered regional, but, as it turned out, hadn't been approved. However, I was given the chance to prove them historically appropriate. So I did my research, and what I found is this. We don't exist. My history is made up of a community whose homes were so poor and unimportant as to be considered unworthy of historic preservation. No famous architect designed the houses of the Tejanos, and there are no books in the San Antonio Conservation Society Library about the houses of the working class community, no photos romanticizing their poverty, no ladies auxiliary working toward preserving their presence. Their homes are gone, their history is invisible.
>
> The few historic homes that have survived have access to them cut off by freeways because city planners did not judge them important. . . . Or they are buildings fenced in by the Plaza Hotel; I wasn't even aware they were part of Tejano history until I began my research into my house colors even though I walk past them almost every day.
>
> Our history is in neighborhoods like the famous Laredito barrio, heart of the old Tejano community and just a block from City Hall: it proved so "historically valuable" it was demolished and converted into a jail, parking lot and downtown

police station with only the *casa* of Tejano statesman José Angel Navarro as evidence Laredito was ever there.

Our past is present only in the churches or missions glorifying a Spanish colonial past. But I'm not talking about the Spaniards here. My question is where is the visual record of the Tejanos? . . .

Frankly I don't understand what all the fuss is about. I thought I had painted my house a historic color. Purple is historic to us. It only goes back a thousand years or so to the pyramids. It is present in the Nahua codices, book of the Aztecs, as is turquoise, the color I used for my house trim; the former color signifying royalty, the latter, water and rain.

But we are a community *sin documentos*. We don't have papers. Our books were burned in the conquest, and ever since then we have learned to keep quiet, to keep our history to ourselves, to keep it alive generation to generation by word of mouth, perhaps because we feared it would be taken away from us again. Too late; it has been taken from us.

In San Antonio when we say historic preservation we don't mean everyone's history, even though the Historic Preservation Office is paid for by everybody's taxes. When they ask me to prove my colors historically appropriate to King William they don't mean Tejano colors. But I am certain Tejanos lived in this neighborhood too. That's what my neighbors have told me. Mr. Chavana, who lives across the street, says his family has been living in this downtown area since the 1830s, and I know he's not lying. He's not allowed to; he's a reverend.

Color is a language. In essence, I am being asked to translate this language. For some who enter my home, these colors need no translation. However, why am I translating to the professionals? If they're not visually bilingual what are they doing holding a historical post in a city with San Antonio's demography? It shouldn't even be an issue.

(CISNEROS, "OUR TEJANO HISTORY," 1J, 5J)

After this eloquent expression she asked people who had houses painted bright colors such as "bougainvillea pink," which lifts the spirits and makes the "heart pirouette," to send in their oral testimonies on disk, paper, video, or audiotapes in order to publish a book to send to the San Antonio

Conservation Society, the San Antonio Public Library, the King William Association, the Historic Preservation Office, and the City of San Antonio. She concludes: "After all maybe somebody else will be inspired and paint their house beautiful South Texas colors, colores fuertes, and nobody would raise a fuss" (5J).

Of course Sandra Cisneros is now widely known as the famous house painter. In the end, she won her battle with the preservationists, who stated that during the course of the battle the colors of the house had faded and were now acceptable.

I detail this story for you because of the way Cisneros elevated the personal into the historical, social, and political. And because of how she continues to inspire the mythology of culture that adds to her growing presence as a cultural representation.

Through all her celebration and fame, Cisneros has remained a loyal friend, never forgetting those who supported her through her struggles. She gives generously to good causes, appears in support of political and social issues, and struggles to be a real person.

However Cisneros is seen by the current interviewer, by the most recent book reviewer, by the journalist who reviews her readings, her audiences continue to be caught up in the emotion of recognizing themselves, their lives, their images, their culture in her stories. While Cisneros was reading "Little Miracles, Kept Promises," one observer wrote: "Ms. Cisneros' interpretation of the culture I grew up in was so vivid and animated that my eyes welled up with tears. The tears were for a longing for days gone by, pride in my culture, and hope for our youth. As I stood in that packed auditorium, 3,000 miles from home I felt myself transfixed to the community I still claim as home. . . . It is my hope that the youth feel a sense of pride, a commitment for their community and culture. There is no better way to show cultural and community pride than by getting involved in the community and for those going to school to demand and strive for the best education possible" (Treviño, 10A).

Finally, one newspaper headline calls Cisneros the "Chicana Bandera." I imagine that means that she is the standard-bearer for all of us. Well, someone is always designated to carry the flag. We see and hear from writers what we want to see, and if a writer touches our hearts it is special. Cisneros might have authored some of her own mythology, but if she has become a cultural icon, it is because we recognize something larger than life in what she writes. And if she enhances her public presentation of self, I say that is added power as well as entertainment.

THIRTEEN

The Tools in the Toolbox

REPRESENTING WORK IN CHICANA LITERATURE

(1999)

In Helena María Viramontes's novel *Under the Feet of Jesus,*
Estrella, the heroine, is fascinated with the toolbox of Perfecto, her stepfather.[1] The young migrant child has followed the route of most migrant
children, going from school to school, seated in the back of the classroom
with indifferent teachers, learning nothing. Estrella has been unable to de-
cipher the symbols of letters, the symbols of reading. For her, words are a
jumble of unintelligible shapes put together, yet she thirsts for knowledge.
Her stepfather's red toolbox becomes a metaphor for the acquisition of
knowledge about the world. It is a knowledge she desperately wants, but
which is incomprehensible without a guide.

> When Estrella came upon Perfecto's red tool chest like a
> suitcase near the door, she became very angry. So what is this
> about? She had opened the tool chest and all that jumbled
> steel inside the box, the iron bars and things with handles, the
> funny-shaped objects seemed as confusing and foreign as the
> alphabet she could not decipher. The tool chest stood guard
> by the door and she slammed the lid closed on the secret.
> For days she was silent with rage. The mother believed her a
> victim of the evil eye.
> Estrella hated when things were kept from her. The teach-
> ers in the schools did the same, never giving her the informa-
> tion she wanted.
> (34)

Perfecto, a man who is able to perform miracles with these tools, understands her desire and sets about teaching Estrella their mysteries.

He opened up the tool chest, as if bartering for her voice,
lifted a chisel and hammer; aquí, pegarle aquí, to take the
hinge pins out of the hinge joints when you want to remove
a door, start with the lowest hinge, tap the pin here, from
the top, tap upwards. . . . Perfecto Flores taught her the
names that went with the tools: a claw hammer, he said with
authority, miming its function; screwdrivers, see, holding
up various heads and pointing to them. . . . Tools to build,
bury, tear down, rearrange and repair, a box of reasons his
hands took pride in. She lifted the pry bar in her hand, felt
the coolness of iron and power of function, weighed the
significance it awarded her, and soon she came to understand
how essential it was to know these things. That was when she
began to read.
(25–26)

Perfecto's tools are those of everyday life, pliers, wrenches, screwdrivers: tools that have a specified function. Simple methods to unravel problems. They are the symbols of how human intelligence can dismantle and remantle the world. Men work with these tools and make sense of their surroundings; they create things and structures. Together, men and tools, it is considered, have made and remade the universe as we know it.

On the other hand, in literature women's work is often disregarded; it seems that the domestic, everyday work of women is of little importance. Ironing, cooking, cleaning house, and taking care of children maintain life and support the family, but are not considered real work. Real work is done outside the house, in offices and big buildings, in the public sector. Real work is to labor and earn money, or to be a professional: a lawyer, doctor, or business executive. In literature we have novels about cowboys and lawyers, professors and workers. These are men who have adventures; and their work is described with meticulous attention to details, giving us a clear idea of how they work and what they do.

In world literature, men's work is validated in every sense of the word, and, yes, even celebrated. A case in point would be seafaring novels, such as *Moby-Dick,* with its intricate descriptions of life at sea and the work sailors do. As Ishmael states at the beginning of the novel,

Again, I always go to sea as a sailor, because they make a
point of paying me for my trouble, whereas they never
pay passengers a single penny that I ever heard of. On the

contrary, passengers themselves must pay. And there is all the difference in the world between paying and being paid. The act of paying is perhaps the most uncomfortable infliction that the two orchard thieves entailed upon us. But *being paid*— what will compare with it? The urbane activity with which a man receives money is really marvelous, considering that we so earnestly believe money to be the root of all earthly ills, and on no account can a monied man enter heaven. Ah! How cheerfully we consign ourselves to perdition!

(MELVILLE, 7)

This perdition is one that women often were able to avoid, because they were not paid for their work. What ensues in *Moby-Dick* is an adventure drama that, in the process of its 532 pages, recounts in considerable detail not only the lives, woes, and heroic/unheroic exploits of its characters, but also massive amounts of information about life on board the ship, the work of catching, skinning, and preserving whale meat and blubber, what the men did to keep the ship in good condition and afloat. Melville's tale pays homage to the work of the working man everywhere, as much as it is a tale of obsession and redemption. His knowledge of whaling, whales, sea life, the winds, the seas, and other facets of the profession have fascinated readers for generations. For example, he discusses aspects of the sperm whale that are scientific and at the same time, it seems, knowledge coming only from experience.

Clearly, one of the narrative strategies in *Moby-Dick* is to claim authority by virtue of the knowledge of this life at sea, the thread of the narrative enriched by the almost overwhelming details of work, intermingled with philosophy and comments about the meaning of life. Although they have struggled to do so, it has been difficult for women writers to claim the same sort of authorial voice, especially that as seen represented in work. The reasons are varied: women's work was not considered a profession, or significant. Their knowledge was considered domestic, emotional, and of little real importance to the public world. And while working-class men were elevated to the status of heroes in the nineteenth century with the rise of the industrial revolution, working-class women were often portrayed as victims rather than heroines.

As we well know, women have always worked and contributed to community and nation building through their work. So it is not the mere representation of work that infuses contemporary Chicana literature; rather it is a new perspective toward that work, a perspective that not only values it but also ennobles it and celebrates it. This perspective is a tool, a strategy that allows contemporary Chicana writers to use their knowledge of domestic work as a way to claim authority in their writing.

Nevertheless, it should be noted that this claim to value through work and meaningful contribution to society is not necessarily a recent one. As early as colonial times female voices resistant to being dismissed as to their worth were recorded in the California Testimonials.

In general, in the early literature of the exploration and colonization of the Southwest we have long accounts of what the explorers did, what they saw, whom they encountered and their work. But women were usually absent from these accounts, or their work was taken for granted. We begin to see Hispana/Mexicanas at work in early testaments of colonization in the West in the Testimonios from the Bancroft Narratives: not in the testimonials told by men, of course, but in those told by the women. The Bancroft Narratives were collected in the 1870s to document the history of California. In the stories told by the Californias, the women proudly interjected stories about their work, hinting that the men they looked after, the priests, the soldiers, and their husbands, would be uncared for both physically as well as economically without their help. As Felipa Osuna de Marrón stated: "Mientras tuvieron preso a mi marido yo con los indios recogí mucho maíz, frijol y otras cosas, y escondí gran cantidad de semilla en los chamizales—así fue como cuando se acabó la guerra tuvimos con qué comer" (in Sánchez, Pita, and Reyes, 51) (While they held my husband prisoner, I, along with the Indians, harvested a great deal of corn, beans, and other things, and I hid a large quantity of seeds in the thicket—thus it was, when the war was over, we had something to eat [translation mine]).

In another story, Eulalia Pérez outlines the work she was responsible for as the "llavera" or head housekeeper of the mission. Among other duties, she outlines the following:

> En primer lugar, repartía diariamente las raciones para la pozolera, para esto tenía que contar el número de monjas, de solteros, gañanes, vaqueros de silla y vaqueros de en pelo— aparte de eso, había que darle cada día sus raciones a los casados. En una palabra ella corría con la repartición de raciones para la indiada, y para la cocina de los Padres. Tenía a su cargo la llave del almacén de ropas de donde se sacaban los géneros para vestidos de solteras, casadas y niños. Después también tenía que atender a cortar la ropa para los hombres. . . . Tenía yo, además, que atender a la jabonería que era muy grande, a

los lagares, a la moliendas de aceituna para hacer aceite, que
yo misma lo trabajaba.
(IN SÁNCHEZ, PITA, AND REYES, 36)

(In the first place she distributed daily the rations for the
stew, for that she had to count the number of nuns, bachelors,
day laborers, cowboys, and cowherds—aside from that every
day she had to give the rations to the married people. In a
word she gave the rations to the Indians and for the kitchen
of the priests. She had the responsibility of the keys for the
clothing storehouse where they took the cloth for the clothing of the single women, the married ones and the children.
Also I had to see to the cutting of the cloth for the men. . . .
In addition I had to attend to the soap manufacturing, which
was extensive, and to the pressing of the olive oil, which I
myself would do.
(TRANSLATION MINE)

Pérez, by enumerating and classifying the amount and details of her work,
insists upon her importance and contribution to keeping the mission economically and socially viable.

Likewise, in the stories collected in the 1930s by the New Mexico
WPA Federal Writers Project, we have tales of the work women did:
weaving, healing, plastering, and building their own houses. We learn that
the women invested in goats and increased the size of their herds while
their men were working outside the home. And we see how women began to design clothes and dye them so they could be different from their
neighbors. In these oral histories the women were quick to point out that
they too had contributed to the development of society and the establishment of both the social and economic base of that society. In a story titled
"Josefa and Her Sons," the hard work Josefa did is articulated, work that
not only included the domestic but also the contributions of women to
house building, work that today would be considered public.

As the oldest child naturally Josefa became mother's helper.
Many responsibilities fell upon her childish shoulders, and the
work of a woman. Her mother taught her all the household
arts and duties that fell to the woman's part in the business of
living as it was in that day. Josefa was taught to cook, prepare
and conserve foods, to plant and tend the kitchen garden, to

safely carry tinajas (pottery vessels) of water and goats' milk upon her head. She learned to weave cloth from the goat's wool and fashion the material she wove into garments for the family. Weave blankets for household use and serapes (shawls) for the family to wear about them in the cold weather. She was taught to make the red dye from an herb that the color might be combined with the natural wool of gray and black to make the blankets more attractive. Josefa could grind the blue corn into very fine meal, she could make tortillas and sopapillas (fried buns) expertly and as well she could plaster adobe walls with mud and lay even smooth adobe mud floors and build fogon compañas (fire places for the family) and keep them in repair and she could help build adobe houses and make the tapanco which was a porch built into the kitchen to be used as a cupboard.

(REBOLLEDO AND MÁRQUEZ, 209)

Thus we can see that in oral histories and documents from the past, when women were given the opportunity to tell their stories, they placed emphasis on the work they did to show their contribution to not only family building, but also to community building.

In the same vein, Chicana writers today create work identities for themselves. We see that in the last twenty years Chicano writers have used their social, cultural, and ethnic history to assert themselves into a narrative from which they had been previously excluded. In particular, Chicana writers have made themselves the heroines of their own stories and the subjects of their own narrations. They have seized their voices where before there was silence, and they have become the voice of authority over what they know. We have bildungsromans (coming-of-age novels), künstlerromans (coming-of-age novels about the writer), and what Annie Eysturoy calls the Chicana bildungsheld—a process in the coming-of-age novel that expands the limitations of those novels for women (133–138). But it is clear that one of the ways in which Chicana writers can claim an authorial voice is by being an expert in work, in their case, women's work, and in all the facets that determine and make up this work. But describing and being knowledgeable about women's work is not enough; in some senses the writers also want to show the importance of this work, and they do so by ennobling it. Thus we have descriptions of the work that parallel those robust descriptions of men on horseback riding unafraid, valiant and proud through the Southwest, or struggling bravely against the elements on a ship in the storm-crossed sea.

Now I examine three contemporary Chicana writers and the ways in which they represent women's work and the women who do the work. These writers are Norma Cantú, Denise Chávez, and Pat Mora.

In *Canícula* (1995), Norma Cantú narrates a semiautobiographic creation that she subtitles "Snapshot of a Girlhood en La Frontera." Although the name of the protagonist is Azucena (Nena), the photographs included in the book are clearly of Norma and her family. *Canícula* is a community and family ethnography of life in border Texas in the 1950s. The narrative voice often slips from a childhood present to a known adult future, and describes in detail perceptions and reminiscences of Chicano/Mexicano life in South Texas. While Nena's father's work was important to the survival of the family, her mother's work was also, although it was often unpaid or underpaid. Yet it is in the details and the memories of the mother's work that we have a lasting impression of the importance of that work to the family and to the heroine.

Azucena's mother began work in the public sphere; as a young teenager she worked in a factory sewing children's dresses: sewing is her profession, one that she continues after she marries and has children, even though it is unpaid. To augment her husband's salary and to acquire the necessities for her family, "she'll sew, for the neighbors, save what she earns and make do" (43). To honor her mother's work, Cantú fills her book with the knowledge she has inherited from her mother, the color and texture of fabrics and dress styles. The descriptions of clothing and the materials from which it is made are constant symbols throughout the narrative, ones that augment the authority of the narrator's voice. Thus we know that her mother, pictured in a photograph, wears a "green evening gown made of the sheerest green organza, looks like gossamer" (42). Later Cantú comments, "Doña Carmen gives me a polka-dotted corte for my birthday, the jelly bean colors dancing on white piqué. . . . In the photo, Dahlia, Esperanza and I wear matching Easter dresses Mami's trimmed at the neck and hem lined with three rows of red, blue, green rick-rack, a different color for each of us" (64). Her mother is such an expert seamstress that she needs no pattern to make clothes; later when Nena, who has learned to sew from her mother, is required to use a pattern in school for a project, she is all "confused": "The empire waist on the sapphire blue chintz dress with the side-zipper never did fit as well as if I'd used Mami's method, but I got an 'A' on the project" (94).

In addition to extolling her mother's skills as a seamstress and her own knowledge of the feel and texture of fabrics, Cantú elevates the status of the profession of beautician in this novel. As she recounts, "The last summer I spend in Monterrey, Mamagrande and Tía Luz send me to the Instituto de Belleza Nuevo León to learn all about being a beautician" (127). Although being a beautician starts off as a "skill," it quickly escalates to a knowledge only a bit short of that of a Nobel Prize scientist: "Every morning we study theory, memorizing scientific names, theories of chemical reactions for permanents and dyes. . . . My senior year at Martin High several friends ask what shampoo I use to get such shine, what spray to get such hold. I brag and at seventeen, begin my unofficial job as hairdresser for friends and family" (128). This work, then, both hers and that of her mother, not only gives them "spending" money that will ease the difficulties of their lives, it gives them confidence in themselves as contributing to the family economy. It is women's work, but work done as a result of training and knowledge.

Denise Chávez uses similar techniques to ennoble women's work in *Face of an Angel* (1994). Her heroine, Soveida Dosamantes, works as a waitress in a Mexican restaurant, El Farol, in a small town in southern New Mexico. The novel describes the texture of Chicano culture as well as the life of Soveida and her family. Chávez also describes the lives of hardworking people and gives us insight into their survival. In fact, Soveida's life and philosophy are ensconced in a book she is writing, "The Book of Service," a sort of "everything I know about life I learned as a waitress" book. The Book of Service is clear and logical; as such it is point and counterpoint to Soveida's life, which is anything but logical. The book has fourteen sections, all of which honor those women who give service. It stands as a metaphor for life, giving practical advice in terms of self-presentation and self-representation. As Soveida states in Chapter 2:

> A waitress has many tools: her head, her feet, her hands, her voice. A waitress's hands are crucial to her survival.
>
> The nails should be clean, not too long, and not painted. . . . Rings will get in the way, usually distract, and will only get stuck with food buildup. . . . So rings are out. Especially wedding, engagement, or friendship. They will only go down the drain sooner or later, and cause some kind of chafing.
> (193)

Women's relationships with oneself, with men, and with the public are commented upon, the various chapters serving as a guide for behavior but also as a code for understanding the psychology of customers and how to deal with them.

In later chapters, Chávez further elevates the work of waitresses, saying, "Remember that you are an actress in a play. Although the play will constantly be changing, you will, under any circumstances, be prepared to assist your fellow actors. And because you are in character, your lines will be easy to remember" (232). Later on, she expands this perspective, giving the profession of waitress even more complications and nuances, as she describes "the Waitress Fugue."

> As a waitress you are required to be a professional public servant, one who is efficient, but not too familiar, an arbitrator and clairvoyant, a formal, not too friendly, confidante, a member of the same basic human family, the directress of order and guardian of discipline, as well as a pleasant, newfound acquaintance.
>
> A waitress must depend on her skills as an actress, mind reader, dancer, and acrobat.
>
> There is nothing like the great synchronized orchestration of the waitress's fugue. . . .
>
> There is the initial organizational preparation, the revving up, and then the steady, expanding circle of contact as the rush sets in. As the demands grow greater, the worlds of the client, waitress, and cook soon intersect and transform into one intricate, complex composition. . . .
>
> If you are a good waitress, you forget your physical self, you become a motion, color, machine, movement itself etched on the elusive, insubstantial canvas of time.
>
> (271)

In fact, the art of being a waitress goes beyond a fugue; it becomes spiritual and holy. The working together of cook and waitress becomes as complex as a baroque symphony, with the waitress playing the central role. It depends on mood, emotion, and psychology as well as the work that is done. It is a profession filled with pride and satisfaction. As Soveida states, "Serving a good meal is like making love. You too would want the mood music and the lowered lights. Not to mention the professional, skilled foreplay" (313).

Even though life itself may be chaotic, confusing, and uneven, "The Book of Service" clarifies, focuses, and instills pride in work and serving others. It sees through problematic relationships in our lives and guides us to an understanding of them as well as how to deal with them. It is profoundly penetrating in its understanding of human psychology. And as Soveida passes the waitress torch to a younger waitress, Dedea, she gives her a copy of her book, saying, "The handbook is about more than serving food. It's about service. What it means to serve and be served. Why is it that women's service is different from men's? I grew up with hardworking women. All my life I have appreciated the work they do" (451).

As in "The Book of Service," Chávez ennobles ordinary work by articulating extensive knowledge of that work, by piling specific detail upon detail of the work involved and by conferring courage upon the women who do the work. A specific case in point is that of Chata, the house cleaner in Soveida's house, who displays fortitude and nobility even as she engages in the most mundane and disgusting task, that of cleaning toilets. Esperanza Vialpando, "Chata," has been cleaning houses for at least twenty years, and she is an expert at it. Soveida works alongside Chata in solidarity, as she says that it never entered her mind to leave Chata alone cleaning the house. However, it is clearly Chata who is in charge, not only of cleaning the house, but in the household organization, "because it's Chata who orders where the knives should be stored and what system will work best in each cabinet" (211). In the following description of Chata's hands and the work they do, again the tools of the house cleaner, Chávez compares them to the hands of Pablo Picasso.

> Chata has the most incredible hands I've seen on a woman. . . . Chata's hands are like Picasso's. They are thick, no-nonsense hands adept at any task. They are hands unafraid and willing to reach out. . . . Chata's hands aren't repelled by moldy food or liquid slosh of any kind. . . .
>
> Chata's hands are no strangers to toxic matter, and continue to dare to plunge into burning water to get the job done. No poison is unfamiliar to these hands, no Drano, no Easy-Off, no lyes, or dyes, or scalding water, or full-strength bleach, because to Chata to feel is everything.
>
> "And because, Soveida, one of the best of God's inventions has to be the fingernail. . . . And when you think about it,

God had to be a woman to invent the fingernail. . . . What
would we do without fingernails? If I had money I'd invent a
cleaning tool, like a scrapy-scrapy thing, made out of fingernails. Nothing tougher."
(211–212)

Through the use of an encyclopedic reiteration of the work involved, such
as in *Moby-Dick,* the specificity of products used and actions required, the
stamina and strength of the women involved, and even the exaggeration
of the language of work, Chávez demonstrates not only the importance
and predominance of the work, but also of the woman who does it. She
becomes as tough a competitor as any lawyer or Wall Street broker, as
staunch an adventurer as any seafaring sailor or alpine climber. Clearly the
narrative voice also acquires authority over the process, the language, and
the person. Woman's work is lifted from the mundane to the sublime.

The last author discussed here is poet, essayist, and narrator Pat Mora. In
her family memoir, *House of Houses* (1997), Mora describes twelve months
of remembering her family, those who are alive as well as those who are
dead. But those who have passed on are still vivid in her memory, and in
House of Houses all family members (dead and living) intermingle with her
memories and her associations, having conversations and putting in both
ghostly as well as real appearances. Throughout the book we see especially
the women at work, talking, philosophizing, remembering. They are intimately connected with senses and smells, with eating and spices, and with
gardens. The descriptions of women and the work they do are so sensual
as to create a virtual texture imbued with synesthesia: multiple sensory
aspects of touch, smell, sight, taste, and sound. This synesthesia permeates
the work to create a virtual orgasm of sensibilities, all connected to women
and their work. Thus Mora elevates women's work, not just into the noble
or the sublime (although that too) but into the sensual. As she says, "So
much of comfort in life is the familiar, the muck from which we've built
this adobe house from the old river of deep memories, the fertile unconscious, memories of a purple tree scent on a warm afternoon, the sound
of a prayer or a sonata, the coolness of old fingers, the taste of a warm
bizcocho, my father's voice" (97). The themes of cooking and gardening
run deep in the book as it is women's domestic work, that of cook and
gardener, that Mora finds particularly sensual. She writes, "But don't the
physical pleasures themselves—tasting the wild orange wind, peering into
the hibiscus' open mouth, hearing the tongued trees, smelling the heat
of rising dough, stroking the plums' red curves—the private body plea-

sures also lure women to those kitchens and gardens? . . . These summer months women are intoxicated by the senses, by honeysuckle and loves real and imagined: old and new loves, unrequited" (158–159).

Finally, of course, the ultimate work is that of writing. Writing heals, remembers, shapes, and creates. Language (as well as a fingernail) is the tool in the toolbox. But writing is like cooking and gardening, like service: it requires time, sustenance, and nourishment. Mora says, "For stories, like plants, need attention and protection, this garden, for example, an accumulation of nurtured possibilities. The fruit and shade trees, flowering plants and herbs survive in this desert oasis because of the attentiveness of the family, its seeds, plantings, cuttings, pinchings, feedings, prunings, and endless, endless watering" (156). In the end, she states, "In our creations, the unconscious surfaces, becomes visible, and in reflecting us, lets us reflect on who we are, offers epiphanies" (272). These epiphanies and these reflections can be seen in the value of women's work.

The response to women's work by Chicana writers has been varied: philosophizing, ennobling, enriching, spiritual and sensual. It is the art of survival, but not just survival, rather a profoundly articulated understanding of that work and of the meaning of work. For after all, it is through that work that we come to make sense of our lives and of our place in the universe. Through work and our representation of it we understand psychology, biology, chemistry, dance, music, sensuality. Through new attitudes toward work and its meaning, the intricate descriptions and valorization of women's work, Chicana writers undo the invisibility of women's contributions and the invisibility of domestic work. Through a description of the knowledge necessary for that work, the writers gain authority, seize agency, and are able to represent their own subjectivity. Chicana writers, the women they write about, and their work enter into another realm: the realm of understanding and valuing themselves.

FOURTEEN

La Nueva Onda—The New Wave

CONTEMPORARY CHICANA WRITING (2001)

Three books written by Chicanas have been recently published or republished. Each of these new editions speaks to both the history of Chicana literature and the contemporary moment. These books are *Romance of a Little Village Girl,* by Cleofas Jaramillo (University of New Mexico Press, 2000); *Puppet: A Chicano Novella,* by Margarita Cota-Cárdenas (University of New Mexico Press, 2000); and *When Living Was a Labor Camp,* by Diana García (University of Arizona Press, 2000).

I will begin with *Romance of a Little Village Girl.* This book was first self-published by Jaramillo in 1955. It was a memoir written by a member of a prominent New Mexican pioneering family in order, as she put it, "to get it right." That is, to clarify, from the experience of an Hispana, what she considered to be history written from an Anglo perspective, one that was distorted. She felt that "American newcomers" did not understand Hispano customs the way they should be understood. In writing about the penitentes, for example, she said, "Due credit is given to the English writers who come to New Mexico and write such interesting books from second-hand information, but I wish here to contradict some of their statements" (Jaramillo, *Shadows,* 64). Her own book is written from lived experiences, wishing to document Hispano culture and history as lived by the people themselves and not interpreted by outsiders. In addition to *Romance,* Jaramillo wrote several other resistance narratives, a book of customs (*Shadows of the Past,* 1941), and a cookbook (*The Genuine New Mexico Tasty Recipes,* 1939). For many years *Romance* has been out of print and available only in special collections in libraries. This revival, thanks to the Paso por Aquí series of the University of New Mexico Press, brings this classic more clearly into the public realm for study and contemplation. In reality, this narrative is a complex personal narrative confronting the disappearance of Hispano culture as she experienced it, family tragedy, and survival in the complex period of change and transformation that was

New Mexico in the early twentieth century, and woven into her own life, which was "vexed by modern dilemmas and concerns." It is also the story of a woman who became the subject of her own narration and created her own subjectivity. Her story is one of faith, struggle, and survival. At the end of the autobiography, the emphasis lies on her involvement in the preservation of culture and tradition and in her self-authorization to do so. She gained the courage to write and to survive from her husband, from her daughter, and from herself. As she tells us, when her husband was dying, she "felt something rush into my hand. Was this undescribable thing something of my husband's spirit that passed into me, through my hand? Was this what gave me the courage and strength needed? Something appeared to be holding me up and leading me. It seemed to say, 'Your baby needs you and there is work for you. Brace up'" (128). Aligning herself with her family, history, and community, she is, at last, able to transcend the sorrows and difficulties of her life and to become whole.

Puppet, by Margarita Cota-Cárdenas, was first published in 1985, one of the few novels, if not the first, in the emerging genre of Chicana literature to be written in Spanish. At the time it was written, language issues were at the forefront of Chicano literature as the writers struggled with complexities of representation, identity, subjectivity, themes, and ideology.

Because it was written in Spanish and published by a small press, *Puppet* had its distribution problems from the start. With no wide distribution system for sending out books, readership suffered. Nonetheless, even with the attendant problems related to small press publication, *Puppet* has become an underground classic. Taught and read in Spanish language and Chicana/o studies classes and by Chicana/o academics, it is one of several Spanish-language Chicana/o classics that is widely known and commented on copiously in the most important venues of Chicano literature, such as conferences, articles, and books, both in the United States and Europe. The fact that Cota-Cárdenas is also well known as a poet (*Noches despertando inConciencias,* 1977, and *Marchitas de Mayo,* 1989) and her poetry is widely anthologized has contributed to recognition of her narrative, even though, until now, it has been difficult to access for non-Spanish speakers. Furthermore, in this bilingual edition, the English version has uniquely incorporated some Spanish so that the reader finds the meaning through an immediate translation or by context. Thus the reader is able to access Chicano cultural reality. This translation, published by the University of New Mexico Press, will allow wider access to the novella and place Cota-Cárdenas where she belongs—as a significant contributor to and initiator of the growing corpus of Chicana/o literature.

Cota-Cárdenas's novel and her poetry are central to the development of Chicana/o literature. Moreover, she has completed the second novel in this series, *Sanctuaries of the Heart,* and has begun on the third.

Like the work of other writers of her generation, Denise Chávez, Helena María Viramontes, Sandra Cisneros, Pat Mora, and Erlinda Gonzales-Berry, Cota-Cárdenas's writing has been a journey of discovery. These journeys have been searches toward understanding what it means to be a woman, Mexicana, Chicana, Americana, in male-dominated societies. These writers slip between two distinct cultures in order to create a fluid third space, and they challenge the norms of both Anglo and Hispano cultures. They are novels that create their own myths and invent alternative forms in which to exist within cultures that are in conflict. They maintain Mexicano/Chicano traditions and at the same time they change them.

The postmodern narration in *Puppet* has made the novella a challenge to the untrained reader. In addition to the fractured narrator, the multiplicity of voices that intermingle, the brutally honest and funny colloquial language that rubs up against official language, the simultaneity of past and present, the history of political oppression of Chicanos by Anglos and by other Chicanos themselves, and the different literary registers that are present in the novel combine to create a cacophony of narration that even Homi Bhabha would be proud of. All these elements are further complicated by a visual text that is punctuated by ellipses, fragmented thoughts, and voices that wander eerily in and out of context. Moreover, we see multiple meta-narratives in *Puppet* as the author dialogues with Sor Juana Inés de la Cruz, Mexico's brilliant seventeenth-century nun, Shakespeare, and Rosario Castellanos, a contemporary Mexican poet, among others. She also dialogues with contemporary newspaper accounts of Puppet's death and oral narratives from Puppet's friends. In the narratives with Shakespeare and Fuentes, which could be read as a dialogue with patriarchal culture, Cota-Cárdenas continually underscores Castellanos's directive that "there must be another way to be."

In addition to these meta-narratives, we have nonlinear time, erasure of the demarcation between popular culture and written literature, a collusion with the reader, and playfulness and exaggeration within the text. These multiple strategies denote a chaos within contemporary culture that the narrator (and the reader in partnership with her) must tread through in order to restore order and enlightenment to the narrative.

Is *Puppet* a mystery? A coming-to-consciousness novel? A political commentary? A novel of social criticism? The story of a woman coming into her own? About writing and creativity? Indeed, it is all of these things and more. That all these aspects are intricately intertwined in the narrative is what challenges the reader, while at the same time yielding itself to multiple interpretations.

Quickly I will give you a brief synopsis, which cannot do the novella justice. The narrative opens with a friend calling the narrator, Pat/Petra Leyva, with the news that a young Chicano, whose nickname is Puppet, has been unjustly shot and killed by the police. This is the impetus for a narrative of grief, resistance, and self-reflection on past and present and on the realm of the private and the public. In the end, the call to action on the part of the community, and the narrator's own resolution of her fears, doubts, and anxieties result in the writing of Puppet's story. At times the narrative is a representation of the dissolution of logic into a chaos caused by fear of the police, the police cover-up of Puppet's death, and slowly, very slowly, the coming together of the community into action. As the narrator faces herself and her own internal subjugation, so too does the Chicano community.

Interwoven into all these narratives is Cota-Cárdenas's gift for language, her ability to capture visually and orally Chicana/o Spanish. Moreover, as always, underlying the narrative is her wicked sense of humor and irony. One final question: Are the events in *Puppet* real? The work is fiction but based on some specific events that took place. But as any Chicano/a can tell you, unfortunately they are more real than they should be. As Margarita Cota-Cárdenas has told me, "Reality is stranger than anything one could make up."

Puppet is a compelling narrative that will lead you into dark situations, but one that ultimately finds redemption. It is, however, a redemption in which all of us need to take part. This excellent translation, done with the author, may help us arrive there.

The final book discussed is new poetry by Diana García, *When Living Was a Labor Camp*. This book takes us into the world of the labor/migrant camp, the Chicano movement and its effect on the migrant workers, the difficulties of Chicanos who were trying to get an education in those days, the Vietnam War, the difficult relationships Chicanas have with Chicano men, and the friendships between women. It discusses all these issues and more, not only poetically but beautifully. Moreover, García has a sense of the ironic, as does Cota-Cárdenas, of the humorous, a perception I particularly like about Chicana writers.

The women in this book want to break out of their poverty, away from families and circumstances that confine them, find that Prince Charming who will love them forever. Quickly, however, they become wise to the disillusionments of the world; they see their husbands die young and their children, for whom they wished so much, pregnant. As they wise up, they do not discard their youthful dreams; they change them. At the end of the book, the narrator leaves us with hope, that love is in the air and fulfillment is already found, or not far behind. The women understand racism, poverty, and they also understand hope. In "These Old Rags," García speaks to the stereotypes of Mexicans as laborers:

> I dig in hard clay dirt,
> freesia bulbs scattered
> at my knees, pause to admire
> rows of landscaped homes,
> a scene a friend once called
> a soap opera set.
> A van pulls up; a voice asks,
> *¿Habla español?*
> I'm puzzled by the accent
> but respectfully I say
> *¿Cómo le puedo ayudar?*
> Prepared to direct him past
> dead-end streets and canyons.
> *Do you live around here,*
> *do you need work?* he asks.
> I rub soil from my hands,
> conscious of my work shirt,
> my sweat-stained face.
> *This is my home. I live here.*
> So clear, so simple.
> Yet again, *Do you need work?*
> I study his button-down shirt,
> knotted tie, propped in a van. . . .
> I know him.
> His son played on my son's
> soccer team. I hesitate,
> review my options.
> I could pretend I didn't hear,
> wait for him to leave.
> My grandfather did.
> He'd stand, hose in hand,
> play a stream of water

on his favorite ash tree,
the trickle speaking volumes.
Or like my dad I could yell
a more satisfying
Who the hell you think
you're talking to!
Then toss some dirt in the air
It's my call.
I carefully reply,
No, but if you need work
I could use a cheap gardener.
(GARCÍA, *Living,* 77–78)

And there are many, many more great poems: "El Comal: My Grand-father's Griddle," a tender tribute to the relationship between her mother and her mother's father; "Las Otras Marías," a comment on the real life of women named María who are not virgins; and finally the voices of many women for whom she writes in "Serpentine Voices":

How many voices can I plum in this poem
Tricky poem, sometimes in the first person "I,"
as in sometimes the story is mine,
as in me the author,
the first-person narrator,
and at times the voice becomes
third person "we,"
plural, not imperial,
because sometimes
we were all voice, girlfriends,
mis amigas, de parte de,
on behalf of all of us,
voices drowning out
that choking silencio,
that persistent marshland of a vacío.
Because we were something.
God, we were something else.
(31)

The strong voices of these three writers are voices that take us through the twentieth century and into the twenty-first. Cleofas Jaramillo, seizing her own subjectivity tentatively and ambiguously, tells us her story and that of her family. She emphasizes the loss of Hispanic culture and memorializes it in a nostalgic way, saving her memories for posterity. Cota-Cárdenas boldly comes to a collective, social consciousness, leaving us a *bildungsroman,* a coming-to-consciousness story. Through the writing of a social political mystery, she takes us through the Chicano movement and through the 1970s. Diana García likewise takes us through the movement, the Vietnam War, and the history of women trying to find meaning and to survive. What we can learn from all these books is that we have a tradition and we have a history; we each need to take responsibility to remember them and to pass them on, and we can do so with creativity and with pleasure. It is through republishing our past writers, translating and reissuing works published during the Renacimiento Chicano, and publishing newly written works (and buying these works so publishers will continue to stock them) that we have created the exciting, vital body of work in contemporary Chicana literature.

FIFTEEN

Size 48D Bras and Men Who Wear Skirts

THE DIALECTICS OF HUMOR
IN DENISE CHÁVEZ'S NARRATIVES (2001)

In recent narratives, *Face of an Angel* (1994) and *Loving Pedro Infante* (2001), written by Denise Chávez, the reader is startled by a surprising, offbeat, bawdy, ironic, often dark humor. Intermingled with serious social commentary and a realistic representation of men and women's lives is a sudden word, line, or description that lightens the narrative and makes us laugh. Sometimes the descriptions seem cruel, and if they were said about us, our feelings would be hurt. At the same time, these descriptions are often so funny they bring tears to our eyes. Chávez plays reality against exaggeration, beliefs against invention, tradition against rebellion. These systems are all underscored by an ironic eye. The playing off of these dialectics of humor makes Denise Chávez's novels readable.

As has been noted by various critics, dark humor and irony are often used by women writers as a way to soften the difficulty of living. A sardonic, ironic humor reflects the ambivalences and uncertainties that women feel as they look for ways to survive. Humor acknowledges that the socially constructed self and its norms are arbitrary and allows us to question that self and those norms.

In an early article on humor in Chicana literature, I found that humor is often a creative solution to overwhelming problems in the relationship of the individual to a rigid society that seeks to make women submissive and passive (Rebolledo, "Walking," 98). It is sometimes used as an in-group message about women's roles, which requires a close examination of gender as well as familial relationships. Often humor serves to debunk traditional myths by which women are subjected to a double standard. For example, men can use dirty language and brag about their sexual prowess while women can or should not. When women touch on taboo subjects, it provokes laughter as well as a sense of scandal (this is a technique often used by Chávez). In that early article, I found that the use of humor by Chicana writers tottered on the line between laughing and crying, that when the tension "that has built up is released in laughter, it is almost immediately followed by a sobering image" (Rebolledo, "Walking," 104). And I asserted that humor in Chicana literature functioned in the following ways:

1. It helped to convey a different point of view, from a female perspective.
2. It struggled against traditional stereotypes, asserting the multiplicities of women.
3. It released the tensions the writers felt about ambivalent or conflictive situations, the most conflictive being whether or not to break away from traditional behavior patterns.
4. It reinforced the writer's identification with the group as a woman and as a Chicana.
5. It functioned as a creative release from anger.
6. It gave insights into the Chicana sociocultural experience.
7. It functioned as a model for change.
   (REBOLLEDO, "WALKING," 104–105)

Since the early 1980s, Chicana writing, particularly the narrative, has developed and matured. In Denise Chávez's work we see the continued evolution of all the above ideas. In addition, she uses humor in her narratives to critique contemporary life and to infuse us with an acute (and sometimes agonizing) sense of our own predicaments. She also challenges the traditional representation of women as passive, accepting, and "nice" by utilizing exaggerated descriptions of women's bodies and all the taboo subjects connected with the body and bringing them out in the open. She exaggerates and probes taboos and presses them to their maximum limit. In many ways she inverts the formula stated above, that of making us cry, by inserting a sobering thought after laughter by doing the opposite. She inserts an amusing idea or thought after a sobering scene.

Let us examine the dialectics of Chávez's various uses of humor.

THE BAWDY BODY

As stated, a clear taboo for women is to speak or write publicly about the realistic, everyday functions of the female body, including menstruation, lactation, sexual responses, and the way in which women prevent pregnancies. Chávez specifically focuses on these female body taboos, articulating them in endless and agonizing details. For example,

Chapter 4 of *Face of an Angel* is titled "Are You Wearing a Bra?" This chapter deals with all the difficulties women have with body image, but it focuses specifically on breasts. Chávez contrasts the idea that society works to hide women's breasts while at the same time specifically targeting them in a sexual way. As Soveida (the narrator) says, "Dolores Loera, my mother, grew up harnessed. As a child, she'd been swaddled in rags; as a young girl, she was confined to dark Victorian blouses with high necklines and long sleeves, as a young woman, she was bound in softened cloth. Her mother . . . thought that every respectable young woman should have her breasts taped down. But it was a losing battle and finally Doña Pancha had to acquiesce when Dolores turned twelve. It was hopeless. Dolores needed a brassière" (*Face,* 19). We learn that indeed Dolores is a large-breasted woman (wearing a size 48D brassiere). Her breasts function as a double signifier: on the one hand they attract men, in particular Luardo, her husband, and on the other hand they often cause Dolores physical pain as "the straps cut into her shoulders, leaving reddened, indented areas. She was prone to headaches, as well as back and neck problems. Sleep was a dilemma. Dolores could never rest on her chest or sides. From the age of twelve, she slept fully on her back, without a pillow" (19). Here Chávez represents the physical pain as well as the psychological inhibitions that large-breasted women suffer. In turn, Dolores is unhappy for her daughter Soveida, fearing that she too may suffer these problems.

Chávez is not content to let the matter rest, however. Later in the novel she brings on another character, Lourdes Torres, Soveida's mother-in-law, who has even larger breasts than Dolores but who also has a completely different attitude toward them. Indeed, Lourdes has a different attitude toward everything physical, and as a mother-in-law, she is a ripe object for ridicule. Seen through the eyes of Soveida, her daughter-in-law, Lourdes becomes a caricature of female vanity. To begin, we are told her hobby is shopping and her "pastime" applying makeup. Here Chávez exaggerates the obsession of many Mexican women, who spend money and time to appear exquisitely made up. As Chávez remarks, "Italian women have nothing over them." The description of Lourdes applying makeup is worthy of a comedy routine:

> —Lourdes Torres eagerly constructed herself daily. She began
> each morning by steaming her face over a pan of boiling
> hot water and chamomile tea. This was followed by a gentle
> scrub with a mild soap called Las Tres Marías that she bought
> from a little shop near the old cathedral in Juárez. The owner,

María Leyba, concocted the soap herself in the back room.
After her morning scrub, Lourdes applied a face cream that
she bought from the same shop, and let her face rest fifteen
minutes while she tweezed, plucked, squeezed, pinched,
rubbed and removed anything that needed to be dealt with.
Then the real artistry began as she applied various shades of
makeup base to her face, to lengthen, highlight, cover up and
generally make more attractive what was already there. This
was followed by adding the powdered rouge in varying shades
to bring the rose to bloom. An eyelash curler helped train
the disconcerting Indian eyelashes upward. Black Cleopatra
eyeliner winged outward as if in salute. A careful and deliberate mascara application came next. This was repeated fifteen
times. The lips were then lined in black eyebrow pencil and
filled in with a lip brush with four alternating shades of lip-
stick and blotted with powder. The whole process took about
thirty minutes.
(176)

Chávez's technique here is to minutely describe, exaggerate, and lengthen
the process most women go to in applying makeup. The point of view of
the narrator is skillfully switched to that of Lourdes as she assesses her state
of beauty and becomes objectified in the process. The contrast between
Lourdes's assessment of what she accomplishes with her makeup routine
and that of other women is emphasized by the fact that most women think
Lourdes looks like a clown.

Immediately after the description of Lourdes's makeup process and her
day spent shopping, however, we are reminded that Lourdes also possesses
two enormous breasts (magnificent ones, in her opinion), which she calls
"Mi atracción." Her chest of drawers is full of lace brassieres of all colors, as
Lourdes understands that men are attracted by female breasts. For Soveida,
Lourdes is a larger-than-life exaggeration of a woman who doesn't hesitate
to give her daughter-in-law advice about her dressing and her makeup, telling her that she has all the potential but none of the follow-through (177).
Yet through the eyes of Soveida, Lourdes is "a cartoon image of Mexican
womanhood" (178). Chávez has captured in the image of Lourdes one of
the stereotypes of Mexican cultural life. She does not ridicule her out of
cruelty; rather she celebrates her eccentricities and, in the process, makes
us laugh. In many ways, Lourdes is a very touching character, blind as to
how she appears to others, but strong and positive in her own way.

In a more serious vein, throughout her novels Chávez represents the reality of female body functions in a humorous way, not only to bring these taboo subjects to the forefront but also to represent a woman's point of view: these supposedly taboo subjects are not taboo to women, for they talk about them all the time. Nonetheless, Chávez pushes the conversations about these subjects to the limit by giving us detailed and inventive descriptions of things we would perhaps rather not read about. One example of this technique is seen in *Loving Pedro Infante*, in which Tere Avila, the heroine of the novel, leaves her diaphragm behind in the hotel room where she has just had a tryst with her lover, Lucio Valadez. The stage is humorously set because everyone knows everyone in the small town, and Tere has to invent a reason to get back into the motel room to recover her diaphragm. When Tere realizes she has left the diaphragm (which she calls "El Demonio"), she shrieks a religious phrase interspersed with profanities, "Ay Dios de mi vida, diosito de mi corazón, chingao!" (*Loving*, 96). This alerts us to her predicament and the linguistic contrasts make us laugh. However, the best is yet to come. As she ruminates on where she might have left it, hoping against hope that she put it away in its "Pepto Bismol pink plastic case," she realizes that she has left it and thus herself exposed: "But no! Oh no! I'd left it exposed, oozing, and swollen, roñoso, a running sore in the face of life, on the soap shelf in the dirty shower stall of the Sands Motel, on the flea-bitten dog-assed side of town behind the tracks. A dripping reminder of my darkest transgression" (97). Underscoring how women really feel about diaphragms, Tere describes in minute detail the intricacies of "El Demonio," how it feels, smells, and her psychological attitude toward it. Most women can relate to the description, even as we shudder to have our feelings revealed.

> God, how I hate folding that thing into my vagina. It has
> the texture of old rubber bands. When it's soft it becomes
> a wrinkly coin purse that winks at me as it buckles out. It
> smiles at me like the one tired gray eye of La Vieja Lerma,
> the cockeyed newspaper vender with the silly grin, her baggy
> striped shorts and pink blouse a perennial clown's outfit as
> she ranges the median strip on Ranchitos Street. . . . I hate
> the medicinal smell of the killer grease, even though there
> isn't supposed to be a smell. I hate the way the jelly feels, not
> something sweet like its name, apricot or raspberry jam, but
> something greasy like a fingerful of Morrell lard, sticky when

I wash my hands making biscochos, remembering too late
that the lard won't come off with water.
(98–99)

One source of humor is the comparison or the connection of the body
with food. Here the diaphragm is first connected to a cake pan, and later
to lard and the making of cookies. However, ruminating on the physical aspects of sex leads Tere on to speculate about her relationship with
Lucio, which will never go anywhere. Thus while we laugh about her
predicament with "El Demonio," we also keep in mind the reality of the
situation and how she will have to face up to sneaking around with a married man.

DEMYSTIFYING SEX

By joking about sex and sexuality, Chávez demystifies romantic notions we might have about these issues. In a Mexican American Catholic culture that is publicly quiet about female sex and sexuality,
some women do share sexual information and secrets. Thus, in *Face of an
Angel,* the women often talk about sex and about men's bodies, in particular their penises. Men themselves are seen as full of folly and foibles, but
the women are more realistic about sex. In a conversation between Pancha
Pacheco, one of Soveida's co-workers, and Soveida, Pancha talks about the
myth that the size of a man's penis makes him a good lover. Pancha says,
"Let's talk about small penis men, Soveida. There are several types. The
Small No-can-do and the Small Can-do. One of my favorite honeys was a
short—in height—cowboy trucker named Squirty Boyesville. . . . A man
of the land, he called himself. Well he knew land, and he knew land. Just
because he had small albondigas, little meatballs, didn't mean he couldn't
simmer the soup to a boil. The man you have to look out for is not the
small link sausage but the Jimmy Dean deluxe. They're usually good kiss-
ers. Period. I call them Mr. Hit-and-miss. Give me my 5′2″ Squirty any
day" (*Face,* 249). The humor here not only resides in the matter-of-fact,
conversational tone of Pancha, but again in the food allusions and the
sexually suggestive cowboy names.

The demystification of sex is furthered by the knowledge that Soveida
learns about sex, not from a doctor or from formal lectures in school,
but from movie previews seen when her Catholic school elementary class

went on a movie field trip. The previews featured women with pointy breasts, and the lay sisters begin shouting, "Don't look, don't look"—to the delight of the students. Soveida tells us that the entire class at Holy Angel was thrilled, not only to have seen the pointy-breasted women dressed in black leather, but to have seen them on a field trip from school (65). We can certainly imagine the shrieking, delighted children even more elated as the horrified nuns try to deter them from "seeing." Later, Soveida learns about sex from a book bought at a garage sale. Finally her education is furthered by reading dirty magazines that one of her uncles keeps in his bathroom.

THE OTHER WOMAN

Mistresses, lovers, and women other than the wife are also a target for Soveida's speculation, wrath, and humor. Her father, Luardo, has been unfaithful to her mother, so Soveida has grown up knowing that men play around. As her mother knows,

> Unfaithfulness was unholy, unclean, and it was a characteristic of someone who was separated from God. And yet, for all the hurts and sorrows of life with Luardo, his absences and lack of interest, Dolores put up with him and always forgave him. . . .
> "He's your father. Someone to be loved, despite his failings. He's weak."
> It was always the other woman who was the villain, the faceless, nameless pelada who lurked in the shadows and hid under the bed. The blame was hers, hers alone. It was her fault, hers and that of her gold-lamé shoes.
> (51)

Later on in the novel, we find Soveida confronting her brother Hector, who is being unfaithful to his pregnant fiancée. She recognizes that not only is her brother an unfaithful man, but all the men in her family have behaved in the same manner, tolerated by their women: "It's no surprise, then, that Hector is *that* way. Luardo had been *that* way. And my grandfather Profe, and his father, too. And his father's father. All of them.

That way. Those Dosamantes" (376). Soveida has at least two relationships, but all the men of her family have a history of being unfaithful to their women.

Looking at this phenomenon from another perspective, we can see that it is Tere Avila in *Loving Pedro Infante* who is the other woman, and we see how she suffers from it. The first time Tere and Lucio make love, Tere tries to pry his wedding ring off while he is asleep. She tells us, "I wasn't going to steal it. I just wanted to see how tight it fit and if the skin on his finger had grown around it. I had to know if there was gunk or food in the grooves. To my dismay, there was no movement with the ring at all. It was on there, good and tight. Lucio was snoring lightly as I left. My calzones were in my purse. There was no way his wedding ring was ever going to be pried loose" (*Loving,* 67).

Tere, at times, feels bad that she is the pendeja, puta, but acknowledges that sneaking around is also exciting, comparing it to a teenager caught smoking in the bathroom. Her life as the other woman has her out of control, as she sees herself she is "gastada, apagada y jodida . . . too busy watching the movie of her life unfold in front of her" (11). She is in love.

However, it is a tawdry story, no "white girl's musical."

> This story is about late-night betrayals, . . . and late-night phone calls. . . . It's been days since you talked con tu honey, so you find a corner in which to park your nalgas and seek him out in the dark with plenty of change. You whisper ay precioso that you love him, only him, that you have to see him, diosito, as you put another fistful of quarters in the phone.
>
> My story is as true a story as they get. There's no turning back, corazón. If you don't want to get burned, don't get in the fire.
>
> (77)

At the same time, as she compares her situation with that of the other women in the Pedro Infante movies, she begins to understand that not only does she pick the wrong kind of men but the system reinforces those traditions, thus further contributing to the oppression of women. Through humor, Tere begins to understand the structures of power and the possibility for changing them. She finds a better way of living and of gaining control over some aspects of her life.

RELIGION

One area as a source of humor is that of religion: in particular, the general public's interpretation of religion and its observations
of religions' servers: nuns and priests. Rather than see nuns and priests
as leaders, aloof and worthy of respect and honor, the people see their
human side and use humor as a way to bring them closer. In *Face of an
Angel,* when Soveida is little, her grandmother Mamá Lupita advises her
to become a nun, hoping that this will save her from the predators she
considers men to be, and from all the trouble men cause. She says, appealing to Soveida's intellectual side, "You like to read. Nuns read all the time
and no one bothers them. They can be quiet. They don't have no one
belching and scratching and making pedos, you know, farts, on the way to
the you-know-what, El escusado" (59). Repeating that she wants to spare
Soveida the "details" about sex, about men, and about life, she piles detail
after realistic detail on Soveida about men and their ways. She contends,
"Men cannot be trained. They're wild bulls or changos: monkeys, I don't
know which. And that's not all. They shed. I could never keep a clean
bathtub. Pelitos por donde quiera. . . . But I want to spare you the details"
(59). Using other arguments, Mamá Lupita tells Soveida that nuns don't get
wrinkles (because they don't have to deal with men) and also that women's
prayers are more powerful than men's because they are more spiritual. Finally, Mamá Lupita confesses that she never wanted to be a nun because
she wanted to become a priest (recognizing that priests had more power
than nuns, even if they were not as spiritual). Women as priests (that is,
the leaders of the church) would be fine, but men as priests are, to Mamá
Lupita, comical. As she tells Soveida, "Priests in the family are a dime a
dozen, Soveida. Everyone know they're jotos and maricones or lusty goats
in search of skirts" (58). Moreover, priests wear skirts, which either hide
their masculinity or emphasize gender.

Religious folk beliefs, such as those of the apparition of the Holy Virgin
or Jesus or some other saint also come in for their share of humor. One
such example is that of "the Holy Tortilla." In Mexican American culture,
the apparition of a religious icon in the real world is met with reverence
as well as with scepticism. The Virgin Mary, Christ, and other sacred
images have been seen on walls, on the floor, and in windows, but especially in tortillas. One day as Soveida is getting ready to take a trip to see
her mother-in-law, her grandmother asks her to stop by to see the Holy
Tortilla. Someone has seen Christ's face in a tortilla and has made a shrine

to it. As Soveida goes to see the Holy Tortilla, feeling foolish, she tells us, "The Tortilla was smaller than I'd imagined. I don't know what I had expected. You could see the black gas-burner grill marks on the Tortilla, which formed the image of a face, and it was definitely someone male. But it was hard to say whether the face was Christ's or any other man's with a full beard. Never mind, to the owners of the Holy Tortilla, the Tortilla was a sacred sign of God's appearance on this earth, the mark of God's grace" (428). In itself, this description is not funny; what is amusing is that Soveida discovers that on the Holy Tortilla are human bite marks, and observes, "Someone hungry and in a hurry had obviously chomped down on the Tortilla before it was observed to be holy" (429).

Thus as religion and religious leaders hold a central place in the life and culture of the novel, they are nevertheless brought down to a human plane through the use of humor.

NAMES AND NAMING

Just as Tere's diaphragm is called "El Demonio," other names in both *Face of a Angel* and *Loving Pedro Infante* are both symbolic and funny. Soveida's last name is Dosamantes (Two Lovers), and that, of course, is what she has. Teresa Avila is named after the famous visionary Spanish nun, Teresa de Avila. Conscious of this fact, and also aware of the contrast, Tere makes a list in which she compares her life to the life of the nun. Calling Teresa de Avila her "tocaya" (namesake), her list is headed "Ways Mi Tocaya and I are alike and not alike." While the list is too long to reproduce here, the humor it provokes dwells not only in the impossible connections that Tere thinks of, but also in the colloquial language that she uses. As usual in her stream-of-conscious way (she calls it the dialogue in her head), when Tere thinks of something, she needs to expand on it. Thus while both she and Teresa de Avila are both single women, Teresa was a saint while Tere is "no saint." Tere notes that the nun never married, while she says about herself, "Married once, although I wouldn't call it Married Married. If that was married, I don't want to ever be married again" (*Loving*, 69). Moreover, while she tells us that Teresa de Avila "Almost went through the Inquisition," she considers herself to have been subjected to an inquisition much worse than the Spanish institution, "Have gone through the proverbial chisme mill of 'interrogations' from the fan club members, especially Ofelia Contreras, a feverish mitotera who has nothing better to do than gossip and destroy reputations" (*Loving*, 70).

Santa Teresa was a mystic while Tere "can't see anything worth shit, liter-
ally and metaphorically."

Later on in the novel, Tere, who is the recording secretary of the Pedro
Infante Fan Club, signs her name as Teresa P. Avila, giving the *P* different meanings as she submits her minutes. At first she tells us it stands for
pendeja (screwed up or stupid), then for puta (prostitute), then for piojo
(head lice). And, of course, ultimately we know that it is also the first letter of Pedro (for Pedro Infante). Actually, Tere is very good at naming: she
calls her friend Irma Granados "La Wirms," Irma's lover and later husband
"El Wes," and the two of them together "Los W's." Irma's cousins (primas) she calls "your preems." The intermingling of Spanish and English
names/words into slang also produces many funny moments.

PEDRO INFANTE AND ROMANCE

In *Loving Pedro Infante* one source of humor is the way in
which Tere carefully describes the multiple roles of Mexican actor Pedro
Infante in his pictures. That Infante is playing a role in the movies is underscored by the careful separation of the role Pedro is playing ("Pedro-as-
Pablo," Pedro-as-Juan) from his own actions. At the same time, underlying the descriptions of those roles is the fact that Tere is trying to deal with
her relationship with Lucio. While describing Pedro Infante's movies, Pedro is seen as a large screen idol recognized as changeable in all his roles,
but also as an actor who, as a person, can do no wrong. As Tere tells us,
"Pedro was the type of man who took care of the women in his life from
Doña Refugio [his mother] to María Luisa to all of his mistresses" (*Loving,*
5). He is sensitive to women and seems to understand them. Clearly Lucio
has none of those characteristics, and although Tere loves him desperately,
she understands too that she always falls in love with the wrong kind of
men. Beyond the sexual act, in their relationship nothing goes right. As
the narrative develops, Tere realizes that even in the movies relationships
never quite seem to work out. In the telling of the movies and the role that
Pedro Infante plays, the comparisons to real-life happenings allow Tere to
understand power structures and to analyze social life, even though she
doesn't necessarily apply it to her own life. For example, while recount-
ing the role of Pedro-as-Pablo in "La Vida No Vale Nada," she tells us
that "Pedro as Pablo is the type of man who will never be faithful to one
woman" (6). And later that one of the characters in the movie, Marta, has
been "sleeping with Pablo's father, one of those aging Mejicanos who have

to prove their barrel-chested manhood by either dying their hair jet black or taking up with a younger woman. She's been chasing Pedro-as-Pablo as well, but he doesn't want anything to do with her, even though she's always throwing herself down on the sand in front of him like a horny, beached mermaid" (15). Thus the movies reveal truths about life, even though they are melodramatic. However, Tere inserts the tale of her own life and relationship with Lucio, which turns out to be as dramatic as that of the movies in the telling. Thus the parody of the movie romance with the passion and drama of Tere's life are synchronic. She recognized herself in the person of Marta, a woman spurned by both the father and Pedro-as-Pablo, saying, "I want to change my dreams, Marta's dreams, but the movie credits roll" (16).

Nonetheless, through the retelling of the movies and of her own life, we realize that Tere is able to work through the predictable narration to forge a meaning for herself where the man doesn't always control the ending. As she tells us, to understand a people, you have to understand their dreams, and in *Loving Pedro Infante* we come to understand Tere, her community, her dreams, and her aspirations.

THE NARRATIVES WITHIN THE NARRATIVES

"The Book of Service"

In *Face of an Angel,* Soveida is the author of several narratives: one is a journal written when she is a child, a second consists of various essays written for her Chicano studies class, and a third, and the most extensive, is a book she is writing, "The Book of Service." This book consists of fourteen short chapters, many of them no more than a page, in which Soveida articulates her thoughts and perspectives on being a waitress. The book is, however, more than a how to serve; it is a commentary on the human condition, professionalism, gender roles, and attitudes toward life. Many of the chapters center on appearance, dress, makeup, voice, function, hands, and the waitress fugue. They also demonstrate the best ways to deal with customers and especially with men. "The Book of Service" tells waitresses how waiting on tables is like living life. Indeed, the essence of its humor relies on its comparisons with life's conditions. One of the most humorous sections is "Meditations on Hair," in which all the people who work in El Farol, the Mexican restaurant, give their multiple opinions on hair. Because, in addition to the restaurant's issues of health, concern with hair is generally seen as a female concern, the contrasting opinions are doubly amusing.

Beginning with "'Surprising how much hair you find on plates.'— Freddie Pacheco, dishwasher," the wait staff at El Farol voice opinions ranging from hair dying (not professional, according to Fermín Fernández, a night waiter) to idiosyncratic hair styles such as that of Pato Portales, the night busboy: "When I first started here, I didn't know what hair meant. Well, it meant I had to cut my hair. It wasn't that long, but it looked good. Now I look like a freak" (*Face,* 390). Using this humorous strategy, Chávez is able to weave into the narrative social values as seen in hair. Disapproval for contemporary sloppiness is illustrated as Pancha Portales, a night waitress, remarks: "Nowadays, it's drugs and sloppiness. The way people go to town, in running shorts or jogging pants, me mortifico, I mean, what's the world coming to? Old ladies at the mall in tennis shoes, women in stretch pants that have done all the stretching that can be done around their bolas and lonjas, and those tank tops, con las chichis sueltas. People can say what they want about me, they probably have, Soveida, but one thing they can't say is, Pancha Portales wasn't ever not neat and clean" (391). And finally we have a hilarious misunderstanding as Eloisa Ortiz, weekend cook, tells Soveida, "I like a man with a smooth chest. Oh, that kinda hair! Hair has nothing to do with it. A bald woman can still make good enchiladas. Huevos rancheros red, side of beans and rice. Whose order is this anyway?" (391).

Denise Chávez is adept at taking a simple image, such as hair, and examining it with a kaleidoscope, extracting every serious and humorous possibility it holds.

The Fan Club Minutes

In *Loving Pedro Infante,* Tere is the secretary of the Pedro Infante Fan Club, and she takes her duties seriously. She faithfully records all the events at the fan club, and they are hilarious as they include all the human disagreements, activities, and future plans of the club, with quite a few of Tere's own opinions mixed in. In the first minutes we read, she signs herself "Secretary Tere Avila, Esquire." Later, as the action in the novel evolves, she has other descriptives, signing herself merely "Secretary Tere Avila," and then "Madrina to the bride." Tere's minutes alternate between a stiff formality and an amusingly detailed contrast, including everything, no matter how inconsequential, that happens at the meetings. The stream-of-consciousness format juxtaposes important occurrences (the report that

Ubaldo, a member, is missing) with the trivial. The Fan Club activities include watching a Pedro Infante movie and then discussing its pros and cons. Tere faithfully reports the sum of the various opinions. Recorded also are the members' votes on various issues, again pro and con. For example, in the discussion of *Los Gaviotas,* a movie in which Pedro Infante plays Juan Menchaca, a Robin Hood, one of the members (Merlinda Calderon) states:

> What got her was the fact that the mother, La Señora Menchaca, didn't tell her son, Juan, that Roberto was his brother, sparing everyone a lot of grief to come.
>
> Ofelia suggested that there wouldn't be any movie if La Señora Menchaca had done that. And not only that, if Merlinda didn't know what was happening in *Los Gavilanes,* it was no surprise she didn't know that her daughter, La Rebecca, was hanging out at Sofia's Mighty Taco with a greasy-headed pachuco from Sunland Park who was full of tattoos and drove a red lowrider car with "Queen of the Night" painted in drippy black letters on the hood.
>
> Merlinda called Ofelia the B-word. Madame President told everyone to SHUT UP.
>
> (*Loving,* 106)

In the club minutes, Chávez weaves past and present memories, grudges, gossip, rambling conversations of events about which the members have a common memory (and vigorous differing perspectives) with a sort of official minute-taking discourse. The narration becomes a parody of minutes while representing the seriousness with which these women approach their "study" of Pedro Infante. This is not meant to make fun of their lives but rather to make ordinary lives larger than life, melodramatic, if you will. This melodramatic element parallels the movies in which Pedro Infante stars. The Fan Club minutes are a master stroke of humor. The voice of the narrator (the minute taker) slips and slides from third person to first person to a collective voice. Moreover, the details included in the narrative allow us to understand the friendship between the members. For example, in the November 29 minutes we read the following:

> We would have started earlier, but the lights went off around 7:15 p.m. when Sista Rocha's son, Carlos Jr., put some nachos in the toaster oven. Too many appliances were going

at once: the washer and her daughter Raquel's hair dryer. We had to wait until Carlos Sr. came home from bowling so he could turn on the circuit breaker. The first fifteen minutes of the meeting were held by candlelight which was very romantic.

The Treasurer's report had to wait until the lights came on. Sista Rocha counted $24.59, which she pulled out from her brassiere. Things are at an all-time low. Former treasurer Onelia González-Johnson's son, Del Wayne, got into her purse and stole the membership dues to support his cocaine habit. We wish Onelia the best of luck in her new job in Amarillo, Texas. We were sad to hear that Del Wayne was sent to La Tuna Penitentiary.

(104–105)

While the club minutes are a spoof off the overly formal records of organizations, they also function as a record on the extra-organizational activities that take place, incorporating verbal interchanges, personal opinions and views of the fan club members, colloquial and street language, as well as recapitulations of the movies and the movie stars' personal lives. The minutes are simultaneously minutes and the subversion as well as amplification of the minutes.

LANGUAGE: ORALITY, BILINGUALISMS, COMPARISONS

Important to eliciting humor in both *Face of an Angel* and *Loving Pedro Infante* is language—in particular, the use of orality, bilingual words, and comparisons. One technique widely used by Chávez is the inclusion of conversational language, including the fusion of other people's conversations in the narration. We have already seen the use of this technique in the Fan Club minutes. When Chávez amplifies the narration with this colloquial narrativity, it often creates an amusing contrast with the narrative surrounding it. This technique stretches the linear narrative so that it is no longer exclusively the voice of one narrator. Likewise, the inclusion of words in Spanish, particularly taboo words or words expressing emotion, add a funny content to the narrative at hand. In the commentaries on hair we see that Pancha tells Soveida "me mortifico" (I get embarrassed), or she talks about "chichis sueltas" (loose breasts, but "chichis" is a slang term). These words and terms are not translated; they speak to the Spanish speaker in the know, and because they are colloquial, familiar terms, they enhance the humor.

Beyond the orality and the colloquial Spanish terms, one other linguistic strategy is the use of exaggerated or outlandish comparisons that enhance amusement. Often the comparisons are between food and aspects of the body. For example, in *Face of an Angel* while Soveida is describing one of her suitors, Albert Chanowski, she tells us, "His eyes were large and bulged like marbles. His right eye wandered off, pulled as it were by something to the side, a vision, an apparition, or an intimation of something coming around the corner from nowhere. Albert called it his fish eye" (233). Later we are told that his hair was "the color of poached salmon."

CONCLUSION

As we have seen, humor functions as a great leveler in the narratives. When human beings are seen with all their good and bad characteristics in a humorous vein, they are no better nor worse than other people. Humor is a way of gaining control over our lives: it helps us to survive, to present injustices, to touch upon taboo subjects, and to mask anger. As Lois Gold has said, "Speaking and writing are . . . aggressive acts, but expressing humor is somehow a more powerful weapon of action, than simply saying 'I think this' " (in Levy, 41). Humor functions as a regenerative strategy, questioning social relations and reshaping them. In both *Face of an Angel* and *Loving Pedro Infante,* the humor allows the women characters to question their positions in an unequal society and find a way to live that allows them to be themselves. It allows them to create their own voices, their own subjectivity. And although these women love men, the real ones and the imaginary ones, in the end it is their relationship to other women that allows them to be all they can be. At the beginning of *Loving,* Tere longed for someone she could talk "deep things" to, someone who would understand. In *Loving Pedro Infante* at the end Tere and Irma are still best comadres (although for a while Irma's marriage to Mr. Wesley threatens to disrupt their friendship), arguing and laughing with each other, "La Lucy y La Ethel" (*Loving,* 215). Tere wonders if the marriage will change their lives together. But the issue is resolved, naturally, through a Pedro Infante movie. Because they are comadres, family, Tere works through her envidia that Irma has found a man to love, one who loves her. As Irma move on to a new life, so does Tere. She comes to the realization that maybe she doesn't want someone like Pedro Infante, or rather like his movie self. As she says, "The game would never end until I grew tired and finally decided to stop. At some point you have to stop" (320).

These female relationships celebrate eccentricities, life's successes and disasters. And to punctuate, Chata, one of the characters in *Face of an Angel* says, "Laughter is good and so are the tears" (*Face,* 217).

Both novels are an extraordinary account of longing and desire—and the exuberant living of life in its sorrows and its pleasures. The humor helps us bear the sadnesses and failures and savor the triumphs.

Cover of Sandra Cisneros, My Wicked
Wicked Ways. *Berkeley: Third Woman
Press, 1987.*

Cover of Sandra Cisneros, My Wicked
Wicked Ways. *New York: Turtle Bay
Books, 1992.*

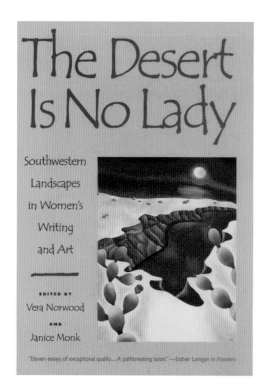

The Desert Is No Lady

Southwestern
Landscapes
in Women's
Writing
and Art

EDITED BY
Vera Norwood

AND
Janice Monk

"Eleven essays of exceptional quality....A pathbreaking book." —Esther Lanigan in *Frontiers*

Cover of Vera Norwood and Janice Monk, eds., The Desert Is No Lady. *Tucson: University of Arizona Press, 1997. Painting by Pola López.*

Cover of Erlinda Gonzales-Berry, Paletitas de guayaba. *Albuquerque: Academia/El Norte Publications, 1991.*

INFINITE DIVISIONS
An Anthology of Chicana Literature

Cover of *Tey Diana Rebolledo and Eliana S. Rivero, eds.,* Infinite Divisions: An Anthology of Chicana Literature. *Tucson: University of Arizona Press, 1993. Cover art: Las Cuatas Diego, by Cecilia Concepción Alvarez.*

Tey Diana Rebolledo & Eliana S. Rivero

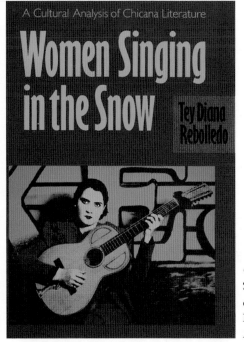

A Cultural Analysis of Chicana Literature

Women Singing in the Snow

Tey Diana Rebolledo

Cover of *Tey Diana Rebolledo,* Women Singing in the Snow. *Tucson: University of Arizona Press, 1995. Cover art: Lydia Mendoza circa 1930, by Ester Hernandez, © 1987.*

CHICANA (W)RITES
ON WORD AND FILM

Edited by María Herrera-Sobek
and Helena María Viramontes

Cover of María Herrera-Sobek and
Helena María Viramontes, eds.,
Chicana (W)rites: On Word and
Film. *Berkeley: Third Woman Press,
1998. Cover art:* Portrait of the
Artist as the Virgin of Guadalupe,
by *Yolanda López (oil pastel on paper,
1978).*

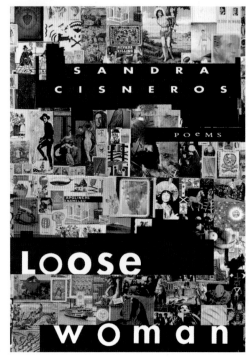

Cover of Sandra Cisneros, Loose
Woman. *New York: Knopf, 1984.*

Our Lady, *by Alma López,* © *1999. Special thanks to Raquel Salinas and Raquel Gutierrez. Courtesy of Alma López.*

Yolanda López, Victoria F. Franco: Our Lady of Guadalupe *(oil pastel on paper, 1978)*.

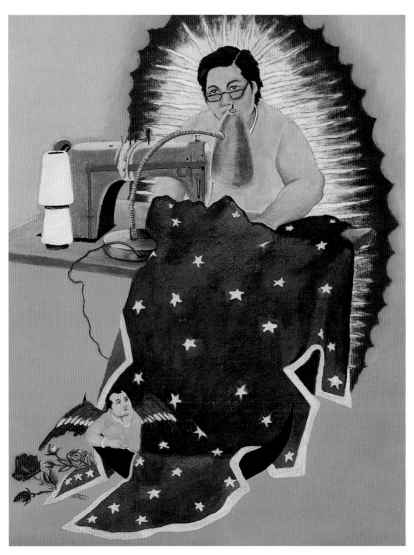

Yolanda López, Margaret F. Stewart: Our Lady of Guadalupe *(oil pastel on paper, 1978).*

La Pastorela, *by Sor Juana Beatriz de la Fuente, 1805. Photo courtesy San Antonio Museum of Art.*

SIXTEEN

*The Archbishop Sees
the Body of the Virgin*

ART, RELIGION, IDEOLOGY,

AND POPULAR CULTURE (2001)

*Un poema escandaloso. La virgen habla por sí misma.
The Virgin Speaks for Herself.*

For TMN

"Scandalous," garumphs the Archbishop!
"Beautiful," sighs the young girl!
Ay! Los católicos viejos, los hombres,
can't keep their eyes off her,
keep printing the image in the newspaper.

"Well, I sort of like it," la virgen says to herself.
"I mean I look modern, moderna, a contemporary image of
    me.
It does bring out my look, the one I gave all those who
threatened my son. La mirada que escondía por el que dirán.

"The roses are quite nice, although I must say that they did
    prick at times.
Tú sabes, those little edges on the thorns not quite cut off.
But a bikini it is not, although really I was quite young and
    look pretty good, if I do say so myself.

"One does have to keep up with the times, after all.
Being an icon is hard enough
without looking placid and frumpy.

"But, if I had had my choice,
pienso que, I think I would have preferred
something in white silk, ajá! seda blanca,
tal vez with a little lace."

On February 25, 2001, an exhibit opened quietly at the Museum of International Folk Art (MOIFA) in Santa Fe, New Mexico. Titled "CyberArte: Where Tradition Meets Technology" and curated by Tey Marianna Nunn, the curator of Contemporary Hispano/Latino Collections, CyberArte consisted of work by four Chicana/Latina artists. It focused on art generated by technology, specifically the computer, or art that used technology parts. The artists were three nuevomexicanas: Elena Baca, a photographer who uses the computer to cut, paste, scan, and capture images; Teresa Archuleta Sagel, who designs weavings on the computer; and Marion Martínez, who creates jewelry, sculpture, and wall hangings utilizing circuit boards and other electronic components. Also included was Mexican-born California artist Alma López, who generates and manipulates images on the computer to make digital prints.

CyberArte generated good reviews without controversy. On February 18 before the show opened, a preview review was published in the local Albuquerque paper, the *Albuquerque Journal,* which stated: "By combining folk elements with state-of-the art computer technology, four Hispana artists have created a body of work that helps break down stereotypes and collapse categories as they pertain to Latino and Hispanic arts and artists." The review noted how Martínez depicted the image of the Virgin of Guadalupe, one of her favorite images: by using "occasional holographic eyes, circuit board or mother board torsos and resistors for decorations, Guadalupe is as beautiful as she is modern" (Van Cleve, F2). Moreover, the critic noted how several of the artists used the computer to get away from toxic substances found in the darkroom or in the environment. Alma López was mentioned for her "Border Series," digital prints commenting on social injustice along the U.S.-Mexico border. In a review in the *Santa Fe Reporter,* Mokha Laget noted the influence of the Catholic Church and its icons on the artists, commenting that the artists faced a challenge in "integrating deeply rooted cultural beliefs with technological innovations." She went on to say that the artists were attempting to carry "religious values through modernistic changes; a startling example being the novinas or e-prayers, to favorite saints on particular websites" (Laget, n.p.). This review praised the exhibit, saying that the "installation may be modest in size, but its themes resonate loud and far."

She was more than accurate. A month after the exhibit opened, several local male Hispanic Catholic activists began to protest the exhibit. They were known for generating controversy in Santa Fe (such as contesting the exhibition of art in a desanctified church, the curriculum in a local high school, and the distributing of birth control information to high school

Our Lady, *by Alma López.* ©*1999. Special thanks to Raquel Salinas and Raquel Gutierrez. Courtesy of Alma López.*

students). They were members of the local Our Lady of Guadalupe parish. Allied with them, and also a member of the parish, was a member of the museum's Board of Regents, a Knight of Malta. The immediate target of the protest was one of Alma López's prints, the image of a young woman standing in the aura of the Virgin of Guadalupe and dressed in a two-piece flowered bathing suit or undergarments, titled *Our Lady*. López stated that she was inspired by an essay by Chicana writer Sandra Cisneros, "Guadalupe the Sex Goddess," where Cisneros explores how she became reconciled to a powerful Virgen de Guadalupe after she was able to recognize her strong indigenous roots and how she came to accept her own sexuality, a sexuality often clothed in secrecy in Mexican American households. In the essay, Cisneros remembers wondering what saints wore under their clothes. Alma López's answer was that the Virgen wore roses, clearly a reference to the roses given to the Indian Juan Diego as proof to the bishop that the apparition was real. López gave *Our Lady* a cloak of Nahuatl symbols reminiscent of Coatlicue, the Aztec goddess and progenitor to the Mexican mestiza Virgin.

This image became known in the news media as "The Lady or the Virgin in the Bikini." It became the magnet for a multitude of reactions, positive and negative, and a pawn in the media toward those attitudes. It engendered protests, prayer vigils, letters to the editors, public meetings,

lawmakers' threats to withdraw the funding from the museum, interven-
tion by the governor of the state, lawsuits, death threats, calls for the res-
ignation of the directors and curator of the museum, anonymous letters,
tears, and many, many reproductions of the print in the newspapers and
on the Internet for all the world to see. The image was internationally
reproduced and a little known artist, Alma López became world famous.
The curator of the show, Tey Marianna Nunn, and the director of the
museum system, Thomas Wilson, were pictured in the *New York Times*
on March 31, 2001 (A9), countless editorials and cartoons were published,
freedom of expression was proclaimed, and censorship evoked as the activists demanded the print be taken down. But the battle became even
more passionately heated when the archbishop of New Mexico, Michael
Sheehan, saw the body of the virgin. Sheehan had been brought in as
archbishop when the previous archbishop, involved in scandal himself, had
not acted effectively to end the uproar caused when several priests in New
Mexico were accused of molesting young boys.

On March 27, 2001, the *Albuquerque Journal* published on the front page
a picture of the archbishop with a headline that read: "Archbishop Says
Art Trashes Virgin, Insults Catholics." He had issued a written statement
saying, "To depict the Virgin Mary in a floral bikini held aloft by a bare-
breasted angel is to be insulting, even sacrilegious, to the many thousands of
New Mexicans who have deep religious devotion to Guadalupe" (Lee, 1).
He went on to compare the image to those such as *Barbielupe* (Barbie as the
Virgin of Guadalupe), or the "Sensation" exhibit at the Brooklyn Museum
of Art, saying "I wish those who want to paint controversial art would find
their own symbols to trash and leave the Catholic ones alone" (A2). Later
the archbishop said that the young woman represented as *Our Lady* looked
like a tramp.

This reaction by a supposedly educated leader of the church was actually quite surprising to many and bears some close examination. It is
certainly true that many New Mexican Catholics are quite traditional (the
member of the Board of Regents actually tried to portray them in a very
patronizing way as "simple"). However, the archbishop's remarks took the
battle onto an even more elevated plane. It became a war of art, gender,
heritage, identity, education, freedom of expression, ossification of culture, and popular culture. It became a struggle over the artistic representation of an image that many felt to be theirs.

Critics asked, how can an educated man such as the archbishop be
so puritanical when Catholic religious art is filled with images that in a
more secular age can be seen as even more erotic and scandalous than *Our*

Lady? At least her body was covered. One newspaper, *Journal North,* published a full-page color reproduction of Jean Fouquet's *Madonna and Child* from the fifteenth century, in which Mary's breast as well as the Christ child's genitalia are exposed. Moreover, it is hinted that the mistress of King Charles VII of France was the model for the Virgin in the painting (Collins, 6).

In many letters to the editor, women and men noted that they found nothing scandalous in the "Our Lady" print and that the church was expressing a double standard, as they often had to put up with naked Christs. As Tom Collins put it, "If the depiction in oil pigment of naked, sacred flesh equals trashing symbols in Catholic iconography, then Renaissance painters, patrons and Popes have already done a thorough job of it and we have nothing to fear from López or her work" (6).

Was it really the body of the young woman that the archbishop objected to? After all, he must have been acquainted with the iconography that Collins referred to. As noted by Leo Steinberg in his book *The Sexuality of Christ in Renaissance Art and in Modern Oblivion* (1996), Renaissance art "produced a large body of devotional images in which the genitalia of the Christ child or of the dead Christ receive such demonstrative emphasis that one much recognize an ostentatio genitalium" (3). That is, this iconography is not meant to be salacious, but rather to reflect the fact that God has become a male human, he nurses from Mary's breast to show us that as a human he must eat, and as an adult he restores us to sinlessness; therefore, he shows no shame (9–14). To illustrate, I refer you to the following pieces of art.

The Portuguese were not scandalized by bare-breasted angels, as evidenced by a painting in the Church of San Francisco in Evora around 1510. Male genitalia are also abundantly evident in paintings, such as in *The Holy Family* (1511), by Hans Baldung Grien, in which the Christ child's genitals are being protected by his grandmother. Moreover, we see a lactating Madonna and child from the workshop of Robert Campin and a crucifixion from the Donatello School, in which Christ's penis is erect, as is evident also in Michelangelo's *Risen Christ* (1514–1520). Finally we have Maerten Van Heenskuck's *Man of Sorrows* (1532) (see Steinberg, 9, 260, 136, 20, 312). All these paintings are fairly explicit, and of course there are many, many more such examples. At times the genitalia were painted out, covered or uncovered according to the whims of the era. And then, of course, there are the many paintings of a bare-breasted, lactating Mary (there are so many images, there is actually a Web site devoted to them).

All these paintings, in the tradition of the Catholic Church, are much more explicit and perhaps even more salacious (even if they are supported by iconographic meaning) than the Alma López print. So why were Catholics and even the archbishop offended? Many women responded to the archbishop's remarks along gender lines. Alma López declared that she is a practicing Catholic and that the Virgin was an important symbol to her. She wanted her to be an icon for the modern world and thus pictured her as strong. The archbishop huffed that if she was a practicing Catholic, he would like to see a letter of support from her parish priest. One letter to the editor said:

> It appeared that the Journal missed the news about the new millennium and instead has chosen to go backward into the 19th century. The work . . . is a powerful and beautiful piece and cannot possibly be seen as disrespectful by anyone other than the most uninformed reactionary. To read the essay by Sandra Cisneros, which inspired the piece and to read the artist's statement . . . would open up a deeper level of understanding of what the artist must have felt as she created the piece, along with the significant history of Guadalupe's presence in her home and her life. . . . It seems obvious to me that a man must have written the Journal's opinion. The López piece is not the static, subservient Guadalupe that most people are comfortable with and used to. She is a living, breathing woman, as is her "angel" who supports her crescent moon. Neither one is a supermodel—both have normal, female bodies—and yes, breasts too. Both seen powerful and self-assured—neither is ashamed of her body. . . . A subservient, enrobed female image is just fine—but a vital, intelligent, earthy female image is a threat. . . . What is ironic and actually wonderful about your attempt to put Guadalupe back in her place is that it illustrates beautifully that she cannot be silenced. Guadalupe, in all of her guises throughout the centuries, has been the protector of the disenfranchised, those without power and those without a voice. She is capable of taking many forms, why not that of a real live woman?
> (WOOD, A5)

Other letter writers following the same vein decided that it was not the rose-covered bathing suit that was offensive; rather that it was "the stance" or "the look." As Kate Nelson wrote in a column: "When I saw Our Lady of the Purported Bikini, what struck me most wasn't the bare belly or the naked legs or even the outcry over a two-piece outfit that Annette Funicello would have found too dowdy for a beach blanket bash. It was the look in her eyes. The same look they train us to adopt as young girls in order to keep ourselves safe. A look that says I'm aware of what's going on around me. That says I'm in charge. That says you can't turn me into your victim" (Nelson, A3). Many people agreed with this assessment, thinking that the look, the stance was not only self-protective and aware but also asserted an independence and self-sufficiency not liked by the archbishop or by the traditional, mostly male, protesters. Linked to a certain misogyny found in Catholic tradition as well as a profoundly held belief that women are in some way unclean, the archbishop was moved to declare the image that of a tart. A touching piece of research by columnists Roberto Rodríguez and Patrisia Gonzales on the artist's model, Raquel Salinas, revealed that she had been raped when young and had great difficulty in overcoming that violation, as rape in many Latino families is relegated to silence. For Raquel, her posing for the picture was a desire "to honor the sacred feminine in a world that daily dishonors women" (Rodríguez and Gonzales, A13). Readers also understood that "as a mujer Chicana, Alma understands the way in which Catholicism has sought to repress and control the body, particularly the native female body. But the body has always been and always will be a site of unruly behaviors; behavior which seeks freedom from the control of self-interested figures of authority that maintain themselves in power through intimidation (you will burn in hell) and crimes to the body" (e-mail from Erlinda Gonzales-Berry, April 27, 2001). And so the argument over gender became a central focus of the controversy.

López herself felt that she was within not only the long tradition of Catholic religious art but within the tradition of Chicana writers and artists who were endeavoring to create new, more positive role models for themselves. As I wrote in a letter to the editor,

> There is a long history in both Chicano art and literature
> of reconsidering the icons and symbols that are present in
> our culture. . . . These reconsiderations are not done with
> disrespect, but rather as a way of revision. These icons are
> so important . . . in order to be able to relate to them in a
> contemporary way. . . . Thus, La Llorona weeps for her lost
> children, lost not because of her but because they are shunned

by society; the children of migrants, the children of the slums
and barrios. La Malinche, who was sold to the Spaniards and
became Cortez's concubine is the translator who struggles to
find meaning in a contemporary world; and the Virgin is a
strong, powerful figure who wears tennis shoes, is independent and active, and who may even wear undergarments.
(REBOLLEDO, "LETTER," A15)

I was referring to the many depictions of the Virgin of Guadalupe in
Chicano art, such as Yolanda López's depiction of her grandmother,
mother, and herself as the Virgin of Guadalupe (see figs. 6.19, 6.20, and
6.21) and Alma López showing the traditional Virgin draped in the cloak
of Coatlicue.

Also important in the discussion was the increasing secularization of
sacred images and their incorporation into popular culture. One mani-
festation of this in Mexico was the controversy over the 1987 Museo de
Arte Moderno showing of a painting by Rolando De La Rosa of Marilyn
Monroe as the Virgin Mary and one of Pedro Infante as Christ in the Last
Supper. The director of the museum, Jorge Alberto Manrique, was asked
to resign. Many of the same sorts of groups and forces that have protested
Our Lady in New Mexico were also at work in Mexico during that time
(Manrique, 1).

Certainly the Virgen de Guadalupe has entered popular culture in both
Mexico and the United States as a comodified item. Utilized as a symbol
of the independence of Mexico and of the United Farm Workers struggle
in the United States, her image is seen on sacred and secular items of public consumption. She is on bottle caps, the hoods of lowrider cars, and tattooed backs (even that of Johnny Tapia, the fighter—who is, as one critic
put it, a man who makes his living by beating up other men in a boxing
ring) (Nelson, A3). Thus the idea of "ownership" of the image became intensified. Protester Juan Villegas stated: "Our Nuestra de Guadalupe does
not belong to the new age interpretation of the millennium century and
never will. Again my generation does not support your point of view
relating to sacred art images being disrespected. You have no right to pro-
voke new thoughts of what type of sacred art images are accepted or not
in my generation. . . . Copyright and the Freedom of Speech laws that
you claim to possess does not apply to my generation. Again these sacred
images belong to the indigenous people of the Americas, not you and/or
your new-age ideology that your exhibit portrays" (in "Four Women and
a Virgin," 6). The debate is characterized by Kate Nelson as "the classic

struggle of women (all women) embracing the power and beauty of themselves, and men in pointy hats, trashing them, telling them to shut up and behave" (Nelson, A4).

One final comment on the controversy. Some critics thought that it went beyond tradition and innovation, beyond gender issues, and into identity politics. As Gonzalez-Berry pointed out, in spite of the supposed tricultural harmony that is proclaimed in present-day New Mexico, it has always been a contested homeland: "For a century, Nuevomexicanos have watched their culture be appropriated, distorted, misrepresented, commercialized" (e-mail message to author). She understands how some Nuevomexicanos are offended by the image, shown in an elite museum from which they have felt excluded. So many years of trying to protect and maintain a cultural identity they feel slipping away has perhaps caused a sort of ossification of culture, that in the name of resistance has become narrow-minded and closed. Thus no change will be allowed. For them, the Virgen will be always submissive with her eyes down, passive and good, ideal and not real.

However, since the controversy I, for one, have found the traditional images of the Virgin disquieting and passive. In my house these traditional representations are turned to the wall.

With the battle carried out in the museum, on the radio, in television and newspapers, the churches, e-mails, and other forms, technology has truly met tradition. And perhaps as one wag put it, "with apologies to Willa Cather, art came for the archbishop."

Finally, Ernest García wrote to the *Albuquerque Journal*: "It seems to me that modern Catholics would do better to plumb the depths of truth that lie at the heart of their faith, instead of the chimera of imagery invented by our predecessors" (A17). It is clear the controversy is here to stay: censorship versus freedom of expression, traditional views versus the desire to find spirituality in something dynamic and modern. Alma López has created a new image of "Our Lady"—one that is essentially the same. However, she has now donned red boxing gloves and is titled *Our Lady of Controversy*!

Part Three

Miscellaneous Essays on Chicana / Latina Literature

SEVENTEEN

Game Theory

A TYPOLOGY OF FEMINIST PLAYERS
IN LATINA/CHICANA WRITING (1985)

What is game theory and how does it apply to feminism, especially Latina feminism? Games are regularized social forms engaged in voluntarily (Huizinga, 78). A game is usually played in a separate sphere, such as a playground, a board, arena, stage, magic circle, or sacred space. To play a game, one participates in an arranged or special set of terms, rules, and limits, with a set of rules made up and accepted by the players. Games imply freedom from normal social conventions or rules. They contain their own course and meaning, but once played, the game "endures as a new-found creation of the mind." It is then transmitted and becomes a tradition of that mind (Huizinga, 9).

An integral part of games is the role that language plays when one considers the game concept as expressed in writing or speech. Language is connected to the game system in that communication, like games, is difficult to master. In order to communicate, one must accept a set of stable rules. Once these rules are mastered, communication may also become a game in which one can triumph (Blake, 14). Language, whether words or numbers, makes possible the creation of game universes because it allows experience to be split into discrete, labeled units. These units are then manipulated by the mind, which arranges and controls the entire sphere of experience (Blake, 65). Thus, on a basic level, language, ritual, and poetry can all be expressed as games/play.

It seems evident through the study of games that games, play, and sport represent "basic values of a given society and seem to fulfill an important function for the learning and maintenance of behavior patterns" (Rappaport, 89). Game playing and the learning of rational game strategy can be important in the development of change. What better tool for a feminist writer to use to educate her readers than a model of feminist game players?

In literature when writers mention games, they often are consciously symbolizing games of strategy in life using the models given above. Most often the game metaphorically describes the power struggle between women and men, but it can symbolize any power struggle. Taking this theoretical model into consideration, I will examine the Latina/Chicana writer's growing awareness of game playing as defined in her literature. Because game players are allowed to make up the rules for the game, or at least to decide on the validity of the rules before playing, the feminist game player has the opportunity for changing the model before play. This change in model or rules may be seen by writers as an educational or ideal tool for changing conventional rules, espousing freedom and setting up new role models. More directly, women can be activated from passive acceptance in socially imposed roles into the recognition that they have choices as to how the game will be played or whether they will play the game at all.

Often, because women don't know or don't understand the rules of games, are unable to secure cooperation from others in the game playing, or simply accept rules by which there is no chance of a positive outcome, they fail to have a positive payoff in the play. For many women options have been limited by the absence of rights, by refusal of others to cooperate in the case of activities which require such cooperation, or by the normative constraints others put on their activities. It is clear that, given the freedom of the player to manipulate and plan strategies within the game, the feminist author can express in her literature her growing consciousness of the power and manipulation struggles involved in games. Changing the role woman defines for herself functions as a model for change for society. Ideally, game theory should be a theory of conflict resolution rather than a theory of optimal decision in the pursuit of self-interest. Women, who have often opted for "other" rather than "self," have suffered victimization and manipulation at the hands of other game players (man, society, bosses). In order to achieve conflict resolution in the form of equanimity and dialogue, feminist game players need to learn strategies in order to reach the payoff they desire.

In Latino literature much attention has been given by literary critics to such famous male game players as Julio Cortázar, Jorge Luis Borges, and Guillermo Cabrera Infante, among others. Little has been given to Latina/Chicana game players, although there are many. This essay will examine the strategies of three Latina writers: Alfonsina Storni, Rosario Castellanos, and Elena Milán, and seven Chicana writers: Inés Hernández, Marina Rivera, Margarita Cota-Cárdenas, María Saucedo, Miriam Bornstein Somoza, Ana Montes, and Alma Villanueva. These writers have at times similar goals and at other times disparate goals, depending on their own strategies.

Games can be divided into three separate groups: (1) games of physical skill, (2) games of chance, and (3) games of strategy, in which players are considered to be "rational" players with "rational" choices. Game theory is concerned with games of strategy only. Models of games of strategy include the following elements:

1. a set of decision makers, called players
2. a set of strategies available to each player
3. a set of outcomes, each of which is the result of particular choices of strategies made by the players on a given play of the game
4. a set of payoffs accorded to each player in each of the possible outcomes.

(LUCHEN, 100)

To these models I would add the basic decision of an individual whether to play the game.

The three Latin American writers studied here represent various aspects of game playing. Alfonsina Storni (Argentina) is clearly a model of game rebellion. In many poems Storni makes us aware of games being played, indicating this by using the words *jugar* (to play), *juegos* (games), and *fiesta* (party), a place where the games are played. The games in her poems are divided into two categories: children's games related to ritual play and adult games of strategy—power manipulations between the sexes.

The *juegos de niños* (children's games) usually involve a loss of innocence on the part of the child, as can be seen in this description of paper boats sailing on a canal, becoming lost in infinity. This recognition of loss, coupled with the child's recognition of death, triggers a trauma that is intricately connected with the loss of illusion suffered in adult games:

Barquitos trabajaba
en nevado papel
Y en el agua soltaba
Tan menudo bajel.

Y navegaba hasta
Que en recodo fugaz
Se interponía: hasta
No los veía más.

Y al perder mi barquito
Solíame embarcar

> Ideas de infinito
> Y rompía a llorar
> (STORNI, 208)[1]

Just as these childhood games touch on essential truths about life, adult seriousness becomes lost in child's play:

> Como los niños iba hacia oriente, creyendo
> Que con mis propias manos podría el sol tocar;
> Como los niños iba, por la tierra redonda,
> Persiguiendo, allá lejos, la quimera solar.
>
> Estaba a igual distancia del oriente de oro
> Por más que siempre andaba y que volvía a andar;
> Hice como los niños: viendo inútil la marcha
> cogí flores del suelo y me puse a jugar.
> (STORNI, 217)[2]

Nevertheless, this loss of illusion is replaced by a recognition that only by the childhood expression of ritual through play can a sense of proportion be retained. The female players in Storni's poems have great freedom of choice as to how they will participate in the game. Once they undergo the initial loss of innocence/illusion, they have freedom to choose to participate in the ritual or not; they become "rational" players. Often, if the player does not accept the rules laid out for her, she chooses not to participate. In "Fiesta," for example, the lyric speaker sees creatures dancing, inviting her to enter the ritual play. The happiness seems false, and she deliberately turns her back on the game:

> Yo me vuelvo de espaldas. Desde un quiosco
> Contemplo el mar lejano, negro y fosco,
> Irónica la boca. Ruge el viento.
> (STORNI, 247)[3]

This invitation into the illusion of the game is, for Storni, the seductive dream because the game, the fiesta itself, is contrived from the promises of love. If she surrenders to the mystique of the prevailing fantasy, she will be cheated. Thus the game is clearly defined as the power struggle between men and women—one in which men always have the winning hand. The only way for a woman to avoid loss is not to let herself be seduced by the

promises made by men. Storni's lyric speakers emphasize this fact over and
over again:

> La casta y honda amiga me dice sus razones:
> —Soy joven, no he vivido. Mi marido? Un engaño.
> Tengo tres hijos, veo rodar año tras año
> En uno como lento sueño sin emociones.
>
> A veces descerrojo, tentada, mis balcones,
> Por ver el hombre fino, el soberbio, el huraño.
> Inútil. Si pudiera curarme de este daño!
> Ay, el amor no es juego que arregle desazones.
>
> Las atenúa, acaso; más los hombres, mi amiga,
> No me valen la pena de un ensayo; desliga
> Mi corazón, cercado, su más viva lisonja.
>
> Tengo el cuerpo perfecto y la boca rosada,
> Para el amor más alto yo fui seleccionada,
> Pero escondo mi fuego bajo un velo de Monja.
> (STORNI, 252–253)[4]

According to Storni, given the morality of a machista society, the
woman who is independent must see that love is a business; she must accept betrayal if she is to have her share. Storni stresses that if woman is to
be seduced by the game of love, it should not be by man but rather by the
illusion that is a part of the game ritual itself. If she accepts the illusion with
the understanding that it is "not real," then she can survive the trickery
and cheating implicit in these games.

Storni's feminist players do not cheat. Indeed, they consider themselves spiritually superior to men. Neither are they arbitrary; rather, they
express their resistance in a society that administers and manipulates their
lives. What women game players must do is reestablish their ability to control their own destiny—that is, they must struggle to become "rational"
players. It is important for these players to achieve a spiritually superior
position. Once there, they can reverse their own victimization by controlling the manipulators. A player can then become the seducer because she
is no longer under male dominance. This game strategy is clearly expressed
in "Romance a la venganza" (A Ballad to Revenge). In this ballad, one
that ironically underplays traditional heroic romantic ballads, the hero
goes off on a hunt for birds (aves), which could also represent innocent

women as with the Virgin Mary (Ave, María): a hunt in which his weapons are a sweet voice and a singing heart (in other words, he is a seducer). He is so successful in this hunt that even the sun becomes distressed and cries blood red tears. A serpent lurking in a tree tries to avenge the birds, but the hunter kills her. However, waiting a few steps away is the lyric speaker:

> Pero aguardándolo estaba
> A muy pocos pasos yo . . .
> Lo até con mi cabellera
> Y dominé su furor.
> Ya maniatado le dije:
> —Pájaros matasteis vos,
> Y voy a tomar venganza,
> Ahora que mío sois . . .
> Más no lo maté con armas,
> Busqué una muerte peor:
> Lo besé tan dulcemente
> Que le partí el corazón!
>   Envío.
> Cazador: si vas de caza
> Por los montes del Señor,
> Teme que a los pájaros venguen
> Hondas heridas de amor.
> (STORNI, 274–275)[5]

The role the feminist game player takes here is an aggressive stance. Using her learned mastery of the game, she also wreaks vengeance for her sisters who have suffered.

The feminist player takes her ultimate vengeance on Don Juan—the male player par excellence in this power struggle. Don Juan is a player whose interest lies only in self-payoff. He therefore destroys and victimizes the unschooled female players in his path. Don Juan's game is precisely the one Storni's players have learned to control. Using illusion to seduce the women, he then debases them by not living up to his promises and boasting of his sexual prowess. Since Storni's players have become educated in the ways of men, they no longer look to them for a reflection of themselves. They can see themselves as they truly are, in their own selves. These modern, educated women (las muchachas leídas) can no longer be reaped; indeed, as Storni predicts, "más no ceden sus rosas. / No despiertes, don Juan" (but they no longer give up their flowers. / Don't wake up, don Juan).

> Y hasta hay alguna artera,
> Jueguetona mujer,
> Que toma tu manera
> Y ensaya tu poder.
> (STORNI, 272)[6]

Storni signals a new age—an age in which women understand how the game is played. Unfortunately, for Storni there are only two options: she can choose not to play if the rules are stacked against her, or she can learn to play using the devious rules created by man.

The work of the Mexican writer Rosario Castellanos can be classified as a model of game equality. Obviously influenced by Storni, she, too, strongly saw the need for women to understand clearly their position in society. Castellanos believed that once women understood the processes that were socializing them into a subordinate position, they could begin to modify them. She saw the need for women to become rational players, defined as one who is able to choose consistently among the possible risky outcomes. This implies freedom and the willingness to take risks.

In "Ajedrez," Castellanos writes about chess, the supreme game of strategy. In the poem there are two players: the lyric speaker and the other— explicitly delineated as a lover and friend, accepting of each other, yet, at the same time, destructive. The title of the poem is significant, because the chess board is one of those sacred spaces or magic circles mentioned. And the magic circle is the place where a harmonious union of the divided self or of the human race should come about after the competition takes place.

In chess the player is required to assume a role that he or she then acts out with the other player. As Philip E. Lewis observed: "The opponents in these games are functionally interdependent, can only exist in coexistence as parts of a system wherein the adversary is also a partner: where the players enter into an openly ambivalent relation" (Lewis, 140). Chess has an established set of rules and tactics that allow the game to endure. The game has also been seen as a substitute for war. Because it has rules, what was chaotic is made orderly. The symbolic parallel of chess to life is unavoidable; the rules of the game set limits and open possibilities. Yet the game of chess is so complex that it is difficult to end. Thus a set of rules for stopping the game, called end game, have been set up.

The two players in Castellanos's poems have not set up the game as Storni's have, that is, according to rules made by men; they have made up their own rules, agreed to respect them, and started the play, "equitativo en piezas, en valores" (292). Unfortunately, the game of strategy has taken on the larger dimensions of the power struggle in life. In addition, this game has a definite flaw. There is no stop rule to end the game; thus the game is transported, symbolically, from the playing field into reality. Since neither player will "give up," i.e., surrender, both have become destructive and are waiting for the final play—the annihilation of one or the other.

And yet this game of strategy takes on another dimension. Because it suspends traditional rules and conventions, both sides are equal—there is no victim/oppressor relationship. The game, with players being equal, could be a constructive one; it could be an invitation to create new combinations. Thus, although the games encourage the urge to "master," these opponents find themselves equal because they began as equals. Blake has pointed out that "the problematical nature of the stop rule in chess, a rule essential to the achievement of finitude necessary to any game, casts into sharp relief the arbitrariness of this rule. For . . . the end of the game is like a brick wall erected at the end of the universe" (Blake, 93). In the meantime, for Castellanos's lyric speaker, there is only antagonism and suspension. On the other hand, the lyric speaker has found a certain freedom that represents the acknowledgment that she is a "rational" player, a role never before allowed her. Freedom becomes synonymous with rationality. She is no longer the victim, as Castellanos's lyric speakers often are.

Another contemporary Mexican poet, Elena Milán, continues this game-playing tradition. Her poetic players are independent women who are mentally as well as morally free from conventional values. Within the framework of poetic rupture with these values, the lyric speaker refuses to play the game according to masculine rules. She refuses to be the object/victim and is saved by her sense of humor and a fine sense of irony, an understanding of the dichotomy of values in the world. In "Decisión," the speaker states: "Facing his laughter which springs forth without restraint, for one second I vacillated between crying and letting myself be infected. And I chose laughter for all times" (Milán, 66). In her poetry, Milán searches for meaningful relationships with men in a society where women are looked upon as sexual and emotional victims, and where those societal values are perpetuated by other women. For example, in one poem the young lyric speaker is told by an older woman, "You must not think, you must not read, if you want to get married" (Milán, 71).

The hypocritical roles women are forced to play are always rejected by Milán's lyric speakers. The games of strategy a woman must know so as not to be engulfed by a male-dominated society also predominate in Milán's poetry. And while the lyric speaker clearly longs for love, she never "conforms" as she resolves the problem of maintaining her own sense of self in an absurd reality.

For Milán the games are not unbalanced, which is a clear indication of the changing role of women in Mexican society. Her lyric speakers set their own rules—rules that are often outside the conventions of society. Her radical voice is ironic and combative and her speakers see themselves as directly engaged in an effort to be themselves under the powerful pressures of an alienating environment. As one lyric speaker comments on her upbringing in Mexican society: "We grew up without refuge . . . dancing with measured step, walking with grace, laughing with discretion, thinking with parsimony, acting conservatively—reactionaries without salvation." (In my house, they were liberals but politics were men's business and it was better that I go make the coffee; Milán, 73; translation mine.)

The lyric speaker knows what is in store for her if she participates fully, sexually, emotionally, and intellectually in life, but she accepts the challenge. As one epilogue to a poem states, "But if I already knew / that all this would happen / how in the devil did I / go and fall? (Cuco Sánchez)" (Milán, 14; translation mine). Often her game players become the aggressors in the game of strategy when, for example, "normal" male-charming techniques are bypassed for more assertive behavior. Such behavior is described in "The Very Complicated Problem of How to Rape a Man." The poem is prefaced by a line from the Nicaraguan poet Ernesto Cardenal, "Tú pudiste inspirar mejor poesía." The poem is structured as a set of instructions for a woman to learn how to function using various aggressive forms to capture the object of her desire. The instructions range from "charro" or cowboy lessons to those for a veterinarian. The male object is seen as an animal to be subdued. The first step is to pick a man you like and then follow through with your "professional" knowledge. The male here is envisioned as a young calf/bull waiting to be harnessed; he is nothing more than an animalized object. Throughout the poem, the advice seeker fails in "getting her man"; the strategy then become one of "desperate" methods,

> maquíllese
> cómprese camisones transparentes
> perfume francés

Y hágase millonaria
o pratique strip-tease.
(MILÁN, 19)[7]

When man becomes the object of the chase, the entire seduction process is not just a game of strategy in which woman is the violent aggres-
sor; the irony resulting from the reversal of roles causes the reader to re-
examine the mythology implicit in role delineation. Milán uses combative
and violent language and concepts as part of the poetic communication of
challenge, nonconformity, and reevaluation of traditional female roles. By
inverting the game strategy, it becomes ridiculous. Undermining machista
values, she searches for humanity in a dehumanized world; her lyric players
have different values in a traditional society.

These, then, are Latin American writers who deal with games and who
are seen as clearly evolving a tradition of consciously given game playing.
Can we see a similar trend in Chicana literature? It seems to me that over
the last twenty years Chicana writers too have developed a sensibility of
using irony, humor, and a consciousness of game playing and have begun
to explore games and their manifestation to the utmost. Let us look at the
game playing of seven contemporary Chicana writers.

Chicana game players refuse to enter Macho/Don Juan games. Don Juan,
in traditional Spanish literature, is the most invoked game player in the
game between the sexes. As stated, his interest lies only in self-payoff with
a negative other orientation. He destroys and victimizes the unschooled
female player in his path. This particular game is one Chicana players have
learned to control. They are no longer innocent, trusting Doña Inéses.[8] As
we have seen in the poetry of Alfonsina Storni, educated, rational players
do not look to Don Juan for a reflection of themselves. The game player
in "Bus Stop Macho" by Ana Montes is approached by a Don Juan who
says, "Ay mamacita, where are you going / A nice, fine looking girl like
you." The woman responds,

Hey you, Macho
where's your head
Times have changed
And your sweet words are dead.
I'm a woman to be loved
Honored and Respected
Yes.
But I'm a person too.

A fellow fighter in a vicious struggle
to liberate our people.
Yes, you too.
Hey brother, change your style
Cause you see—
There's a lot of women who think like me.
(MONTES, 24–25)

From the sexual game playing the speaker takes the stakes to the social
and political arena, challenging the male not only to respect her sexually,
but to treat her as an equal in the social and political struggle. Once the
overtly sexual macho game playing is squelched, the covert one must be
dealt with. To reach equality in the creation of new models is what game
playing is about. Yet at times for the early Chicana writers the struggle to
become a "rational" player seemed hopeless, as Inés Herández Tovar humorously shows in "Chifladones."

I don't know which
is more amusing
or more absurd
the fact that you
call this love
or the fact that
I accept it as such.

He: "The day you beat me
at a game of pool
I'll know we're equal."

She: "The day you choose
to wash the dishes
I'll know we are."

Monogamy is not practiced
by either the culture
that rejects it
or the one that purports
to accept it.

Quién eres tú
pa' que me hagas
sufrir tanto?

> Y quién soy yo
> pa' que te escriba
> poesía?
> (HERNÁNDEZ TOVAR, 44)

Chicana game players recognize that often a strong opponent searches for a weaker opponent for a certain win. In "Even," Marina Rivera warns her opponent of her growing knowledge of strategy.

> You look for her
> someone you could crack
> down the noseline
> between the breasts
> and lower see
> brown organs, brown blood
> brown bone even
>
> these words you want
> are a game and those of us
> who have learned the game
> have triangular hearts
> which spin, gyrate
> toward white, toward brown
> toward ourselves most often
> our way; to gather
> edges like dry wood
> make a bed, a bridge
> lie on it
>
> our lives are mouths
> no matter how
> the jaw placed
> the teeth don't seal
> they buckle here
>
> we point them out
> so when you point
> at our lives
> you get it straight.
> (IN FISHER, 408)

And María Saucedo acknowledges that if a woman feels she has no fenses, she will be defeated. She must find strength, she must continu struggle in the game if she is to win.

> And la Mujer sat on
>   the curve
> And cried: "I am only a woman!
>   "I am defenseless and can do nothing!
>   "Desgracia la mía ser mujer!"
> Y se ahogó en sus propias
>   lágrimas y self-pity.
> Y encontraron su cuerpo
>   cuando se secó el lago de lágrimas
> Y dijeron ellos: "La pobre se ahogó . . .
>   ni modo . . .
> Y siguieron caminando nodding their heads.
>
> Y La Mujer sat on
>   the curve.
> Y dice: "Pinche concrete curve, cala mucho!"
>   Se levantó y caminó
> . . . se tropieza con una piedra . . .
> Y dice: "Pinche piedra, me machucó el dedo!"
>   Echando madres siguió and
>   she bumped into a lamppost . . .
> Y dice: "Pinche lamppost . . . qué harto dolor me dejó!"
>
>   PERO
> Ella siguió y siguió . . .
> Llegó a la casa . . .
> Y se puso a hacer tortillas y Revolución.
> (SAUCEDO, 112)[9]

Miriam Bornstein Somoza equates participation in the playing of games with freedom of expression, particularly in the writing of poetry. An integral part of game concept is language. Communication, like games, is difficult to master. In order to communicate, one must accept a set of stable rules. Once these rules are mastered, communication itself may also become a game in which one can triumph (Blake, 65). Thus

language, ritual, and poetry can all be expressed as games. Bornstein Somoza says,

> considero que fui parte del circo
> aplaudí a lo romano ante jugadores cristianos
> me divertí con gladiadores futbolistas
> y la virgen de la macarena amarré como todos a un
>   comercial
> que por sólo un minuto
> interrumpía mi programación
> pero un día
> al asesinar la manaña
> con el sofocante rumor de las calles
> los zumbidos de caras indiferentes
> a cada paso me topé conmigo misma
> ellos son yo
> son yo misma
> y desde entonces
> me dieron ganas de ser bruja
> y jugar a la vida con poemas.
> (BORNSTEIN, 6)[10]

In order to be a rational player, a woman must have a clear sense of
who she is. She must not search for her reflection or her sense of self in
other players. She must, however, if need be, look to others, both men and
women, for cooperation in strategy planning. Thus another writer, Alma
Villanueva, bases her game-playing strategy (the growth of self-identity)
through a sense of connectedness with other women. In her long poem
Mother May I? she refers to a children's game where the children ask the
mother for directions, "Mother, may I take a giant step?" Villanueva explores the child giving birth to herself, becoming the mother. The process
begins as play:

> the pretend
> place
> is bed, we
> lay together, you
> tell me stories
> about when you were
> little and you were

bad, I
laugh and laugh
and we
are both 5
and no one's
the mother, we
hid from the
grown ups,
playing
. . . . . .
I think one time we
never switched back and I stayed
your
mother and I stayed
bigger and I stayed
stronger, to take
care of you,
mother, we
forgot the world is bigger than
our bed.
(VILLANUEVA, 11−12)

Once the birthing has taken place, self-knowledge gives the child the ability to play, strategize, to make choices. The child is ready:

I've
learned the ropes
I've
cultivated my gardens
I've combed my shores
I've
played house
played god
created universes
in my kitchen
in my womb
and when I
hide I
play mother
to my own little girl. I

was always
good at
make believe. all
I ask is
    may
I play?
(VILLANUEVA, 36—37)

Like the poets who preceded her, Margarita Cota-Cárdenas is clearly aware of the loss of innocence necessary to play games in society and the need for women to put forth their own rules of the game. Cota-Cárdenas's lyric speakers are often children playing games in their imagination. These games serve to keep the bogeyman away: that is, they form a protective device against the real world. The self within needs to be nurtured, so the game players resort to "pretend" games, thus creating another more manageable and sustaining environment. As Huizinga states, "The child is making an image of something different, something more beautiful or more sublime or more dangerous than what he usually is" (Huizinga, 13—14).

As the child can "pretend," so can the adult change her world into a desired one using the same methods. This is the case in "Mejor fingimos" (Let's Pretend):

qué chiste
        tener que morir un poeta
        para ser apreciado

por qué no jugamos

        cierra tú los ojos
        y yo
            me acuesto aquí
                en esta camita de piedra
        y al ratito
            como en la Biblia
            me levanto
(COTA-CÁRDENAS, *Noches,* N.P.)[11]

In addition, for Cota-Cárdenas, the adult game player must not participate in a game she defines as one-sided or in which she has no choice, even if it means her own destruction:

Soliloquio travieso

mucho trabajo   ser flor
a veces
   solitas
     y en camino
concentramos muy fuerte   así
   arrugamos la frente
     para marchitarnos antes
y al llegar al mercado   ji ji
     no nos pueden vender.
(*Noches,* N.P.)[12]

The implicit mischievousness suggests that this player has deliberately chosen the role of "spoilsport" to ruin the "payoff" for her opponent. For this game, the strategy chosen (to be a withered flower and not a beautiful one) gives her a "negative payoff" on the one hand, in that she grows old and withered, but it also has a positive payoff for her inner self: she remains true to her own values. This, then, is the true test of the game—the true mastery. If you can handle the illusions and the strategic trickery of the other player or players, and if you can master the idiom or language of the game, then you are truly a rational player. To master the language of the game seems to indicate demythifying the traditional values perpetuated by society in order to give a player a chance. The demythification of the opponent and a correct assessment of her/his own true power are important elements in this game transcendence; they can lead to alternative actions. In "Justo Será" (It Must Be Just), Cota-Cárdenas states:

días   semanas   meses
   sin saber de
     poetizados espasmos
todo por creer
     en los caballeros-andantes
   aquel pinchi bato
y su mitificado horse
     coming down the camino-brick-road
   with a mecate-rope
   around his pescuezo-neck
que nunca

nunca
llega
(*Noches,* N.P.)[13]

The new role model for the woman player is explicitly delineated by all these feminist game players. She is a rational player who makes rational choices, having demythified her opponents to operate within a sphere of freedom. To begin, the rules of the game must make the players equal. If they do not, the players have two choices: they may choose not to play or they may manipulate men in the ways women have been manipulated in the past. Manipulation, however, is not seen as a positive value in this game playing; it perpetuates values not adhered to by feminist game players who are striving for direct confrontation and communication.

Games require application, knowledge, skill, courage, and strength. Once a woman acquires these, she can then make her own decisions as to what payoffs she considers valuable. It is illuminating that feminist game players traditionally do not want to concern themselves only with their personal payoffs. They want to engage in a focus of self and other, where the self will not be betrayed because she has been unable to play the game.

The elements that feminist game players must understand and participate in are: (1) demythifying the opponent, (2) supporting other feminist game players (to be used later in larger cooperative confrontations), (3) becoming "rational" in the ways in which women are manipulated, (4) searching for the ideal but also equal combinations of self and other, (5) remaining true to your own self, even if the payoffs are destructive, or (6) remaining outside of the game. As Cota-Cárdenas states:

busca tu nombre
dentro de ti misma
CHICANA
crea tu propia palabra
tu esencia   TU

. . . .

sé homenaje a tu raza   crea tu propio cosmos
CHICANA   HERMANA   MUJER
ahora actúa por
TI
(*Noches,* N.P.)[14]

EIGHTEEN

Art and Spiritual Politics

SOR JUANA BEATRIZ DE LA FUENTE—
A FEMINIST LITERARY PERSPECTIVE (1995)

Here am I, a literary critic who studies and researches Latin American women writers and Chicana writers, at a conference of artists and art historians.[1] My task is to discuss a painting by Sor Juana Beatriz de la Fuente, a *pastorela*, a piece of "folk art" painted, so the label tells us, in 1805.

I am neither an art critic nor an art historian, and little is known about either the painting or the painter. And so, as we literary critics, especially those of us who indulge in cultural studies, are wont to do, I intend to engage in both cultural studies and in a symbolic analysis of the painting utilizing as my authorities what I know about nuns in convents from the sixteenth to the nineteenth centuries, especially nuns in Mexico and Spain. I will discuss the literary heritage left by nuns, the way in which they had to deal with the dominant discourses (read "patriarchal church fathers"), their oppressions and triumphs, and how Sor Juana Beatriz de la Fuente and her painting fit into this cultural background.

To begin, I am told by Dr. Marion Ottinger of the San Antonio Art Museum, where the painting is housed, that, although there is no information on Sor Juana Beatriz, the painting came from Morelia and Sor Juana Beatriz was probably a cloistered nun. The fact that she uses the name Sor (sister) also corroborates the fact that she was cloistered. As we know, residing in a convent was often the only alternative to marriage for many women in colonial Mexico. And for some women, being in a convent run by women, where emphasis was placed on the spiritual, was a positive way of existence for them. If the nuns came from the upper class, life in a convent could be very rewarding. In general, convents were built in urban areas (not in fields and isolated places where the women could be victims of assaults) and were singularly completely self-sufficient. The buildings themselves were often small walled fortresses, where in effect there were two chapels, one open to the public and one private for the nuns. The *locutorios*

La Pastorela, *by Sor Juana Beatriz de la Fuente, 1805. Photo courtesy
San Antonio Museum of Art.*

(visiting rooms) were separated from the general public by wooden *rejas*
(bars), but the nuns could receive visitors freely. Moreover, the nuns lived
in their own apartments, which, if not double-storied, contained several
rooms, as they had servants to serve them. Some of these servants were lay
sisters or women who wanted to live a religious life but who did not have
the dowry or means to maintain themselves. But those who did have the
means often retained economic control as they oversaw properties, gardens, and orchards seen as essential to the well-being of the order (Marcela
Gutiérrez, 240–245). In fact, some of the more rigorous orders underwent
many modifications that were imposed by local customs, economic necessity, and the varying evolutions of criteria decided upon by the founders
and keepers of the orders. One of the most important changes occurred

during the seventeenth century when Archbishop Payo de Ribera allowed the nuns to live in individual cells, to administer their own income, and to make use of the rents of their capital investments (241).

In colonial Mexican society, the nuns utilized the mystic aureole of their life of sacrifice and devotion and the social prestige of belonging to prestigious or distinguished families with their own personal merit of culture, ingenuity, and gracefulness as well as their affable and courteous comportment in order to achieve both political and social goals. They specialized in being excellent hostesses; they showered their guests with musical recitals, literary recitals, congenial conversation, and especially with their sweets and desserts, brandies and wines—culinary specialties for which each convent was renown (242). Thus their participation in ordinary life had a double axis: they were respected and admired because of their absence since the cloister signified their renunciation of ordinary pleasures, and also because of their presence, their affectionate relationships with viceroys, prelates, ladies of the court, the clergy, and young visitors of both sexes.

As Electra Arenal and Stacy Schlau have pointed out in their book *Untold Sisters,* while nuns were "instruments of the enforcement of the social order by the religious and royal elite; nevertheless, the relatively peaceful structure of their contemplative life, separate from men, gave them some autonomy," and they made important contributions to the "vibrant and tragic criolla and mestiza culture that emerged from conquest and colonization" (Arenal and Schlau, 337).

Some nuns were illiterate but others were educated, especially in acceptable liturgies, lives of the saints, and Catholic tradition. In fact, the requirements to profess as a nun were often rigorous, as they should be able to read in order to pray the orations and the officio of Our Lady, and they should be able to write their name in order to sign their desire to profess, but in reality there were many nuns who had knowledge beyond the required and in the convents were secretaries, historians, and writers (Marcela Gutiérrez, 240). They have left poetry, plays, and devotional materials.

Several recent books have theorized about the importance of the writing of women in convents in Spain and Latin America in the sixteenth, seventeenth, and eighteenth centuries. As mentioned, Arenal and Schlau in *Untold Sisters* and Jean Franco in *Plotting Women* have been among the first to try to place the discourse of these women within the framework of male narration. Franco sees the writing of nuns during this time as a struggle for interpretive power. During the colonizing centuries, religion and its various discourses was one of the most powerful "master narratives." But during the Reformation and as the church felt its hold over reason threatened by the emerging new scientific thought, the more it began to look to religious sentiment to revive its "flagging spirituality." Women were in truth prohibited from speaking or writing in the public sphere, which would have been the confessional or the pulpit, the two locations privileged by the church. But at the same time that women were unable to participate in the rational, public sphere of discourse, a more intuitive, direct form of knowledge, that of mysticism, was one that was accepted by the church; in fact, it had strong defenders who claimed it constituted a higher and more immediate form of knowledge than scholastic theology (Franco, 5). According to Franco, "Mysticism was a knowledge that bypassed book learning and whose claims to truth had to be judged in part by its emotive effects—levitation, rapture, groans and sighs" (xiv). Women were adept at mysticism because of their perceived "lesser rationality," which came from the realm of feeling—therefore, the clergy "unwittingly created a space for female empowerment" (xiv).

These nuns were able to escape from their physical environment and selves. Since they could not engage in public discourse, many women "bypassed rationality to enter into mystical communion with God, converse directly with the Saints and the Virgin, and obey the dictates of inner voices" (5). The nuns who had visions and other out-of-body experiences had to be carefully watched and recorded: one means of recording their experiences was to order them to write these experiences, carefully supervised by their confessors and church mentors. We therefore have a written account of notes, records, and life histories of these women, accounts that today represent a rich store of imaginative and fantasy literature. Imagine, women who were cloistered, enclosed in orders, and separated from the world; women who saw painful figures of martyred saints and of Christ in the church; women who inflicted penitence on themselves or fasted often—these women writing their imaginations. These women whose experiences were not written anywhere became the authors of powerful representations in their visionary writings. Often they were self-effacing: "Yo la peor del mundo" (I, the worst in the world), writes the brilliant Sor Juana Inés de la Cruz; "Yo, gusano del mundo" (I, the worm of the world), writes another. Yet Sor Juana soars and has visions of a world of the intellect. Some nuns said that Christ, or alternatively the Virgin Mary, had personally told them their secrets and that they were speaking for them: thus the visionary nuns assumed the authority they needed, through the direct mystical experience no one could contradict, in order to speak, to narrate, and to write. Not only did God communicate secrets to them but they were transported to distant places (a holy parallel to the flight of witches);

they saw visions and hallucinated (6). In dreams and visions, then, these women went beyond their cells and convents, flying across time and space; at times they went to hell and viewed life and the dangers (as well as the seductions of purgatory), or they were transported to heaven to converse with Christ and angels and saw the future. They were able to penetrate all secrets, including sexual temptations, which often appeared. Franco claims that these flights were "the feminine equivalent of the heroic journey of self-transformation" (6).

Because the visionary experience was a subjective, emotional one, these women tended to put themselves outside clerical control. Their writing, however, was carefully regulated and watched; their confessors controlled how much they should write and often told the women to destroy their writings as an act of obedience. With the advent of the Inquisition, the writing nuns had to be careful of what they wrote, that it not be heretical, and it is clear that they were well aware of these dangers. One indicator that they knew of the danger that could befall them is precisely how they seized authority (by declaring that what they were writing was told to them by God, the Virgin, or other sacred voices) and by denying it at the same time: *they* were not the authors of the writing, merely the instruments of a higher authority/spirit.

As an example of these perspectives we have Sor María de Agreda (1602–1665), a Franciscan nun who founded a convent in Agreda, Spain. As a child she was often ill; when she became a nun "the Lord subjected her to severe trials . . . the devil, surmising she was to accomplish great things, raised all hell against this woman. Some frightening things took place" (Carrico, 4). Her inner life seems to have been full of diabolical temptations (her family was an extremely religious one; witness the conversion of their castle into a convent), including persistent sexual ones. The manifestations of this inner life were to be seen in trances, visions, and even levitations. An autodidact, like Sor Juana, she had obviously read Pliny, the accounts of the Franciscan fathers in the New World, as well as any other material she could obtain. However, to be an intellectual nun was not only an unwomanly attribute but also to be subject to the Inquisition, so Sor María de Agreda engaged in a subversion that many religious women writers were forced to utilize, a subversion I call the discourse of hysteria. That is, these women could not admit that they were thinkers and creators of intellectual or academic work; they therefore stated that the Virgin Mary or Christ himself had appeared to them in a dream or a vision and that they were only the medium through which the message was being transmitted to the general public. In their dreams they sometimes *became* Christ or the Virgin Mary, or even sometimes the very devil him-self. (The devil appeared quite often in these visions, quite sexually tinged, as he was the representation of the primary temptation.) Sor María de Agreda wrote a book titled *The Mystical City of God,* in which she detailed the life of the Virgin Mary, especially the nine months that Mary had spent in her mother's womb. This book was condemned by her confessor for its language as well as for its content, and she was ordered to burn it, along with the diaries she had kept of her bilocations to New Mexico (1630), where she claimed to have appeared to the natives, spoken to them in their own languages, and converted them to Christianity. Because of her visions and her bilocations she had become friendly with King Philip IV of Spain, serving as a sort of spiritual confessor to him. They corresponded faithfully for over fifteen years (with more than 600 letters). Although her manuscript was condemned by the Inquisition, Sor María had already sent the king a copy of *The Mystical City of God;* thus the manuscript was saved. Her discourse of hysteria eventually allowed her to claim that she had not written it with her own will, that she was only the subject of a dream or of a vision. In addition to her other writings, Sor María de Agreda also wrote a cosmology of the world as well as some philosophical tracts. What is interesting about her cosmology is that here she attempts to enter into the realm of "science" of rational thought, as opposed to that of her ecstasies, confirmed by the church. Her knowledge of the world, of course, is not revealed by reading and study, but rather by an out-of-body vision that God takes her on in order to show her the nature of the world. Church fathers were particularly thwarted by this subversion because in order to reject it, they would have had to claim that there were no such things as apparitions and visions.

Of course the most brilliant woman during the colonial period in Mex-ico was Sor Juana Inés de la Cruz (1651–1695), who not only was a gifted writer and musician but a woman who dared enter into the public sphere. In her *Respuesta* she gives us an enthralling as well as verbally brilliant picture of her life as she defends herself against the attacks of the Bishop of Puebla, who scolded her for engaging in a critique of a sermon writ-ten forty years earlier by a Portuguese Jesuit, Father Antonio de Vieyra. In the *Respuesta* she defends education for women, displays her brilliance in Latin, cites a long list of learned women as her authorities, introduces cooking as a science, and claims that Aristotle would have been a better philosopher if only he had known how to cook. Clearly in a patriarchal society that felt that women should not be engaging in debates in the public sphere, especially religious women, Sor Juana had transgressed. She eventually put away her books and spent the last few years of her life taking care of her fellow sisters before dying from an epidemic at the age of forty-four (Peden, 1–50).

In order to examine their lives, often nuns were ordered to write *Vidas,* careful examinations of their thoughts and their spiritual life, and then in the name of obedience they were ordered to burn them. So an educated nun could write, and certainly she would be able to paint, considered along with sewing, embroidery, playing a musical instrument, and cooking to be a female accomplishment, all for the benefit of the convent. In the great convents of Puebla and Guadalajara that I have seen, in addition to paintings with religious themes, such as the lives of the Virgin, Christ, or the martyrs, there are a series of paintings of the nuns themselves. These portraits are of them just before they go into the convent or of them as novices in the convents. The habits are often extraordinary and the detail to the dresses amazing. The paintings that the nuns saw everyday in the convent and the church would clearly be of religious themes, good versus evil, morality plays, the martyrdom of various saints. Many of these paintings came from the baroque period and were full of violence, blood, and dreadful evil creatures who tempted the good.

This particular *pastorela* painted by Sor Juana Beatriz (you see, I have finally come back to her) is an interesting painting for various reasons. Pastorelas were often morality plays in which the shepherds, after seeing the star, start off to Bethlehem to bring presents to the Christ child. Pastorelas are usually performed just before Christmas in Mexico and are prevalent today. The characters in the traditional pastorela include a hermit, a lazy shepherd (Bartolo), a beautiful shepherdess (Gila), Michael the Archangel, or a guardian angel, and, of course, the Devil. In the pastorela it is important that the shepherds (along with the Three Kings) see the Christ child for themselves in order to publicly validate his birth for the people. The Devil, of course, tries to tempt the hermit to seduce Gila in order to prevent the shepherds from reaching the Christ child and validating his presence. However, good wins over evil and the shepherds eventually reach the Christ child. While this painting does not duplicate exactly the theatrical pastorela, it contains many of its elements. The action takes place outdoors, under a tree representing the Tree of Life, and is a pastoral scene. Christ represents the pastor and we are the sheep or the lambs of Christ. The moral of the story is certainly evident, with the young man (who could represent the lazy shepherd) asleep in a chair underneath the tree. His guardian angel hovers anxiously over him, while an adult Christ with his hammer, symbol of Christ's crucifixion and subsequent resurrection, is about to strike a bell hanging from one of the branches of the tree, representing Christ's power to scare the evil spirits away. The traditional figures of Mary, Christ, and the guardian angel seem very static; the mobile figures are the *calavera* (Death), who with his scythe is twisting his bones in an awkward way, and the wonderful Devil with his evil red tongue, hairy body, and monkeylike figure, swinging on a vine (suggestive of the serpent) below the student. Fortunately the Tree, which appears to overshadow the background, is very healthy and the viewer can only come to the conclusion that the sleeper will awaken to a spiritual consciousness and be saved.

Although elements of baroque painting with its highly contrastive colors between light and dark affect this painting, except for the Devil and the skeleton, the painting is highly neoclassical in style. But the exuberant Mexican use of color is also evident. Christ, the Virgin, the guardian angel, and the sleeping youth are very European in face and color. In fact, the painting lacks any regional or national stamp beyond that of the Devil. The Virgin does not appear to be the Mexican Virgin of Guadalupe and the rest of the iconography seems traditionally European. In fact the representation of Christ reflects his representation in a literary text written by an *ilustra* (an illuminated one), Ana de Aramburu:

> Your color is beautiful, but like a gentleman's, pink and proud. Your eyes are beautiful, peaceful, humble red. Your eyes rob hearts, Lord, your face, Oh Lord, is very honest, Lord, your beautiful red hair hangs down to your waist, You have a coral mouth, so small and beautiful, very pink, Lord, your cheeks. It is true that your height is a meter and half, isn't that so, my Love? You have a fine body, thin, with small feet, How terrible to see your foot touch the ground, your hands are long, your nails well shaped, your brow wide. Is there anyone who doesn't love you? Just looking on you engenders love, your humility, your honesty, your patience, you are very peaceful . . . I will give you my heart so that you will impress your passion onto it.
>
> (FRANCO, 71)

But it is, after all, the Devil who is the most interesting figure. He is so grotesque, his mask so fearsome (and humorous at the same time), that his conception in this piece is quite amazing. It also greatly resembles a description of the devil by María de San José in her vida (1703). First she describes her joy in taking communion and in being united with Christ; "This is the Lord whom I desire to serve. I intend nothing else, but to please Him. I want no happiness, nor rest, nor any other good, but only to do His will; for if this Lord is indeed powerful, as I see, experience, and know Him to be: then why should I not trust in this Lord, who shall remove me, for my good, from all these trials?" (Arenal and Schlau, 384). Later she describes the following:

> I walked back to the room where my mother and sisters were. And as I passed the staircase, I encountered the devil, who was seated on the bottom step in human form, like a naked mulatto. He was gnawing at one of his hands. Just as I saw him, he raised a finger as if to threaten me and he said to me: "You are mine. You will not escape my clutches." I saw this more with inward vision than with my bodily eyes. The words he said to me sounded in my ears: I heard them spoken. But comforted and aided by Him who can do everything, who is God, I managed to enter the chamber where my mother was.
>
> (385)

Thus the painting of the pastorela very much follows a European tradition, but we encounter a frightening tempting devil figure very much in the perspective of a nun's imagination.

To conclude I would like to leave you with the following thoughts and questions. It is interesting to note that we know the name of the painter of the retablo, Sor Juana Beatriz de la Fuente, as most retablos were unattributed and unsigned. Interesting, too, that it was a woman and a nun who painted it, and in so doing managed to insert herself into a public (albeit for women) space. The painting thus gives us a glimpse of an artistic legacy left by women. Although the icononography of the painting is European and traditional, she nonetheless inserts the Virgin along with Christ in the traditional battle of good and evil. The calavera and the devil are perhaps the only two figures that reflect regional or national popular culture (or Mexicanness), if you will. And perhaps the student sleeping, dressed in the traditional dress of the *estudiantina* (student theatrical group), is not a male at all. The painter, a nun, could not specifically paint herself into the public discourse of temptation, but perhaps the student youth could represent her human self that was seeking salvation.

HOMELAND AND EXILE IN MARJORIE
AGOSÍN (1997)

I first met Marjorie Agosín when we were both young as-
sistant professors around seventeen or eighteen years ago (well, Marjorie
was young, and I was a bit younger than I am now). I knew her first as
a budding poet, and then several years later she traveled to Reno, Nevada, where I was teaching, to show us *arpilleras,* the cloth tapestries sewed
by Chilean women whose family members, husbands and children, were
among the "disappeared." After the military takeover of 1973, the social
and political situation in Chile was chilling, oppressive, scary. People inside and outside of Chile were afraid to talk about what was happening;
they were shocked and fearful of reprisals. And this young academic was
traveling to universities all over the United States talking about the disappeared, showing and selling the arpilleras to raise money for the women
who made them.

   Since that time I have followed Agosín's career, and I have continued
to be impressed by the scope of her work, her fine poetry and literary
criticism, her social and political commitment, and the variety of themes,
function, and passion seen in her work. As I prepared this paper, I was
struck by her enormous productivity and her enormous passions, and how
profoundly she believes in the act of writing as empowerment, of memory,
and of freedom. For she is not only a poet of irony, metaphysics, and
desire, a literary critic of Latin American women writers, an essayist published in leading Latin American and American journals and newspapers,
but more recently has written narrative texts that combine biography and
autobiography in her book *A Cross and a Star.*

   Let me quickly give you an overview of Agosín's work. Marjorie Agosín
has written sixteen books of poetry, her first two being *Chile* and *Conchalí,*
her most recent, *Dear Anne Frank* and *Council of the Fairies*: she is a prolific
writer. Her poetry has evolved over the years, as one might hope in a ma-

ture poet, but within that evolution many concerns remain the same. The idea of women's silencing and how to break through that silence is a central issue for Agosín. At the same time she understands the paradox of women's silence as signifying resistance, for example, as when a woman refuses to break her silence when she is tortured to reveal names of supposed collaborators; thus silence becomes a positive under certain circumstances. Agosín has taken classical myths such as the legend of Penelope and of Robin Hood, and subverted, undermined, and revised them. Relationships between men and women also come under close scrutiny: whereas men were ironized and satirized in her early poetry, passion, desire, and fulfillment of the mature sexual self are evident in her book *Hogueras* (Bonfires). In this book, which surpasses even Pablo Neruda's *Versos del Capitán* in erotic love poetry, woman's body and sexual desire are described as the godhead. In her passion woman is central, not man. Another unifying theme is the idea that women are made up of and covered by smoke, that in their suffering, anguish, passion, and death by fire, there is always a phoenixlike regeneration. When women live under patriarchy and oppression, "los paises de humo," they are still illuminated by the light and passion within:

> Y tú
> despojada
> abierta
> herida
> eres
> iluminada
> un faro
> en
> los mares del sur
> (AGOSÍN, *Women of Smoke,* 114)

> (and you
> dispossessed
> open
> wounded
> are luminous
> a light house
> in
> the seas of the south.
> (TRANSLATION MINE)

Carmen Naranjo states in the preface to *Women of Smoke,* "In Marjorie's poetic discourse there are no pitiful cries or hysterical accusations: there is a language of women who live and suffer, who love and whose stories unfold in the raw reality of smoke, a metaphor for their subjugation and the discrimination that plagues them" (7).

In her literary criticism (thirteen published books) Agosín has been one of the few literary critics to concentrate on women writers who write about political and social oppression. She has made known to a larger public authors who were virtually ignored, such as Alicia Portnoy and María Carolina Geel, as well as writing important works about more well known authors such as María Luisa Bombal, Gabriela Mistral, and the Chilean singer Violeta Parra. She has not shied away from discussing difficult issues such as the torture, violation, and rape discussed in creative fiction, nor has she dismissed women's popular arts such as sewing, ceramics, painting as mere domestic tasks. In them she has seen political and social implications and has elevated these commonplace aspects of women's creativity to include their symbolic value. She acknowledges, for example, the influence of the *arpilleristas* on her own life: "I am profoundly grateful to the Chilean arpilleristas who taught me the value of life, the value of left-over scraps: who taught me persistence and a true desire of justice for all. From these women I learned to listen and then to tell, and in spite of all the adversities, I learned to hope for a more just and human society. It is to these women that I dedicate this book as well as to my mother who taught me that even though I had bread and a roof over my head I must never forget those who don't" (*Scraps of Life,* ix).

Again she has stated, "The work of the arpilleristas, those wives and mothers of the disappeared who, very early in the morning, to take advantage of natural light, begin to embroider with their tired and wounded hands the histories, the everyday living, everyday living that contains disappearances, mutilations, tortures. They who are submerged in memory create with luminosity the history of their children, of the children of a divided country so that they will never forget that they are" (*Literatura,* 104).

Agosín has also edited twelve anthologies. In her anthology of Latin American women writers, *These Are Not Nice Girls,* Agosín focuses on aspects of rebellion, resistance, and subversion of women writers. Agosín has also written five books of narrative fiction. Lately she has combined the biographical and autobiographical in *A Cross and a Star,* a story about her mother's experience of being a Jew in a German (largely Nazi) town in southern Chile and, of course, the experience of being an exile. This is

Agosín's story, too, because as a Chilean Jew living in the United States, she is triply exiled, her heritage coming from a family of exiles. The stories of her family surface over and over again in Agosín's writing: in poems, in short stories, in biography.

An overriding alignment in Agosín's work is with women who survive, no matter what it takes—women who live with passion, integrity, wildness. She is attracted to gypsies, and wild, mad women. Her lived experiences, and those of her family, have made her side with the homeless, the exiled, the marginal. She reveals all this in a poem titled "Dedication."

> I am irreverently
> partisan to
> lost causes
> to those wild, barefoot
> women
> imagining themselves a setting sun,
> a canvas of light
> in the air's openwork
> embroidery.
> Like a mad woman I love
> the unwary,
> the beggars,
> who watch over
> the sunsets,
> the sublime rose-tinted sky
> by the edges of the roads.
> I dedicate myself to things lost,
> to those without homes,
> to those sick,
> dying of cold and cancer,
> to the guerrilla fighters
> in love with peace.
>
> I am what I am:
> improper,
> happy,
> bold
> in my desires,
> a friend of beggar woman,

an enemy of eggplant,
quince preserves,
the military.
(*Toward,* 12)

Often Agosín's writings are unsettling. They shift from poetic discourse to political discourse in subtle ways. And they can be disconcertingly direct and profound, forcing her readers to reflect on situations they might rather avoid. In *Zones of Pain,* perhaps her most political book of all, Agosín relentlessly focuses on the pain and suffering women have endured, but these poems are delicately embroidered in poetic language. As she says in her prologue:

> The disappeared women slipped in among dreams. They would watch me, at times they would wake me up caressing me, more than anything else they would ask me not to forget them. That's how these Zones of Pain kept growing. The women buried but still alive wove the fabric of my words that in the humility of helplessness sought for clear places and voices.
>
> The zones of pain represent the wandering of buried women and the wandering of searching mothers. The zones of pain are ours, are dark, and at times too easily slip the mind. For those reasons I wrote them down, because I wish to accompany my dead sisters.
> (*Zones,* 2)

In "Beyond the Dawn" she writes;

> Beyond the dawn
> clothed in fog,
> they asked her
> why are you weeping?
> whom are you seeking?
> —she only said to them
> give me back my
> daughter.
> (4)

Agosín constantly asks us to reflect on our own actions toward the dispossessed, the exiles, and human rights. In "The Most Unbelievable Part" she writes,

> The most unbelievable part,
> they were people like us
> good manners
> well-educated and refined.
> Versed in abstract sciences,
> always took a box for the Symphony
> make regular trips to the dentist
> attended very nice prep schools
> some played golf . . .
>
> Yes, people like you, like me
> family men
> grandfathers
> uncles and godfathers.
>
> But they went crazy
> delighted in burning
> children and books
> played at decorating cemeteries
> bought furniture made of broken bones
> dined on tender ears and testicles.
>
> Thought they were invincible
> meticulous in their duties
> and spoke of torture
> in the language of surgeons and butchers.
>
> They assassinated the young of my country
> and of yours.
> Now nobody could believe in Alice through the looking glass
> now nobody could stroll along the avenues
> without terror bursting through their bones
>
> And the most unbelievable part
> they were people
> like you
> like me

yes, nice people
just like us.
(12)

Calling into question how human beings, supposedly "normal" with "normal" values and sentiments, could capture and torture other human beings forces us to consider whether we too could behave in a similar manner. And she asks us to remember and to call those dispossessed of human rights, the poor, the Indian, women, the disappeared:

I am the disappeared woman,
in a country grown dark,
silenced by the
wrathful cubbyholes
of those with no memory.

. . . .

Don't conspire with
oblivion,
tear down the silence.
I want to be
the appeared woman
from among the labyrinths
come back, return
name myself.
Call my name.
(28)

Now I address four aspects of exile and homeland in the work of Marjorie Agosín. The first is the sense of loss and of exile of people who have been dispossessed because of political or social reasons. This includes not only the Jews during the Second World War, but takes on the additional representation of people, particularly women, who have had to leave their homes and have lost their families because of natural phenomena such as earthquakes, or political phenomena such as oppressive and cruel military governments. The second is her representation of the political and religious refugee, the Jew as the wanderer. The third aspect is how Agosín inherits the alphabet and then is challenged to use that alphabet to create a language by which to remember, and, finally, how Agosín goes about creating and reconstructing a homeland in the text.

In thinking about homeland, one thinks about attachment to a national culture, to land and landscape, to religion, to language. But Agosín and her family have been denied national and cultural identity time after time. In fact it seems that a history of Agosín and her extended family would be one that occurs between holocaust and holocaust. The first holocaust is the persecution of the Jews and their exile and extermination by the Nazis during the Second World War. Agosín's immediate family fled to Chile and most survived, always living with the guilt of survivors and with the dreadful knowledge of the fate of those who did not. For this reason Agosín empathizes with the figure of Anne Frank. One theme in her work is the tattoos on the arms of women, hidden under long gloves. The tattoo becomes the icon for those who survived, their suffering is often "tattooed on the memory." Another theme is that of the train. Whenever Marjorie or any member of her family boards a train, they are never sure where that train will take them. This refers to the many Jews who were taken to labor or extermination camps thinking they were going someplace else. The other holocaust is what occurred in Chile after the fall of Salvador Allende in 1973 and with the military takeover of General Pinochet. This time it was not religion that was targeted, but students, intellectuals—everyone. The result was the same: torture and annihilation. Thus the idea of homeland for Agosín is problematic since it became a homeland of repression, torture, and the disappeared: her homeland is often populated with a sense of guilt, injustice, and exile. At the same time it is a beloved and longed-for region. As Agosín has said, "I think about my country and it hurts me. It is a borrowed region of vast plateaus, knolls and snow-capped peaks" (*Cross,* 97). The grief over what was happening in her homeland is articulated in "Questions":

> They asked me
>   with the false innocence of the privileged:
>   if in my country we skied.
> I answered them with that not so
> false innocence
> of survivors:
> sometimes,
>   that it is an extravagant sport
>   for the rich of the region,
>   and that our children
>   had never seen snow.

> They asked me:
>   Then what did we do
>   in my country?
>   I answered them
>   boldly:
>   we dig up the dead
>   in order to bury them.
> (*Toward,* 9)

Moreover, because Agosín is herself an exile, a Chilean living in the United States, she is separated from language and family. And when she has returned to Chile, it was a country in fear, turmoil. As Agosín says, "I have come back to an imprisoned country" (*Scraps,* 1). She states,

> As a woman
> I have no country
> only rocks
> and rivers
> an illusion
> without city walls.
> (*Women of Smoke,* 114)

Yet homeland is homeland, and there is always the longing to return. In "Forgetting" she writes:

> Exiled brutally
> I left behind countries,
> left behind midnights
> in sleepless
> cities.
> All
> I took along were two
> or three words,
> the darkness of the
> streets,
> some bread crumbs
> for the return home.
> (*Toward,* 114)

Her dispossessed people are not only wandering Jews but all those dispossessed human beings in the world; having lost everything, they become detached from place, possessions, and even people. In "Wise Woman" the poetic speaker states,

> I
> Fully aware
> I got used
> to losing
> things:
> old
> gifts,
> jewelry in the back of some drawer,
> lackluster hair dried out by the sun.
>
> II
> I never tried to recover
> anything
> not even the houses I dearly loved;
> I learned to detach myself from things
> with a humble tranquility,
> with a certainty
> that nothing
> was ever really
> ours.
> (120)

In fact, a sense of loss is one of the distinguishing features in Agosín's work—but it can be redeemed and reconstructed through memory and writing. In a short piece, "The Blue Teacups," the narrator tells of a moment in Stockholm when, as if in a dream, she is drawn to a dark place—a wake—where only belongings of a dead woman remain. She is taken by blue teacups with golden edges. Discovering that the cups belonged to a Jewish woman from Hungary who never, in all her travels, let go of them, the narrator brings the teacups to her home in Boston. For her they have become the symbol of exile: "They have traveled, have been buried in earthquakes, and have survived the loss of children and homes. I cannot stop looking at them. I find my eyes full of the roads of my great-grandmother Helena. The one who had to leave her house, her feather pillows, her histories and her memories one morning because she was Jewish" (*Women of Smoke,* 21). The teacups acquire meaning precisely because they represent exile, "I care for them and love them because I preserve the water of so many exiles in them" (20–21). And in "Candelabras" Agosín reconstructs her grandmother's plight:

> My grandmother
> Helena,
> the lady of Vienna,
> the wandering dancer,
> only brought
> from her city
> silver
> candelabras,
> the family linen
> and the pallor
> of padlocks
> buried
> under her bleeding
> skirt.
> (*Toward,* 76)

Like the blue teacups, the candelabras are something Agosín cherishes, saying, "I now keep the Viennese candlesticks in my home and although I don't pray, I talk to God and get angry with Him and ask him about those who have no homeland" (*Cross,* 143). The few objects remaining become symbolic of the totality of loss: home, family, religion, place.

Those who have no homeland become wanderers, and so Agosín becomes the traveler and refers to her family as "The Wanderers." In a short piece by that name she recounts all the journeys of the women in her family—her grandmother who crossed the Andes on a mule, her mother who had to leave Chile for "many relentless and complicated reasons," and herself: "and so, by fate, I became and am a wanderer. I, too, have just given birth to a child. I, too, will have to invent a country for him. And if my child asks me where I am from, I will tell him that I carry a country within myself. Like all women, I carry my home in my hair and carry love in my body full of spirits and pilgrimages" (*Women,* 26). For herself she tells us, "How much I have won and lost in my voyages. However, above all else I maintain my language and the capacity to be astounded before horror. The garden of my house is like the heart of a savage girl" (*Cross*, 92).

Of course, life survives loss and exile, life becomes reconstructed— her grandmother carried her bronze padlocks across the oceans where she "planted flowers and found a new place to hang her keys." But loss and exile must be remembered and told, just as those tortured and disappeared must be remembered. "My quest" says Agosín, "resides in finding a language by means of these writings that resuscitate the dead, a language that speaks, makes them appear and feel" (*Literatura*, 11). Through the stories and memories of her family, the exiled, the disappeared, and because of the holocausts and deprivation of human rights, she has inherited the alphabet. But inheriting an alphabet is not enough. With that alphabet she must create a language adequate to express what the alphabet demands. What she must do is find a language that can speak and remember adequately.

The alphabet and language have been learned from women telling stories. There was Carmen Carrasco, displaced from her home in the Chillán earthquake of 1956, telling Agosín's mother, Frida, stories about magic and superstition. "She always began by telling us that we should preserve a respect and silence for the storyteller because if we didn't her words would turn into black birds" (*Cross*, 115). She also told her that it was "necessary to speak of the dead who suffer in order to perpetuate their life" (119). There was Frida's grandmother, Helena, who "would recreate her Viennese landscapes, adamant and without forgetting that in those same forests they burned her Jewish girlfriends" (133). Language has both its homeland connotations and its political connotations. In Agosín's mother's house the languages spoken were German, Russian, Yiddish, and later Spanish: "For Helena all that remained from Germany was its language, that same language that obliged her to strip and to tie up her hair so as later to have it shaved off, that same language that forbade her to go to the movies and to school, to touch the trees and go out into the street. That's why I like Spanish. It tastes like something sweet and remote, and although it has a relationship with the word for inquisition, it is a language for love and not for prohibiting or giving orders or incinerating the hair of my Grandmother Helena" (149–150).

The most important storyteller of all is Frida Agosín, Marjorie's mother. In *A Cross and a Star* it is sometimes hard to discern exactly who is speaking; as Agosín tells us, "I gathered together her words. I didn't invent anything or perhaps I invented everything. Sometimes her voice rolls up like my own in order to confuse itself with the language of love" (4). Later she writes:

> One day I began to listen to my mother and she told me about her years in southern Chile before and after the Second World War. Bewildered, she told me to tell her sacred and dark, painful and stirring story.
> For a long time I approached her words, like warm blankets and dangerous roads. Sometimes their silence made me stop before the proximity of horror.
> This is the story of foreigners and exiles and it doesn't matter if I forgot your name because you are also in the dark dwelling of memory, crossing the dangerous thresholds of all bygone times.
> (98)

Inheriting the alphabet gives Agosín the tools to make a language that will express her sense of injustice and of human dignity and human rights. She tells us, "Of all languages, I prefer that of love" (174). As her texts shift between holocaust and holocaust, her language is not only of love, but also of survival, "We survived exiles, foreign tongues and jibes from the daily inferno" (177). It is the language of memory and of remembering. With this language Agosín constructs beauty and painful remembrance at the same time. She tells us, "Memory like a chest of magical echoes, like a compass in a familiar closet. I graze my memory not knowing if I tell what I invent or if I invent what I tell. I wish to talk about a mythical and mythmaking country on the southernmost tip of the planet. It is called Chile. A fertile and generous land, it is a country of deluded wanderers and poets" (1). And when she was once asked if she had a community in the United States, she commented on the powerful grip of homeland, "My community is located in the streets of my childhood, in doorsteps full of old women and birds. That is where I am constantly drawn, for inside myself I have never left home" (*Women of Smoke*, 29).

Thus homeland, for victims of the holocaust, like for Chilean political exiles, becomes a reconstructed entity. It exists in memory and in language, it exists in nature and remembering people one loved. It exists in the imaginary and the real where "life in all its natural beauty can lust and grow," say Celeste Kostopulos-Cooperman in the introduction to *A Cross and a Star* (xvii). It reconstructs those who have disappeared by naming them again and again. For it is the naming and in finding that alphabet and that language adequate to the naming that the disappearance can be reconstructed and made real. And so it is in the language of survival, remembrance, and love that even a problematical homeland can be imagined and transcended.

TWENTY *Questioning Nepantla*

THE LAND IN BETWEEN — GEOPOLITICAL
TYRANNIES AND OTHER BORDER
COMPLEXITIES (2002)

The Border, Border Theory, Border Studies, the border-
lands, la frontera, los fronterizos. A broad complex subject with many perspectives, many meanings. Does it mean side by side or face to face? Is it a
barbed wire fence that delimits, or an invisible line that shifts? Is there such
a phenomenon as a border identity? Is the physical border between the
United States and Mexico a true dividing line, or is it an amorphous space
that does not truly separate? The title blurb for *Across the Border Lies,* by
Paul Flores, states, "The contemporary U.S. Mexican Border may divide
the first world from the third, but for those who live beneath its shadow,
la frontera often unites what it was meant to separate."

For the last ten years or so, interest in the border has grown and attention has focused on the concerns about the border. Books and articles explore the complexities of the border, including a perceptive article by Arturo Aldama, "Millennial Anxieties: Borders, Violence, and the Struggle
for Chicana/o Subjectivity." Along with the critical articles there has also
been a plethora of creative writing by Chicanas and Chicanos as well as
Mexicanos and Mexicanas about living on the border and crossing the
border. Some books that come immediately to mind are Norma Cantú's
Canícula (1995), Alberto Urrea's *Across the Wire: Life and Hard Times on the
Mexican Border* (1993), and Ricardo Aguilar's *A barlovento* (1999). In their
review essays, Juan Bruce-Novoa, María Socorro Tabuenca, Luis Mendoza, and Alberto Ledesma (among others) have comprehensively cata-
logued and analyzed much border literature. In "The U.S.-Mexican Border in Chicano Testimonial Writing: A Topological Approach to Four
Hundred and Fifty Years of Writing the Border" (1996), Bruce-Novoa
traces some of the earlier literature that views the border from both the
Mexican as well as the U.S. side; he begins with explorer Cabeza de Vaca
and ends with contemporary writer Alberto Urrea. In "Viewing the Bor-

der: Perspectives from the 'Open Wound' " (1996), Tabuenca reviews contemporary Mexican authors who write on the border and raises some perceptive questions about what a border writer is. Mendoza discusses writers from Texas in "The Border between US: Contact Zone or Battle Zone?" (1994), and Alberto Ledesma analyzes the literature of immigration in "Undocumented Crossings: Narratives of Mexican Immigration to the United States" (1998). Here I do not intend to review the literature already amply discussed; rather I want to question the idea and representation of the border in the contemporary moment.

When Debra Castillo asked me to prepare a paper on the border, in particular "border identities," she said it would be part of a tripartite dialogue on "proscribed identities" for a session on prose fiction. The word "proscribed" is quite a harsh word, meaning prohibited, denounced, to banish or exile. This would fit in with the sense that people on the border have been marginalized, sent to the edges, and disappeared. While in some senses the creation of a border identity, particularly a migrant one, might fit that definition and it is particularly true in a historical sense, I would prefer to see border identities as inscribed identities—that is, written or engraved, enrolled as on an official list. Another definition of "inscribed" would be to draw or delineate (one figure) within another figure so that the inner lies in the boundary of the outer at as many points as possible.

We have certainly been conscious of the border in terms of economic and linguistic cultures, but perhaps it was not until Gloria Anzaldúa articulated the border as an open wound in *Borderlands* (1987) that Chicano literary scholars became so painfully aware of the truth of that statement. Her concept of "la nueva mestiza" was an open category that invited participation from a large group of people, because it blurred the boundaries of identity "through the process of having to cross over and negotiate through the limitations" (E. Hernández, 11). When asked why her book was so widely accepted, Anzaldúa stated:

> One of the reasons that *Borderlands* has been so well received is because it allows people from all cultures to read themselves into the text and it articulates an identity and a category and a reality that the cultural mestiza can be anyone. We are faced with the fear that if we open up our hearts and embrace our visitors they will take over our house. Not only that, but that they will be disrespectful to us in our own house. How can you say that this is our house, but it is also their house, with-

out inviting a takeover? How much do you make accessible
to the other, and how often do you say, "Stop right there?"
(11)

Taken broadly and metaphorically, this is quite true, so that now everything is a border—wherever the notion of opposites, limits, delineation,
and conflict take place, it fits into the understanding of border. Perhaps because of this broadly focused perspective Guillermo Gómez-Peña declared,
"The border as metaphor has become hollow. Border aesthetics have been
gentrified and border culture as a utopian model for dialog is temporarily
bankrupt. But the border as a region of political injustice and great human
suffering still exists. The border remains an infected wound on the body of
the continent, its contradictions more painful than ever" (8–9).

Because borders are present everywhere, I want to clarify that here
I am not talking broadly about borders, about Ireland or Serbia or Af-
rica. Here I articulate the border/la frontera as being the U.S.-Mexico
border, measuring some 1,600–2,000 miles (depending on who is doing
the calculations) as the focus of my discussion. In fact, I should say Mexi-
can-U.S. borders. On the Internet, if you call up borders, one interesting
entry is a map of the U.S.-Mexico border with stars locating the various
cities on both sides that face each other. As you click on the stars different information comes up stating facts about those cities. At each contact
place, then, different cultures have sprung up in relation to one another,
to their regions and their relationship to the nation centers. Matamoros/
Brownsville, Nuevo Laredo/Laredo, El Paso/Juárez, Tijuana/San Diego,
all have their own border identities. We must take into consideration that
many of these cities are large (and growing even larger) metropolitan areas,
but there are small towns and rural areas on the border also. These borders
are not monolithic essential cultures. We must talk about the plurality of
border cultures and borderlands, and then discuss their specificities.

What defines these borders? Is it nation, culture, language? Is the border violence? Is it seen clearer from one side than the other? Does the
perspective of the border change according to gender? Is the border only
one? Are there spaces in between that can be distinguished from the spaces
that delimit? Questioning Nepantla is to question the geopolitical representation of the border from many sides: the social, the political, certainly
the economic, the cultural, the spiritual. Where do these borders and borderlands begin and end? Are there internal borders that reflect the actual
borders? How is the border represented by the United States, by Mexico?

Who is a border writer, as Tabuenca asks? Those who write about the border from the center of Mexico or the center of the United States, those for whom the border is an abstract concept? Or is a border writer one who writes from and on the border?

There is one area on which many critics agree: the writers who write from and on the border, on both sides, but more particularly from the Mexican side, have been truly marginalized. Perhaps the Chicano/a writers, for whom the border and immigration across the border is such a central part of their writing, are more well known. Mexican writers writing from the border, escritores fronterizos, such as Ricardo Aguilar, Rosinda Conde, Rosario San Miguel, and others, are not known either in Mexican or U.S. literary circles. I am in complete agreement with Socorro Tabuenca, that for us to truly understand the meaning of these borders and their representations we must study and contemplate the messages that these writers, of and from both sides, ask us to consider.

At this point I would like for you to contemplate the following perspectives that I see arising from border literature about, on, and from the border. I am not trying to essentialize these representations, realizing that they exist in complex and complicated forms; rather I am trying to clarify for myself some of the multiple areas that these subject identities can occupy.

One subject identity that has been explored in some depth is the emigrant/immigrant subject. In the introduction to their book *Culture across Borders,* David Maciel and María Herrera-Sobek assert that historical, sociological, social, and gender studies are the issues that have dominated immigration studies on both sides of the border. They claim that the cultural elements of Mexican immigration and the cultural/artistic manifestations that this immigration process has inspired have not received the academic inquiry that they merit. Recently many testimonial narratives about the immigration experience have appeared, such as Ruth Behar's *Translated Woman* (1993) and Ramón "Tianguis" Perez's *Diary of an Undocumented Immigrant* (1991). In fact, it is perhaps the immigrant subject that has been paid the most attention over the years, starting with *Las aventuras de don Chipote o cuando los pericos manen* (1928). Clearly the immigrant as seen from the perspective of the United States is someone who is here to work, to perform the most menial labor, and cheaply, and to be sent back to Mexico when there is no longer need for that labor. The immigrant is often vilified, "otherized," made invisible, only to become important when once more there is need for his or her labor. Seen from the Mexican side, these representations are called *bracero* narratives (more recently

paisano narratives to mitigate the negativity the word *bracero* might con-
jure up). In them Mexico is often romanticized while the United States
is vilified, forming a highly nationalistic narrative discourse. Thus border
literature can include immigrant literature, but it also can be different
from it as it may include perspectives of a settled population whose life is
informed by what is happening en el otro lado. While the great majority
of these migration narratives come from a working-class perspective, an
early narrative, that of Olga Beatriz Torres, *Memorias de mi viaje,* tells of a
young girl's experience in the United States after her family (clearly upper
class) flees Mexico during the Mexican Revolution. Her clearly Mexican
identity begins to be inscribed with the notion of a changed relationship
to the world, similar to that which Juan Bruce-Novoa claims happened to
Cabeza de Vaca during his travels through what is now the southwestern
United States.

However, the outsider status felt by most border crossers, particularly
the undocumented ones, is clear. Claire Fox claims that the symbols of the
fence and the river, which strive to keep "aliens" out, are mirrored by the
terms locally used to name such persons: mojados, alambristas (wetbacks,
wire crossers/cutters). The moments of crossings form the experience.
They become crossers, used to being chased. Ledesma claims that while
reading the bracero, paisano narratives we must pay attention to whether
they are documented or undocumented workers, a key perspective in the
understanding and representation of their attitude to the border.

Given the ever-increasing militarization of the border and escalating
criminalization of Latinos in the United States, Luis Mendoza feels that
any "simplified notions about identity politics" become impossible (129).
This is especially true given the events of September 11 and the intensified
vigilance on the border.

On some levels migrants have been made the national enemy; they are
portrayed as drug dealers and pushers, they are illegal, they take work away
from true Americans, they claim benefits and Social Security (they don't
deserve), and in general are stereotyped negatively. While we know these
claims are not true, they impact the lives of those migrants. Thus these
narratives "often deal with prejudice, ill-treatment and poor wages, and in
general present the bracero experience as a wretched and unbearable one"
(Maciel and Herrera-Sobek, 43).

On the other hand, María Herrera-Sobek demonstrates that many Chicano narratives are often different from the bracero narratives, because the
Chicano narratives are written by those who have chosen to stay in the

United States, and they portray their experiences as positive often focusing on the reasons that "compelled emigration" out of Mexico (Maciel and Herrera-Sobek, 80). In terms of gender, the Chicana immigrant narratives bring another perspective to the variable. They enable women to redefine traditional Mexican gender roles and to gain personal agency without the patriarchal social order (Ledesma, 84). In fact, Chicana narratives are often tales of growth, independence, and change.

There are many border narratives in which the inferiorization of the Mexican immigrant leads to linguistic and physical violence. Many undocumented workers crossing the border become victims of the coyotes who take them across, of thieves who confront them on their way, and of the Border Patrol itself. Women are particularly vulnerable to violence and rape. This violence not only occurs to those who are crossing the border, but also to those women living and working on the border. One case in point is the violence and mayhem being perpetuated against women in Juárez, mostly maquiladora workers, young women who have been raped and murdered, their bodies abandoned in fields. A December 14, 2001, article in the *Albuquerque Journal* stated that at least sixty-seven women have been slain in Ciudad Juárez in the past eight years, and although the police have imprisoned several men, women continue to be killed and left in the same manner (D8). This terrible scenario, protested by women's groups in Juárez, continues to be ignored by authorities in power, who seemingly have been unable to find the perpetrators. As Arturo Aldama and others tell us, violence on the border is caused by poverty, politics, unequal power relations, lack of education, disenfranchised youth: an entire social text of violence. It is a text that can no longer be tolerated or ignored and is a text that is inscribed in many border narratives.

Another perspective of the border is the Negotiating Border Subject. Here we see clearly represented in the literature a subject who resides in a place of contradiction. Anzaldúa's new mestiza resides there, as do the narrative and poetic subjects of many Chicano/a Mexicano/a works. As Alberto Ledesma points out, while many Mexican immigrant narratives deal with racial and class struggles that they experience in the United States, Chicano/a immigrant narratives "concentrate their attention on the redefinition of identity, on the constant adjustments that Mexicans now living in the United States need to negotiate their cultural surroundings" (88). On the Mexican side, the fronterizos are often called vendidos or felt to have a lack of "Mexican" identity. These subjects are constantly negotiating their nationality, their languages, their cultural values. One case in point (out of many) is Elva Treviño Hart's *Barefoot Heart: Stories of a Migrant Child* (1999), where coming back from a trip to Mexico, she tells us:

> When we got to the border, I spoke to the border patrol in perfect English, putting on my American persona again. I had spoken only Spanish for days. I had dreamed in Spanish, eaten in Spanish, prayed in Spanish. Suddenly, talking to the American guard in English, I felt like a gringa with brown skin.
>
> A few miles north of Laredo, there was another inspection point. The guy poked his head inside the car window and asked, "Y'all American citizens?"
>
> "Yes, Sir" I answered, the way Texans expect you to.
>
> But inside I wondered who we were, and especially who I was.
>
> (HART, 204)

This question of negotiating identity is echoed many times by border writers. Raquel Sentíes says,

> "Soy de la frontera,
> de Laredo,
> de un mundo extraño
> ni mexicano, ni americano
>
> . . . .
> Soy como el Río Grande,
> una vez parte de México,
> desplazada.
> Soy como un títere
> jalado por los hilos
> de dos culturas que chocan entre si.
> Soy la mestiza, la pocha, la Tex-Mex,
> la Mexican-American, la *hyphenated,*
> la que sufre por no tener identidad propia
> y lucha por encontrarla . . .
> (SENTÍES, *Soy,* 91–92)

And Pat Mora states, "I live in a doorway between two rooms" (*Borders,* 20).
Rarely analyzed, however, is this subject from the Mexican point of view. One excellent narrative, *A barlovento,* by Ricardo Aguilar, clearly

delineates the ambiguity, the shifting locus and the perplexity of contrasting life as lived on the border.

> Qué se siente ser mexicano? Cómo le explico a un extraño
> sin caer en los estereotipos comunes y en las nostalgias pedes-
> tres. Hoy que considero mi situación de mexicano exiliado,
> tengo por fuerza que decir que yo fui mexicano pero en otro
> tiempo . . . los cambios de gusto, tacto y olfato ante esta
> cultura menos agreste, menos angular, más a gusto, más desar-
> rollada tecnologicamente, lo hace a uno diferente. Ahora que
> repasamos lo sucedido desde el 68 y examinamos la reali-
> dad del México de ahora, poscolonial, posmoderno, caído,
> abatido ante una multitud de hechos críticos, se nos colora
> la memoria. Siento como que además de aquellas situaciones
> enormemente agradables que ya dije, allí al lado, seimpre
> ha estado lo grotesco, lo peligroso, lo horrible, allí, frente
> a la manifestación de la hermosura arquitectónica, musical,
> costumbrista, culinaria, artística está la muerte, la vejación, la
> violación, la violencia constante y continuá de los mexicianos
> hacia otros mexicanos.
> (94–95)

Although there are many more border subjects that could be analyzed, I want to finish this discussion by mentioning border identity as
seen through positive memory. The child narrator of *Canícula,* by Norma
Cantú, constructs her identity through her border crossings and those of
her family. Although the center of her life is Laredo, everyday realities
dictate that the child and her family undergo multiple border crossings.
These crossings constitute her multilateral, polyglot cultural experiences
that shape the young narrator's sense of self. The history of U.S.-Mexican
relations as well as of her family's immigration, stabilization, struggles, and
life on the border shape the narrative. As the narrator tells us in the section
"Crossings,"

> Bueli and Mami and Papi crossed the bridge on foot from
> one Laredo to the other, they took turns carrying me, or
> maybe only pushing my blue stroller. Chirinola, our dog,
> came too, papers and all. It was 1948. For Bueli, the move
> brought back memories, mental photographs gone now,
> except for the stories she told: how in 1935 she and Maurilio,

my Texas-born grandfather, and their two young daughters
packed all their belongings and drove their pickup truck
down from San Antonio. They felt lucky; most deportees left
with nothing but the clothes on their back—sent in packed
trains to the border on the way to Mexico, even those who
were U.S. citizens. She told of crossing from one Laredo to
the other and losing everything—Buelito's pride and joy,
a black Ford pickup truck and all their belongings—to the
corrupt customs officials at the border. Tía Nacha still talks
of how weeks later she saw a little girl wearing her dress—a
mint green dress she'd hemmed herself with pastel blue
thread, a memorable dress so unlike the ugly, drab, navy-
blue uniforms of Sacred Heart Elementary School. But there
was nothing to be done, except cry and go on. And in 1948
crossing meant coming home, but not quite.
(5)

Fronterizo poet José Manuel García-García reiterates this idea:

> Frontera que está en todas partes,
> Margen que desplaza su idioma multiple,
> Tiempo exilio de raiz a piel de llanto.
> Eternos extranjeros,
> De vez en cuando regresamos,
> sin puntos de partida
> hacia el comienzo.
> Border that is everywhere,
> margin that displaces its multiple language,
> exile time from origin to weeping skin.
> Eternal foreigners,
> from time to time we return,
> with no starting points
> towards the beginning.
> (GARCÍA-GARCÍA, 106−107)

For Pat Mora the border is once again that startling contrast where two
unequal worlds met, where "children go to sleep hungry and stare at stores
filled with toys they'll never touch, with books they'll never read. . . . what
I miss about the sights and sounds of the border is, I've finally concluded,
its stern honesty. The fierce light of that grand, wide Southwest sky not

only filled me with energy, it revealed the glare of truth" (*Nepantla*, 14). Her poetry and narratives reveal how sharply that glare manifests itself in her thinking about los dos lados.

In *A barlovento* Ricardo Aguilar recounts, from a different perspective than that of Cantú, the story of his family and the living of everyday life, recorded in minute detail, on the border, specifically Ciudad Juárez. Aguilar writes in his autobiographical mode, "la gente habla mucho de lo que es o no es la frontera y más se es chilanga descúbrelotodo y sábelome-jorque nadie para engrandecerse ante los demás, la verdad es que uno que de veras la conoce de primera y muy primera mano se da cuenta de ella, aquí, en la minucia (Aguilar, 208). Notable here, too, is the resentment felt towards "Chilangos," residents of Mexico City who see themselves as the center and the fronterizos as ignorant and marginalized. His is a novel of middle age, the coming to consciousness about life when in your fifties. The protagonist walks constantly and notes the specificity of the cities he is walking in, using Juárez as his point of reference. Thus Juárez becomes the central site of comparison. Juárez, a small town in his youth, has grown enormously in the intervening years because of migration, urbanization, and Mexican public policy. Just as the protagonist is growing old and de-crepit, suffering with illness and coping with aging, the city demonstrates the same decay. By recording in copious minute detail the everyday life of everyday people in Juárez, Aguilar strives to capture the sights, smells and people of the city. One talisman of his youth and memories of Juaritos is a two-story house that he cherished. Today it is the site of a hospital, and he watched as the construction of the new building slowly engulfed the house until it was swallowed up.

Aguilar is not romantic about the border, about the problems and de-lights of Mexico, but he also recognizes the problems and delights of the United States; thus the novel is a constant shifting back and forth between perceptions of both nations and of living in the land in the middle. While living in the United States life is more tranquil, he nevertheless misses the vibrancy, energy of his Juárez, even though the city is every day trans-forming itself. Through Aguilar's eyes we see and admire the skill of the bootblack, taste and appreciate the beauty of the fruitstand, the luscious colors and smells of the sweet shop: "en el ventanal se asoman unas cocadas de color dorado medio quemaditas, greñudas blancas color rosa mexicano, unos rollos de guayaba tamaño puro a la Churchill, cristalizados de limón, naranja, guayaba, calabaza, biznada y camote, alegrías de semilla de ama-ranto pegadas con miel y sus acompañantes obleas de colores chillantes, el dulce que los aztecas consumían para las fiestas del nacimiento de Huitzilpochtli" (217). And so on, you get the point. As he has told us, the realization of the border is in its details, in life lived by ordinary people.

I could go on and on. I haven't talked about language, about anger, about myth and mythmaking, about politics, or public policy from both sides, nor about politicians. However, I would like to finish with this observation. In a perceptive novel about maps and mapmaking, *The Mapmakers' Dream,* James Cowan writes, "In order to complete an exact map of the world, I must learn to look at the problem from another perspective. Instead of trying to define each continent in a way that fixes its reality so that all might agree with my interpretation, I need to be more circumspect in my assertions. Each of us has the right to speak of his coastline, his mountains, his deserts, none of which conforms to those of another. Individually we are obligated to make a map of our own homeland our own field or meadow. We carry engraved in our hearts the map of the world as we see it" (Cowan, 131). Perhaps we can carry the same analogy to the border, the border as seen from the perspective of the person who had engraved the image of the border through his or her experiences and carries that image in her or his heart. But it is also true, as Cowen tells us, "When I began this map I was intent on realizing a certainty, and now the reverse has proved to be true. No continent or people have turned out to exist except in relation to themselves. Their geographic location has also proven to be deceptive. The inescapable conclusion is that the true location in the world, of its countries, mountains, rivers and cities happens to be in the eyes of the beholder" (134). And so, perhaps the true perceptions of these borders and their interrelationships lie in the eyes of those who experience them and live in them.

NOTES

1. THE CHRONICLES OF PANCHITA VILLA: EPISODE ONE (1993)

1. This essay was originally published as "The Chronicles of Panchita Villa: A Chicana Guerrillera Literary Critic," in Jeanne Campbell Reeseman, ed., *Speaking the Other Self: American Women Writers* (Athens: University of Georgia Press, 1997), 79–90.

2. I have modified the translation.

3. When I read this paper at the Conference on American Women Writers in 1993, several Chicana colleagues came up to tell me they had received identical letters. This means the editors blanketed everyone but did not contact them personally.

3. WOMEN WRITERS, NEW DISCIPLINES, AND THE CANON (2000)

1. This essay was originally published in *Legacy* 19, no. 1 (2002): 14–17. Reprinted by permission of the University of Nebraska Press.

4. THE POLITICS OF POETICS: OR, WHAT AM I, A CRITIC, DOING IN THIS TEXT ANYHOW? (1987)

1. This essay is reprinted with permission from the publisher of the *Americas Review* (Houston: Arte Público Press—University of Houston, 1987).

8. LAS MUJERES HABLAN:
CREATIVITY AS POLITICS (1996)

1. This essay was first published as the introduction to *Las Mujeres Hablan: Exhibition and Symposium Catalogue,* edited by Connie Gibbons and Tina Fuentes (Lubbock: Lubbock Fine Arts Center, 1993).

11. "MI VIDA LOCA": SYMBOLIC SPACES
IN THE CONSTRUCTION OF IDENTITY
IN CHICANA LITERATURE (1998)

1. See Chapter 9, "Mujeres Andariegas: Good Girls and Bad," in Rebolledo, *Women Singing in the Snow.*

13. THE TOOLS IN THE TOOLBOX: REPRESENTING
WORK IN CHICANA LITERATURE (1999)

1. This essay was first published as "The Tools in the Toolbox: Representing Work in Chicana Writing" in *Genre* 32, nos. 1 and 2 (Spring/Summer 1999): 41–52. Reprinted by permission of the University of Oklahoma.

17. GAME THEORY: A TYPOLOGY OF FEMINIST
PLAYERS IN LATINA/CHICANA WRITING (1985)

1. I used to make little boats
from snow white paper
And onto the water I let loose
these small vessels.

And they navigated until
a sudden bend
imposed itself: then
I never saw them again.

Upon loosing my little boat
I was always seized
by ideas of the infinite
and would burst into tears.
(TRANSLATION MINE)

2. Like a child I went towards the east, thinking
that with my own hands I could touch the sun.
Like a child I went, along the round earth
Pursuing there, so far away, my wild solar fancy.

I was equidistant from the eastern gold
no matter how much I continued to walk;
I did what children do: seeing my search useless
I picked flowers from the earth and began to play.
(TRANSLATION MINE)

3. I turn my back. From a corner stand
I contemplate the sea distant, black and frowning
Ironic mouth (inlet). The wind roars.

4. My honorable and dear friend told me her reasons:
—I'm young, I haven't lived. My husband? A deceiver.
I have three children, I see year after year roll by
I'm like a slow dream without emotions.

At times I open, tempted, my balconies,
in order to see the elegant man, the proud man, the
     diffident man.
It's useless. If only I could cure myself of this dis-ease!
Oh, love is not a game that arranges one's uneasiness.

I paid attention, at times, but men, my friend,
are not worth an essay, my heart, fenced in,
untangles the most lively flattery.

I have a perfect body and a rosy mouth.
I was selected for the highest sort of love.
But I hide my passion beneath the veil of a nun.

5. But I was waiting for him
A short distance away . . .
I tied him with my long hair
And dominated his anger.
Once he was tied I told him
—You killed so many birds,
I am going to avenge them
Now that you are mine . . .
But I didn't kill him with weapons.
A much worse death I found:
I kissed him with such sweetness

That his heart broke in two!
  Message
Hunter: if you go hunting,
In the Mountains of the Lord
Be aware that birds are avenged
By deep wounds of love.

6. Young well-read women
in this century of ferment
Die of boredom
with no one to pick them.
More beautiful than ever,
O great fanciers of dainties, they are.
But they no longer give up their roses.
Don't wake up, don Juan.
The lunar adventure
has not stopped in vain;
Your punishing hand
will not find fortune.
And there is even an artful,
playful woman,
who, imitating your ways,
tries out your power.

7. Because this poem is not well known, I cite the complete poem here (translation mine).

El complicadísimo problema de como violar a un señor

    Tú pudiste inspirar mejor poesía
        Ernesto Cardenal

Instrucciones previas:
  aprenda a florear la reata
  tirar con rifle y escopeta
  manejar éter y cloroformo
  y un poco de judo o de karate

Escoja un hombre de su agrado
y algo más de su agrado
  en especial uno que le ocasione
  escalofríos en la melena
  y calor en los pies
  Uno que no la vea

o siga tan calmado
después de remirarla

¿Hecho? Pues adelante

Primer ensayo
    Sígalo
    cronometre el tiempo que está solo
    y en el momento elegido actúe
    Aproveche su experiencia charra
    llácelo manéelo átelo como a un novillo
    ¿Está a punto?
    A la carga
    Si este método no resulta
    debido a la posición del atacado
    dispónganse a intentarlo nuevamente

Segundo ensayo
    Cargue su rifle de narcóticos
    ¡CUIDADO!
    Un error de puntería
    podría ser desastroso

    Dispare
    Ya
    Esto no funciona
    El método lo inhibe demasiado

    No se dé por vencida
    Recomience después de desechar
    todos los dormitivos

    Habrá que usar de sutilezas

Tercer ensayo
    Visite a su veterinario
    compre la droga
    Ingéniese para que su objetivo
    se la trague
    Espere que haga efecto
    y plántese delante

    Si él no la ataca
    dé el caso por perdido
    y encuentre otro ejemplar

Regrese al primer ensayo
   Si también fracasa
   nada de histerismos

todavía quedan
los métodos desesperados:
maquíllese
cómprese camisones transparentes
perfume francés
Y hágase millionaria
o pratique strip-tease

The Very Complicated Problem of How to Rape a Man

> You should have inspired better poetry
> Ernesto Cardenas

Previous instructions:
     learn to twirl the lariat
     shoot with rifle and shotgun
     use ether and chloroform
     and a bit of judo or karate

Pick a man who pleases you
or more than pleases you
     especially one who causes you
     to have shivers up your spine
     and makes your feet feel warm
     One who doesn't even look at you
     or calmly continues on
     after looking at you

     Ready? Well continue

First Exercise
     Follow him
     calculate the time he is by himself
     and at a moment you select act
     Utilize your charro experience
     rope him, throw him down, tie him like a calf
     Is he ready?
     Charge

     If this method doesn't work
     given the position of the subject
     get ready to try again

Second Exercise
        Fill your rifle with narcotics
        BE CAREFUL!
        An error in aim
        could be disastrous

        Shoot.
        Now
        This isn't working
        The method inhibits him too much

        Don't give up
        Try again after throwing away
        all the sedatives

        You will have to be subtle

Third Exercise
        Visit your veterinarian
        buy the drug
        Be ingenious so that your object
        swallows it
        Wait for it to take effect
        and plant yourself in front of him

        If he doesn't attack you
        give the object up as lost
        find another subject
Return to the first exercise
        If this also fails
        don't get hysterical

There still remain
the desperate methods:
make yourself up
buy transparent nightgowns
become a millionaire
or practice strip tease

8. Doña Inés is the innocent and trusting young woman Don Juan seduces.

        9. And the woman sat on
                the curve
        And cried: "I am only a woman!"
                "I am defenseless and can do nothing!"
                "What a misfortune to be a woman!"

And she drowned in her own
    Tears and self-pity.
And they found her body
    When the lake of tears dried up
And they said "the poor woman drowned herself. .
    What can you do . . ."
And they continued walking nodding their heads.

And the Woman sat on
    the curve.
And she says: "Damn concrete curve, it really digs into me!"
    She got up and walked,
. . . and she bumped into a rock . . .
And she says: "Damn rock, I stubbed my toe!"
    Cursing she continued and
    she bumped into a lamppost . . .
And she says: "Damn lamppost . . . what a lot of pain it gave me!!!"
    BUT
She kept on and on . . .
She arrived home . . .
And she began to make tortillas and Revolution.

10. I believe I was part of the circus
I applauded like the Romans before the Christian players
I amused myself with the football gladiators
and the Virgin of the Macarena
With the rest I allied myself to the commercials
which for just a moment
interrupted my programing
but one day
upon assassinating the morning
with the suffocating noise of the streets
the bussing of indifferent faces
at every step I bumped into myself
they are me
they are myself
and since then
I wanted to be a witch
and play at life with poems.
(TRANSLATION MINE)

11. what fun is it
    to have to die a poet
        to be appreciated

why don't we play
    close your eyes
       and I
           will lie right here
              on this little bed of stone
         and in a little while
           as in the Bible
            I will rise

12. *Mischievous Soliloquy*

it's hard   being a flower
    at times
        when we're all alone
          and on the way
we concentrate real hard   like this
        we wrinkle up our foreheads
           to wither up beforehand
and when we get to market   ji ji
        they can't sell us.

13. days   weeks   months
    without knowing
        poeticized spasms
all for believing
    in knights-on-horseback
        that darn guy
and his mythified horse
    coming down the camino-brick-road
    with a mecate-rope
    around his pescuezo neck
that never
    never
      gets here.

14. look for your name
      within your own self
Chicana
    create your own word
      your essence   YOU
. . . .
be a credit to your race   create your own cosmos
CHICANA   SISTER   WOMAN
    now act for
     YOU

18. ART AND SPIRITUAL POLITICS: SOR JUANA BEATRIZ DE LA FUENTE—A FEMINIST LITERARY PERSPECTIVE (1995)

1. This discussion was an interdisciplinary experiment in which scholars from various disciplines were asked to discuss a work of art about which little is known. This paper was presented at the College Art Association Meeting in San Antonio in 1995.

BIBLIOGRAPHY

Agosín, Marjorie. *Conchali*. New York: Senda Nueva de Ediciones, 1980.

———. *Council of the Fairies*. Falls Church, Va.: Azul, 1997.

———. *A Cross and a Star: Memoirs of a Jewish Girl in Chile*. Trans. by Celeste Kostopulos-Cooperman. Albuquerque: University of New Mexico Press, 1995.

———. *Dear Anne Frank*. Hanover: University Press of New England, 1998.

———. *La Felicidad*. Santiago: Editorial Cuarto Propio, 1991.

———. *Hogueras/Bonfires*. Trans. by Naomi Lindstrom. Tempe, Ariz.: Bilingual Press, 1990.

———. *La literatura y los derechos humanos: Aproximaciones, lecturas y encuentros*. San José: Editorial Universitaria Centroamericana, 1989.

———. *Scraps of Life: Chilean Arpilleras*. Trans. by Cola Franzen. Trenton, N.J.: Red Sea Press, 1988.

———. *These Are Not Nice Girls: Poetry by Latin American Women*. Fredonia, N.Y.: White Pine Press, 1994.

———. *Toward the Splendid City*. Tempe, Ariz.: Bilingual Press, 1994.

———. *Women of Smoke*. Trans. by Naomi Lindstrom. Pittsburgh: Latin American Literary Review Press, 1988.

———. *Women of Smoke: Latin American Women in Literature and Life*. Trans. by Janice Molloy. Trenton, N.J.: Red Sea Press, 1989.

———. *Zones of Pain*. Fredonia, N.Y.: White Pine Press, 1988.

Agreda, María de. *Mystica Cuidad de Dios*. Madrid: En la Impr. de la Causa de la Venerable Madre, 1765.

Aguilar, Ricardo. *A barlovento*. Torreón, Coahuila: Editorial del Norte Mexicano, 1999.

Alarcón, Norma. "Traddutora, Traditora: A Paradigmatic Figure of Chicana Feminism." *Cultural Critique* 13 (Fall 1989): 57–87.

Alarcón, Norma, Ana Castillo, and Cherríe Moraga, eds. *Third Woman: The Sexuality of Latinas*. Berkeley: Third Woman Press, 1989.

Aldama, Arturo. "Millennial Anxieties: Borders, Violence, and the Struggle for Chicano Subjectivity." *Arizona Journal of Hispanic Cultural Studies* 2 (1998): 41–62.

Allen, Paula. "Sandra Cisneros: S.A.'s Literary Luminary Ignites." *San Antonio Express-News Magazine,* January 17, 1993, 6–15.

Anaya, Rudolfo. *Bless Me, Ultima.* Berkeley: Quinto Sol Publications, 1972.

Anzaldúa, Gloria. *Borderlands/La frontera: The New Mestiza.* San Francisco: Spinsters/Aunt Lute, 1987.

———. *Prietita and the Ghost Woman/Prietita y La Llorona.* San Francisco: Children's Book Press, 1996.

Arenal, Electra, and Stacy Schlau. *Untold Sisters: Hispanic Nuns in Their Own Works.* Albuquerque: University of New Mexico Press, 1989.

"Author Defends 'Periwinkle' Home amid Neighbors' Gripes." *The Monitor,* July 29, 1997, 6D.

Avakian, Arlene Voski, ed. *Through the Kitchen Window: Women Explore the Intimate Meanings of Food and Cooking.* Boston: Beacon Press, 1997.

Bacharach, Deborah. "Beware, Honey." *Sojourner* 20, no. 11 (July 1995): 3.

Behar, Ruth. *Translated Woman: Crossing the Border with Esperanza's Story.* Boston: Beacon Press, 1993.

Berez, Kim. "National Writers Voice Project Comes to Chicago." *Letter eX.,* February/March 1994, 7–9.

Bhabha, Homi. "Unpacking My Library . . . Again." In *The Post-Colonial Question: Common Skies, Divided Horizons,* ed. Lain Chambers and Lidia Curti, 199–211. London: Routledge, 1996.

Blake, Kathleen. *Play, Games, and Sport.* Ithaca: Cornell University Press, 1974.

Bornstein Somoza, Miriam. "Para el consumidor." In *Siete Poetas.* Tucson: Scorpion Press, 1978, 6.

Bruce-Novoa, Juan. "Canonical and Noncanonical Texts." *Americas Review* 14, nos. 3–4 (Fall–Winter 1986): 119–135.

———. *Retrospace: Collected Essays on Chicano Literature.* Houston: Arte Público Press, 1990.

———. "The U.S.-Mexican Border in Chicano Testimonial Writing: A Topological Approach to Four Hundred and Fifty Years of Writing the Border." *Discourse* 18, nos. 1 and 2 (Fall–Winter 1995–1996): 32–53.

Cabeza de Baca, Fabiola. *We Fed Them Cactus.* 1954. Reprinted with an introduction by Tey Diana Rebolledo. Albuquerque: University of New Mexico Press, 1994.

Carbonell, Joaquín. ". . . érase una niña escritora." *Rayuela,* April 6, 1992, 1.

Campbell, Kim. "Book Publishers Say 'Hola' to US Hispanic Market." *Christian Science Monitor,* April 20, 1995, 9.

Cantú, Norma. *Canícula: Snapshots of a Girlhood en la Frontera.* Albuquerque: University of New Mexico Press, 1995.

———. "Writing at the Crossroads: Un lenguaje y una realidad fronteriza." Paper delivered at the Latin American Studies Association Conference, March 16, 2000.

Carrico, James A. *Life of Venerable Mary of Agreda.* Stockbridge, Mass.: E. J. Culligan, 1960.

Castellanos, Rosario. *Poesía no eres tú. Obra poética: 1948–1971.* Mexico City: Fondo de Cultura Económica, 1974.

Castillo, Ana. *Goddess of the Americas/La Diosa de las Américas.* New York: Riverhead Books, 1996.

————. *The Invitation.* San Francisco: A. Castillo, 1979.

————. *My Father Was a Toltec.* Novato, Calif.: West End Press, 1988.

————. *So Far from God.* New York: Norton, 1993.

Chávez, Denise. *Face of an Angel.* New York: Farrar, Straus and Giroux, 1994.

————. *Loving Pedro Infante.* New York: Farrar, Straus and Giroux, 2001.

Cisneros, Sandra. *Bad Boys.* San Jose, Calif.: Mango Press, 1980.

————. *Hairs/Pelitos.* New York: Alfred A. Knopf, 1994.

————. *The House on Mango Street.* Houston: Arte Público Press, 1983.

————. *Loose Woman.* New York: Alfred A. Knopf, 1994.

————. *My Wicked Wicked Ways.* Berkeley: Third Woman Press, 1987. Reprint, New York: Turtle Bay, 1992.

————. "Our Tejano History Has Become Invisible." *San Antonio Express-News,* August 17, 1997. 1J, 5J.

————. "Who Wants Stories Now?" *New York Times,* March 16, 1994, 17.

————. *Woman Hollering Creek.* New York: Random House, 1991.

Cixous, Helene. "The Laugh of the Medusa." In *New French Feminisms,* ed. Elaine Marks and Isabelle de Courtivron, 245–264. New York: Schocken, 1980.

Collins, Tom. "Across a Line: Amid an Outcry from the Catholic Church, 'Our Lady' Presents a Serious Homage to Artist's Religious Faith." *Journal North,* March 30, 2001, 6.

"The Color Purple." *The Monitor,* July 29, 1997, 1D.

Córdova, Josephine. *No lloro pero me acuerdo.* Dallas: Taylor Publishing, 1976.

Corpi, Lucha. *Máscaras.* Berkeley: Third Woman Press, 1997.

Cota-Cárdenas, Margarita. *Marchitas de mayo. Sones p'al pueblo.* Austin: Relámpago Press, 1989.

————. *Noches despertando inConciencias.* Tucson: Scorpion Press, 1977.

————. *Puppet: A Chicano Novela.* Austin: Relámpago Books Press, 1985. Trans. by Barbara D. Riess and Trino Sandoval. Reprint, Albuquerque: University of New Mexico Press, 2000.

————. *Sanctuaries of the Heart/Sanctuarios del corazón.* Tucson: University of Arizona Press, 2005.

————. *Siete Poetas.* Tucson: Scorpion Press, 1978.

Cowan, James. *A Mapmaker's Dream.* New York: Warner Books, 1996.

Danini, Carmina. "Cisneros Promises Fight for Her Purple Abode." *San Antonio Express-News,* August 1, 1997, B1, B7.

De Hoyos, Angela. *Arise, Chicano! and Other Poems: Chicano Poems for the Barrio.* San Antonio: M&A Editions, 1975.

————. *Chicano Poems: For the Barrio.* San Antonio: Dezkalzo Press/M&A Editions, 1975.

———. *Selected Poems/selecciones*. Introduction by Evangelina Vigil. Corpus Christi: Dezkalzo Press, 1989.

———. *Woman, Woman*. Houston: Arte Público Press, 1985.

Dion, Marc Munroe. "Whispers from a Brave Author." *Kansas City Star,* June 2, 1991, 3.

Durke, Martha. "Real Issue behind Purple House Is Tolerance." *San Antonio Express-News,* August 12, 1997, 6B.

Espada, Martín, ed. *El Coro: A Chorus of Latina and Latino Poetry*. Amherst: University of Massachusetts Press, 1997.

Eysturoy, Annie O. *Daughters of Self-Creation: The Contemporary Chicana Novel*. Albuquerque: University of New Mexico Press, 1996.

Fisher, Dexter. *The Third Woman*. Boston: Houghton Mifflin, 1980.

Flores, Paul. *Across the Border Lies*. Berkeley: Creative Arts, 2001.

"Four Women and a Virgin." *Bob Magazine* 1, no. 5 (May 2001): 6.

Fox, Claire F. "The Fence and the River: Representations of the US–Mexico Border in Art and Video." *Discourse* 18, nos. 1–2 (Fall–Winter 1995–1996), 54–82.

Franco, Jean. *Plotting Women: Gender and Representation in Mexico*. New York: Columbia University Press, 1989.

García, Diana. *When Living Was a Labor Camp*. Tucson: University of Arizona Press, 2000.

García de Lara, José. "Neighbors of Cisneros Adore Purple House." *San Antonio Express-News,* August 13, 1997, B4.

García-García, José Manuel. "Poemas de un habitado sueño, IV." *Entre Líneas II.* Juarez: Universidad Autónoma de Ciudad Juárez, 1998.

Garza, Melita Marie. "Sandra Speaks." *San Antonio Light,* December 30, 1992, D1.

Gibbons, Connie, and Tina Fuentes, eds. *Las Mujeres Hablan: Exhibition and Symposium Catalogue*. Lubbock: Fine Arts Center, 1993.

Gilman, Charlotte Perkins. *The Yellow Wallpaper*. Boston: Small, Maynard, 1899.

Gómez-Peña, Guillermo. "Death on the Border: A Eulogy to Border Art." *High Performance* 58 (1991): 8–9.

Gonzales-Berry, Erlinda. "Carlota Gonzales." In Rebolledo, ed., *Nuestras Mujeres,* 35–36.

———. E-mail message to author, April 27, 2001.

———. *Paletitas de guayaba*. Albuquerque: El Norte Publications, 1991.

Greenberg, Mike. "Authenticity Is Always Fresh, Never Frozen." *San Antonio Express-News,* August 13, 1997, B1.

Guerra, Carlos. "Color of Purple Obscures Bigger Historic Issue." *San Antonio Express-News,* August 7, 1997, B1.

Gutiérrez, Marcela Tostado. *El álbum de la mujer: Antología ilustrada de las mexicanas*. Vol. 2: *Epoca colonial*. Mexico City: Instituto Nacional de Antropología e Historia, 1991.

Gutiérrez, Ramón A. "Marriage and Seduction in Colonial New Mexico." In *Be-*

tween Borders: Essays on Mexicana/Chicana History, ed. Adelaida R. Del Castillo, 447–458. Encino, Calif.: Floricanto Press, 1990.

Guzmán, Martín Luis. *Memorias de Pancho Villa.* Mexico City: Ediciones Botas, 1938–1940.

Hammond, George P., and Agapito Rey. *The Rediscovery of New Mexico, 1580–1594.* Albuquerque: University of New Mexico Press, 1966.

Hart, Elva Treviño. *Barefoot Heart: Stories of a Migrant Child.* Tempe: Bilingual Press, 1999.

Hernández, Ellie. "Rethinking Margins and Borders: An Interview with Gloria Anzaldúa." *Discourse* 18, nos. 1–2 (Fall–Winter 1995–1996): 7–15.

Hernández, Salomé. "The Present-Day U.S. Southwest: Female Participation in Official Spanish Settlement Expeditions: Specific Case Studies in the Sixteenth, Seventeenth, and Eighteenth Centuries." Ph.D. diss., University of New Mexico, 1987.

Hernández Tovar, Inés. "Chiflazones." *Con Razón, Corazón.* Austin: I. H. Tovar, 1980?, 18.

Herrera-Sobek, María, and Helena María Viramontes, eds. *Chicana (W)rites: On Word and Film.* Berkeley: Third Woman Press, 1998.

Hodge, Frederick Webb, George P. Hammond, and Agapito Rey, eds. *Fray Alonso de Benavides' Revised Memorial of 1634.* Albuquerque: University of New Mexico Press, 1945.

Huizinga, Johan. *Homo Ludens: A Study of the Play Element in Culture.* London: Hunt, Barnard, 1950.

Jaramillo, Cleofas. *The Genuine New Mexico Tasty Recipes.* 1939. Rev. ed., Santa Fe: Seton Village, 1942.

———. *Romance of a Little Village Girl.* San Antonio: Naylor, 1955. Reprinted with an introduction by Tey Diana Rebolledo. Albuquerque: University of New Mexico Press, 2000.

———. *Shadows of the Past (Sombras del pasado).* Santa Fe: Seton Village, 1941.

Joysmith, Claire. "Entrevista a Sandra Cisneros." *El Nacional,* September 26, 1993, 4–7.

———, ed. *Las Formas de Nuestras Voces: Chicana and Mexicana Writers in Mexico.* Berkeley: Third Woman Press, 1995.

Katz, Jesse. "Purple Passions Swirl about Texas Abode." *Los Angeles Times,* August 11, 1997, A1.

Kaufman, Gloria, and Mary Kay Blakely, eds. *Pulling Our Own Strings.* Bloomington: Indiana University Press, 1980.

Kilgore, Susan Jane. "Through Medusa's Eyes: American Women Writers and the Figure of the Mad Woman." Ph.D. diss., University of New Mexico, 1985.

La Chrisx. "La Loca de la Raza Cósmica." In Rebolledo and Rivero, eds., *Infinite Divisions,* 84–88.

Laget, Mokha. "The Spirit of Technology: Cyber Arte Is a Small Show with a Lot to Say." *Santa Fe Reporter,* February 26–March 6, 2001, 26.

Ledesma, Alberto. "Undocumented Crossings: Narratives of Mexican Immigration to the United States." In Maciel and Herrera-Sobek, eds., *Culture across Borders,* 67–98.

Lee, Morgan. "Archbishop Says Art Trashes Virgin, Insults Catholics." *Albuquerque Journal,* March 27, 2001, 1, A2.

León Portilla, Miguel. *Pre-Columbian Literature of Mexico.* Norman: University of Oklahoma Press, 1969.

Levy, Barbara. *Ladies Laughing: Wit as Control in Contemporary American Women Writers.* Amsterdam: Gordon and Breach, 1997.

Lewis, Philip E. "La Rochefoucauld: The Rationality of Play." *Yale French Studies* 41 (Summer 1968): 133–147.

Littledog, Pat. "Hollering Loud: An Interview with Sandra Cisneros." *Texas Observer,* August 23, 1991, 4–7.

Lomas Garza, Carmen. *Family Pictures/Cuadros de Familia.* San Francisco: Children's Book Press, 1990.

Luchen, Gunter, ed. *The Cross-Cultural Analysis of Sport and Games.* Champaign, Ill.: Stipes Publishing, 1970.

Maciel, David R., and María Herrera-Sobek, eds. *Culture across Borders: Mexican Immigration and Popular Culture.* Tucson: University of Arizona Press, 1998.

Madison, D. Soyini, ed. *The Woman That I Am: The Literature and Culture of Contemporary Women of Color.* New York: St. Martin's, 1994.

Manrique, Jorge Alberto. "Ataque al Museo de Arte Moderno." *Luna Córnea,* no. 11 (January/April 1997): 1.

Martínez, Demetria. *Breathing between the Lines.* Tucson: University of Arizona Press, 1997.

Martínez, Elizabeth, ed. *500 Years of Chicano History in Pictures.* Albuquerque: Southwest Organizing Project, 1991.

Martínez, Katynka Zazueta. "An Afternoon with Sandra Cisneros." *TWANAS,* June 8, 1995, 12, 15.

Martínez, Rick. "Cisnero Scenario Will Repeat." *San Antonio Express News,* June 22, 1995, 31A.

———. "Genius Lives in Gawdawful Places like Texas, Too." *Houston Chronicle,* June 23, 1995, 31A.

McIlvain, Jamie. "Voice of an American Mexican." *The Monitor,* March 11, 1994, 1A, 12A.

Melville, Herman. *Moby-Dick or the Whale.* New York: Oxford University Press, 1947.

Mendoza, Luis Gerard. *Historia: The Literary Making of Chicana and Chicano History.* College Station: Texas A&M University Press, 2001.

———. "The Border between US: Contact Zone or Battle Zone?" *Modern Fiction Studies* 40, no. 1 (Spring 1994): 119–139.

Meyers, Christene C. "Writers Refuse Stereotypes." *Billings Gazette,* October 13, 1994, B1.

Meyers, David, and Dina Fisher. "Book Review: Sandra Cisneros at the Poetry Center, December 16, 1992." *Letter eX.*, February 1993, 2.

Milán. Elena. *Circuito Amores y Anexas*. Mexico City: Editorial Latitudes, 1979.

Miles, Barbara. "Critics Miss Cisneros Theme." *San Antonio Express-News*, June 1995, 4.

Milner, Jay. "Rare Talent." *Lufkin Daily News*, June 2, 1991, 10.

Molina, Rafael. "Sandra Cisneros, artífice de la literatura Chicana." *Cultura: La Jornada*, June 18, 1995, 26.

Montes, Ana. "Bus Stop Macho." *Comadre* 1, no. 1 (1997): 24–25.

Mora, Pat. *Agua Santa/Holy Water*. Boston: Beacon, 1995.

———. *A Birthday Basket for Tía*. New York: Macmillan, 1992.

———. *Borders*. Houston: Arte Público Press, 1986.

———. *The Desert Is My Mother/El desierto es mi madre*. Houston: Arte Público Press, 1994.

———. *House of Houses*. Boston: Beacon, 1997.

———. *Listen to the Desert/Oye al desierto*. New York: Clarion, 1994.

———. *Nepantla*. Albuquerque: University of New Mexico Press, 1993.

———. *Pablo's Tree*. New York: Macmillan, 1994.

Mora, Pat. "Retrieving our Past, Determining Our Future." Unpublished essay. Later published in part as "Used Furniture" in *Nepantla*.

———. *Tomás and the Library Lady*. New York: Alfred A. Knopf, 1997.

Nakao, Annie. "The Voice of the Latina: Sandra Cisneros' Tales Speak to the Hearts of Women." *San Francisco Examiner*, January 11, 1993, C1, C4.

Nelson, Kate. "Our Lady of All This Fuss Can't Rock a Faith Built on More than Scorn." *Albuquerque Tribune*, April 5, 2001, A3.

Niggli, Josephina. *Mexican Village*. Introduction by María Herrera-Sobek. Albuquerque: University of New Mexico Press, 1994. First published by the University of North Carolina Press, 1944.

Norwood, Vera, and Janice Monk, eds. *The Desert Is No Lady*. New Haven: Yale University Press, 1987. Reprint, Tucson: University of Arizona Press, 1997.

Obejas, Achy. "Sandra Cisneros: Return a Hit, Miss Affair." *Chicago Tribune*, December 19, 1993, 124, 129.

Paredes, Raymond. "Review Essay: Recent Chicano Writing." *Rocky Mountain Review* 41, nos. 1–2 (1987): 124–129.

Peden, Margaret Sayers. *A Woman of Genius: The Intellectual Autobiography of Sor Juana Inés de la Cruz*. New York: Columbia University Press, 1989.

Pierce, Caroline. "Cisneros Scattershoots with Wicked Wit." *Caller-Times*, September 21, 1992, E7.

"Purple Politics." *San Antonio Express-News*, August 1, 1997.

Quintana, Alvina E. *Home Girls: Chicana Literary Voices*. Philadelphia: Temple University Press, 1996.

Rapoport, Anatol, ed. *Game Theory as a Theory of Conflict Resolution*. Bingham, Mass.: Kluwer, Boston, 1974.

Rebolledo, Antonio. *La llama y el indio y otros cuentos.* Mexico City: Gráfica Panamericana, 1949.

Rebolledo, Antonio, and Edward Eyring. *Amanecer.* Vols. 1 and 2. Albuquerque: University of New Mexico Press, 1944.

Rebolledo, Tey Diana. "Abuelitas: Mythology and Integration in Chicana Literature." In *Woman of Her Word: Hispanic Women Write,* ed. Evangelina Vigil. Houston: Arte Público Press, 1983, 148–158.

———. "The Bittersweet Nostalgia of Childhood in the Poetry of Margarita Cota-Cárdenas." *Frontiers* 5 (1980): 32–35.

———. "Letter to the Editor." *Albuquerque Journal,* March 30, 2001, A15.

———. "The Maturing of Chicana Poetry: The Quiet Revolution of the 1980s." In Treichler, Kramarae, and Stafford, eds., *For Alma Mater,* 143–146.

———. "Signatures of Landscape in Chicana Writing." In *The Desert Is No Lady: Southwestern Landscapes in Women's Writing and Art,* ed. Vera Norwood and Janice Monk, 96–124. New Haven: Yale University Press, 1987.

———. "Walking the Thin Line: Humor in Chicana Literature." In *Beyond Stereotypes,* ed. María Herrera-Sobek, 91–107. Binghamton: Bilingual Press, 1985.

———. *Women Singing in the Snow: A Cultural Analysis of Chicana Literature.* Tucson: University of Arizona Press, 1995.

———, ed. *Nuestras Mujeres: Hispanas of New Mexico. Their Images and Their Lives, 1582–1992.* Albuquerque: El Norte Publications, 1993.

Rebolledo, Tey Diana, Erlinda Gonzales-Berry, and Teresa Márquez, eds. *Las mujeres hablan. An Anthology of Nuevo Mexicana Writers.* Albuquerque: El Norte Publications, 1988.

Rebolledo, Tey Diana, and Teresa Márquez, eds. *Women's Tales from the New Mexico WPA: La Diabla a Pie.* Houston: Arte Público Press, 2000.

Rebolledo, Tey Diana, and Eliana Rivero, eds. *Infinite Divisions: An Anthology of Chicana Literature.* Tucson: University of Arizona Press, 1993.

Reeseman, Jeanne Campbell, ed. *Speaking the Other Self: American Women Writers.* Athens: University of Georgia Press, 1997.

Rhodes, Hal. "Three Rights Make a Left: Virgin in Floral Bikini Comes for the Archbishop." *Crosswinds,* April 5–12, 2001, 6.

Richelieu, David Anthony. "Readers Still Seeing Purple in House Uproar." *San Antonio Express News,* August 12, 1997, B1.

Rivera, Marina. "Even." In *The Third Woman: Minority Writers in the United States,* ed. Dexter Fisher, 407. Boston: Houghton Mifflin, 1980.

Rivera, Tomás. *Y no se tragó la tierra.* Berkeley: Editorial Justa, 1983.

Rodríguez, Roberto, and Patrisia Gonzales. "Model in Photo Collage Says 'Our Lady' Symbol of Struggle." *Albuquerque Journal,* April 25, 2001, A13.

Romero, Mary. "Class-Based, Gendered, and Racialized Institutions of Higher Education: Everyday Life of Academia from the View of Chicana Faculty." *Race, Gender, and Class: Latina/o American Voices* 4, no. 2 (1997): 151–173.

Ross, Lena, ed. *To Speak or Be Silent: The Paradox of Disobedience in the Lives of Women.* Wilmette, Ill.: Chiron Publications, 1993.

Ruiz de Burton, María Amparo. *The Squatter and the Don.* Edited with an introduction by Rosaura Sánchez and Beatrice Pita. Houston: Arte Público Press, 1992.

————. *Who Would Have Thought It?* Edited with an introduction by Rosaura Sánchez and Beatrice Pita. Houston: Arte Público Press, 1995.

Sánchez, Rosaura, Beatrice Pita, and Bárbara Reyes, eds. *Crítica: A Journal of Critical Essays. Nineteenth-Century California Testimonials.* San Diego: University of California, 1994.

Sandoval, Emiliana. "Las Mujeres." *Pasatiempo* (Santa Fe), April 30–May 6, 1993, 28–31.

"Sandra Cisneros: Cuando me pedían que hablara de cisnes, hablaba de ratas." *La Vanguardia,* May 20, 1992, 12.

"Sandra Cisneros: Giving Back to Libraries." *Library Journal,* January 1992, 55.

Saucedo, María. "Sobre la liberación de la mujer." In *Fiesta in Aztlán: Anthology of Chicano Poetry,* ed. Toni Empringham, 112. Santa Barbara: Capra Press, 1982.

Schouten, Liesbeth. "Cheek to Cheek, Chiquita, Latino-amerikaanse Literatuur in de VS." *Onze Werld,* July–August 1992, 67.

Sentíes, Raquel Valle. *Soy como soy y qué.* San Antonio: M&A Editions, 1996.

Shuru, Xochitl E. "La loca in *Loose Woman*: From Female Insanity to Female Empowerment." Unpublished paper, 1995.

Silva, Elda. "Local Author Recipient of Value Grant." *San Antonio Express-News,* June 13, 1995, 1.

Steinberg, Leo. *The Sexuality of Christ in Renaissance Art and in Modern Oblivion.* 2d ed. Chicago: University of Chicago Press, 1996.

Storni, Alfonsina. *Obra poética completa.* Buenos Aires: Sociedad Editora Latinoamericana, 1968.

Tabor, Mary B. W. "A Solo Traveler in Two Worlds." *New York Times,* January 7, 1993, C1, C10.

Tabuenca, María Socorro. "Viewing the Border: Perspectives from 'the Open Wound.'" *Discourse* 18, nos. 1–2 (Fall–Winter 1995–1996): 146–168.

Torres, Olga Beatriz. *Memoria de mi viaje/Recollections of My Trip.* Albuquerque: University of New Mexico Press, 1994.

Treichler, Paula A., Cheris Kramarae, and Beth Stafford, eds. *For Alma Mater: Theory and Practice in Feminist Scholarship.* Chicago: University of Illinois Press, 1985.

Treviño, Isaac, Jr. "Don Pedrito Subject of Reading in New York City, Published Book." *Falfurrias Facts,* July 18, 1991, 1, 10A.

Trujillo, Carla. *Living Chicana Theory.* Berkeley: Third Woman Press, 1998.

Urrea, Luis Alberto. *Across the Wire: Life and Hard Times on the Mexican Border.* New York: Anchor Books, 1993.

Van Cleve, Emily. "Modern Art: Artists Use Computer Technology to Create Traditional Images." *Albuquerque Journal,* February 18, 2001, F1, F2.

Venegas, Daniel. *Las aventuras de don Chipote, o cuando los pericos mamen.* Mexico City: SEP-Cultura, 1984.

Vigil, Evangelina. *Thirty an' Seen a Lot.* Houston: Arte Público Press, 1984.

Villanueva, Alma. *Mother, May I?* Pittsburgh: Motheroot, 1978.

————. *The Ultraviolet Sky.* Tempe: Bilingual Review Press, 1988.

Villegas de Magnón, Leonor. *The Rebel.* Ed. Clara Lomas. Houston: Arte Público Press, 1994.

Viramontes, Helena María. *Under the Feet of Jesus.* New York: Dutton, 1995.

Walsh, Rebecca. "Writer Cisneros Lends Power to Chicanas." *Salt Lake Tribune,* October 2, 1994, E4.

Wood, Mary Antonia. "Letters to the Journal." *Albuquerque Journal,* March 30, 2001, A15.

Yerkes, Susan. "King William Seeing Red over Purple." *San Antonio Express-News,* July 29, 1997, D1, D10.

————. "Now We Know Why It's Called Purple Passion." *San Antonio Express-News,* July 30, 1997, G1.

————. "Purple Passion and the Art of Saying 'No.'" *San Antonio Express-News,* August 9, 1997, G1.

INDEX

bildungsheld (liberating self-creation),
53, 144
bildungsroman (coming-of-age novel),
57, 144
Bilingual Review/Press, 14, 43, 59, 106
bilingual writings and bilingualisms, 106,
172–173
Black women, 17, 21
Bless Me, Ultima (Anaya), 58
"The Blue Teacups" (Agosín), 223–224
body, 159–163, 215
Bombal, María Luisa, 216
border identities, 228–238
Borderlands (Anzaldúa), 54, 99, 229–230
"Border Series" (López), 176
Borges, Jorge Luis, 73, 188
Bornstein-Somoza, Miriam, 107, 188,
199–200
bracero narratives, 231–232
Breton, André, 129
Brown, Dolores, 7–8
Bruce-Novoa, Juan, 41, 71, 228, 232
brujas (witches), 67, 85, 88–89, 208
"Bus Stop Macho" (Montes), 196–197

Cabeza de Baca, Fabiola, 51, 60, 62, 86
Cabeza de Vaca, 228, 232
Cabrera Infante, Guillermo, 188
California Testimonials, 51, 142–143
Caló, 106
Campin, Robert, 179
"Candelabras" (Agosín), 224
Canícula (Cantú), 52, 70, 71, 145–146,
228, 235–236
canon: Bruce-Novoa on, 41; and Chicana
literature, 13–23, 26, 36–39, 41; and
Chicano literature, 41; feminist canon,
13–23, 26
"Canonical and Noncanonical Texts"
(Bruce-Novoa), 41
Cantú, Norma, 39, 45, 52, 70, 71,
145–146, 228, 235–236
Capirotada press, 59
Caracol (Snail) press, 58
CARA show, 67
Cardenal, Ernesto, 195
Carrasco, Barbara, 92, 93, 94

Carrasco, Carmen, 225
Castellanos, Rosario, 7, 35, 153, 188,
193–194
Castillo, Ana: Chicano critic on, 46; in
feminist canon, 14; in public press,
126; writings by, 51, 59, 64–67, 106,
116, 120–122
Castillo, Debra, 229
Catholic Church, 175–183, 205–213. *See
also* religion
Cautiva Inditas, 82–83
Cenicienta Syndrome, 29
Centro de Escritores de Aztlán, 43
Cervantes, Lorna Dee, 58, 97–98, 100,
106
Chávez, César, 62
Chávez, Denise: and Arte Público Press,
36; on body taboos, 159–163; Chicano
critic on, 46; friendship between
author and, 39; humor in writings
by, 158–174; on names and naming, 167–168; narratives within the
narratives of, 169–172; novels by, 52,
86, 153, 158–174; on other woman,
164–165; in public press, 126; on religion, 166–167; on sex and sexuality,
163–165; work represented in novel
by, 52, 146–149
Chicana academics, 15–22, 26, 29–33
Chicana artists and artwork, 59, 60,
70–71, 92–94, 175–183
"The Chicana Bandera: Sandra Cisneros
in the Public Press" (T. D. Rebolledo),
124–138
"Chicana Creativity and Criticism"
symposium, 41
Chicana critics: biases of, 46–47; and descriptive thematic analysis, 44; and dichotomous ideology, 47–48; directions
of critical perspectives, 51–53; entire
text inclusion by Rebolledo, 43–44;
functions of, 43–45; honesty by, 46;
isolation of, 54; as literary historians,
44–45, 51–52; and living authors,
45–46; new models for, 54–55; and
politics of poetics, 40–48; problems
of, 15–22, 26, 43–48, 53–55; and